44541 856

Governments, Citizens, and Genocide

ALEX ALVAREZ

Governments, Citizens, and Genocide: A Comparative and Interdisciplinary Approach

INDIANA UNIVERSITY PRESS

Bloomington and Indianapolis

Portions of this book, most notably parts of chapters 1, 3, and 5, have appeared in earlier form in the journals *Social Science History, Sociological Imagination,* and the *Proceedings* of the international conference on the "Bosnian Paradigm."

This book is a publication of

Indiana University Press
601 North Morton Street
Bloomington, Indiana 47404-3797 USA

www.indiana.edu/~iupress

Telephone orders 800-842-6796
Fax orders 812-855-7931
Orders by email iuporder@indiana.edu

The paper used in this publication meets the minimum requirements of American National Standard for Information Sciences—Permanence of Paper for Printed Library Materials, ANSI Z39.48-1984.

Manufactured in the United States of America

Library of Congress Cataloging-in-Publication Data

Alvarez, Alex.
    Governments, citizens, and genocide : a comparative and interdisciplinary approach /
Alex Alvarez.
        p. cm.
    Includes bibliographical references and index.
    ISBN 0-253-33849-2 (cl : alk. paper)
        1. Genocide.   I. Title.

HV6322.7 .A58 2001
304.6′63—dc21

                                                          00-057501

1 2 3 4 5   06 05 04 03 02 01

For My Children

Ingrid, Joseph, and Astrid

May you live in a safer, saner world.

Contents

Acknowledgments

This book could not have been written without a great deal of personal and professional support, for which I am profoundly grateful.

I first wish to thank Susanna Maxwell, the Dean of the College of Social and Behavioral Sciences at Northern Arizona University, who has provided a tremendous amount of moral and material support for my work. I also want to express my gratitude to Ray Michalowski and Marilyn McShane, who in their capacity as Chairs of the Department of Criminal Justice were incredibly helpful and encouraging. They have also been instrumental in creating a departmental culture that is tremendously supportive of faculty research efforts. Ray, thanks for your time and insight. Marilyn, you are the most enthusiastic and giving person I have ever met; thanks for everything.

I also wish to extend my gratitude to Marilyn Grobschmidt at Indiana University Press for her assistance and work on behalf of this project. I also want to thank all others at Indiana University Press who helped make this book a reality. Special thanks to the copyeditor, Shoshanna Green, who did a remarkable and thorough job, and Jane Lyle and Sue Havlish for their able help. My appreciation also to Dr. Frank Chalk, for his time and effort in reviewing this manuscript. His comments and advice were outstanding.

Many friends and colleagues were generous with their time and helped out by reading various drafts of the manuscript or of different chapters. Their comments were invariably thought-provoking and informative. Specifically, I wish to recognize Dr. Phoebe Morgan, Dr. Barbara Perry, Dr. Margaret Vandiver, Dr. Marilyn McShane, Dr. Mark Beeman, Dr. Geeta Chowdry, Dr. Jeff Ferrell, Dr. Neil Websdale, Dr. Nancy Wonders, Dr. David O. Friedrichs, Jamie Carr, and Pamela Steen-Kurz, and give special thanks to Christiane Schubert for her excellent suggestions. They were invaluable. Thanks as well to the office staff at N.A.U., Ingrid, Cathy, Helena, Mary, Joanna, and Adam. You're the best!

I want to particularly recognize my friend and colleague Neil Websdale, a kindred spirit if ever there was one. Our discussions and conversations keep me sane. Thanks also to Mark Beeman, who helps me maintain perspective and balance. I wish to acknowledge my good buddy Mahesh Nalla for all his support and assistance over the years. I am also indebted to my close friend Ronet Bachman for her unconditional friendship. We have been through a lot together since graduate school.

I owe much to a man who has been a tremendous inspiration and role model for me. That man is my father, Leroy Alvarez. From him I learned my love of books, history, and learning. His love and support mean more to me than I can ever articulate. Thanks, Dad.

I am eternally grateful to my wife, Donna, whose love and strength are a never ending source of wonder for me. She is the strongest person I have ever met. I have learned that I do not accomplish anything alone. In a very real sense *my* accomplishments are *our* accomplishments. Donna, I love you.

Finally, thanks to my children, Ingrid, Joseph, and Astrid, who don't realize how much they have taught me. My love for them knows no boundaries.

Governments, Citizens, and Genocide

Introduction

The failure of the international community to tackle the problem of genocide is reflected by the failure of the academic community to contribute much to our understanding of the problem. The study of genocide has remained marginal to academic discourse.

—Michael Freeman[1]

Silence is the real crime against humanity.

—Sarah Berkowitz[2]

This book presents a comparative and interdisciplinary discussion of the crime of genocide. Given the increasing pervasiveness of genocide in this century, it is surprising that social scientists have so seldom applied their efforts to the study of this particular type of criminality. The social sciences, devoted as they are to the analysis of social phenomena, have much to offer the discourse on genocide. This is especially true of the discipline of criminology, since it is a scientific discipline that specifically and exclusively studies crime and criminals.

On the whole the social sciences have been largely blind and mute where genocide is concerned. In 1979, for example, Helen Fein surveyed eighty-two introductory sociology textbooks and found that most ignored the concept or at best briefly mentioned it in a paragraph or two.[3] More recently, Zygmunt Bauman admonished,

> When compared with the awesome amount of work accomplished by the historians, and the volume of soul searching among both Christian and Jewish theologians, the contributions of professional sociologists to Holocaust studies seems marginal and negligible. . . . This alarming fact has not yet been faced (much less responded to) by the sociologists.[4]

Even today, "sociological attention to this topic has, at best, grown from almost nonexistent to barely existent."[5] Herbert Hirsch echoes this comment when he asserts that social scientists either do not understand or do not accept the importance of genocide research.[6] While there have been a few noteworthy exceptions to this omission, genocide has remained largely outside the mainstream of contemporary social science.[7] This is surprising, to say the least.

Given the criminological posture toward crime and criminality, it is remarkable that no specific criminological explanations have been applied to genocide even though it has been defined as a crime by various organizations, such as the United Nations, since the 1940s. While various theoretical explanations have been applied to the analysis of genocide, almost none have referred to the large body of theory and research expressly developed to explain criminal acts and actors, even though genocide clearly falls into this category.[8] I raise this issue because I believe it to be of central importance in developing a more complete understanding of genocide. The failure of social scientists in general, and criminologists in particular, to address themselves to the study of genocide is not of significance only for scholars interested in abstract debates; rather, it has broad implications for the ways in which the public conceives and understands genocide. The failure of social scientists to develop a research agenda on genocide reveals much about common attitudes toward and preconceptions of genocide and crime.

Since genocide is social action, it involves the social construction of meaning. Max Weber suggested that "Action is social insofar as, by virtue of the subjective meaning attached to it by the acting individual (or individuals), it takes account of the behavior of others and is thereby oriented in its course."[9] Therefore, the ways in which genocide is portrayed by social scientists can serve to shape opinion and policy and in turn heighten concern and spur action. The scholarly analysis of genocide may assist in turning the empty rhetoric of "never again" into a promise and a reality. For example, criminologists have begun to recognize that our choice of behaviors to define and study as crime can dramatically affect popular perceptions and definitions of crime, and, consequently, social policy. Gregg Barak has recently argued that criminologists need to shape and guide mediated images of crime and crime control in a process he terms "newsmaking criminology."[10] According to Barak,

> Newsmaking criminology refers to criminologists' conscious efforts and activities in interpreting, influencing, or shaping the presentation of "newsworthy" items about crime and justice. More specifically, a newsmaking criminology attempts to demystify images of crime and punishment by locating the mass media portrayals of incidences of "serious" crimes in the context of all illegal and harmful activities; strives to affect public attitudes, thoughts, and discourses about crime and justice; . . . allows criminologists to come forth with their knowledge and to establish themselves as credible voices in the mass-mediated arena of policy formation; and asks of criminologists that they develop popularly based languages and technically based skills of communication for the purposes of participating in the mass-consumed ideology of crime and justice.[11]

In other words, newsmaking criminology seeks to inform and shape popular conceptions of crime and issues related to criminal justice. Inclusion of genocide as a substantive area of social science and criminological research will assist in this process of shaping understanding and increasing awareness of genocidal crimes. Conversely, failure to address this topic is not without consequences. Ray Surette points out that "A number of criminologists have stated that the media's ignoring of certain types of crimes and criminal cases is as damaging as what is actually reported."[12] This disregard, then, may in fact facilitate a diminished sense of the importance of genocide.

In some ways, the effect of this academic neglect may be comparable to the damage done by those who deny the Holocaust. While I am by no means suggesting a moral equivalency between those who, for various reasons, omit reference to genocide and those who actively work to mislead and repress truth, I am asserting that both behaviors have somewhat similar results. That is, the failure of social scientists to adequately address the study of genocide contributes to perceptions and attitudes that, through exclusion, minimize the importance and significance of genocide. This is essentially what Holocaust denial is all about. In the words of Smith, Markusen, and Lifton:

> by absolving the perpetrators of past genocides from responsibility for their actions and by obscuring the reality of genocide as a widely practiced form of state policy in the modern world, denial may increase the risk of future outbreaks of genocidal killing.[13]

When scholars actively deny genocide, the implications are even more dramatic. Smith, Markusen, and Lifton assert that

> Where scholars deny genocide, in the face of decisive evidence that it has occurred, they contribute to a false consciousness that can have the most dire reverberations. Their message, in effect, is . . . mass murder requires no confrontation, no reflection, but should be ignored, glossed over. In this way, scholars lend their considerable authority to the acceptance of this ultimate human crime. More than that, they encourage—indeed invite—a repetition of that crime. . . . By closing their minds to truth, that is, such scholars contribute to the deadly psychohistorical dynamic in which unopposed genocide begets new genocides.[14]

I therefore argue that the failure to study genocide, to call attention to this form of crime, to make conscious and self-conscious choices about the objects of research attention, results in a diminished sense of concern and urgency, thus facilitating its perpetration. Bruno Bettelheim once warned that "If we remain silent, then we perform exactly as the Nazis wanted: behave as if it never did happen."[15] Similarly, Herbert Hirsch argues that silence will ensure the repetition of genocidal crimes.[16] It seems that, in some ways, the behaviors that are not studied are as important as those that are. Totten and Parson note that

> Certain scholars and activists seem to have come to the conclusion that, if there is ever going to be any hope at all of stanching genocidal actions, then they (and not governments) are going to have to be the catalyst behind such hope.[17]

It is in this spirit that this book is written. There is no crime in the twentieth century that has been more costly, more devastating, and more global in its impact than genocide.

Explaining the Lack of Scholarly Attention

At this point it may be useful to explore the reasons for the unwillingness of the social sciences to tackle this issue, since the explanations reveal much, not only about social scientists, but about the general public as well. There are several possible explanations for the curious exclusion of genocide from the social science realm of inquiry. One possible explanation is that geno-cide is simply too overwhelming and complex a topic for many social scientists. Perhaps, as Peter Hayes suggests, they suffer from the

> apparent awe most researchers feel in the face of the Holocaust. Confronted by the extent and viciousness of the massacre, scholars have trouble finding words ade-quate to describing what happened, let alone analyses equal to accounting for it.[18]

This does not, however, explain the apparent willingness of scholars in other disciplines to study the "incomprehensible," nor does it explain why criminolo-gists in particular have often analyzed other monstrous crimes without appar-ent difficulty. Therefore, we must look elsewhere for an explanation. There seem to be several reasons for the apparent reluctance exhibited by social scientists and criminologists to study genocide.

The first reason relates to what Frank Williams has termed "the demise of the criminological imagination."[19] Borrowing and revising C. Wright Mills's term, Williams asserts that empirical scientism has put far more emphasis on measurement and technique than on theory. Williams explains that "we are more concerned with measurement itself than with speculation about the sub-stance being measured."[20] The process has become more important than the un-derlying reason for the process. He continues this line of reasoning and asserts,

> In short, empirical scientism has raised methodology and large datasets above theory development. Social science journals have become repositories of statistical analyses and methodological commentaries. The field itself has moved to spend a greater amount of time in evaluation of existing theory than was done at any other point in this century. Unfortunately, because of the inability to adequately opera-tionalize these existing theories, we have become discouraged with our pursuit of understanding: Originality has inversely suffered, and a great deal of interest in theory has been lost.[21]

If Williams's assessment is accurate, it may help explain why criminologists have focused predominantly on what have been perceived as more traditional crimes to the neglect of other crime types, such as genocide. Rather than wad-ing out into uncharted behavioral and theoretical waters, criminologists have stayed with the familiar and easily identifiable predatory crimes that have long been the staple of mainstream criminological research. Focused on mainstream street crimes such as robbery, rape, and burglary, criminologists have been con-tent to exclude more problematic behaviors, such as genocide.

It may also be that social scientists have chosen not to analyze genocide be-cause of a perception that it is a foreign phenomenon, exclusive to other socie-ties and times. Most scholars tend to focus solely or predominantly on social phenomena within their own countries. Some of this may be attributed to the difficulty of cross-national research, in which issues of definition and reporting make the work exceptionally difficult.[22] Part may also be a result of a natural ethnocentric focus among researchers who see the problems of their society as more relevant, interesting, or significant than those of other nations. Genocide, however, is not necessarily a foreign phenomenon. For American scholars, for example, history reveals clearly documented cases of genocide against various Native American tribes by European colonists and settlers.[23] In fairness, it should be noted that not all tribes were subjected to genocidal policies, nor was the U.S. government always genocidally inclined. Nevertheless, there are documented cases of certain tribes being deliberately infected by means of disease-laden blankets in what are rightly perceived to be some of the first instances of biological warfare.[24] Other tribes suffered from blatantly ethnocidal policies intended to destroy their culture, such as the practice of removing Indian children from their parents and placing them in boarding schools where they were forbidden to practice their native languages and customs.[25] The explicit goal of these schools was to "civilize" Indians through a process of forced assimilation. In short, the United States has in its history destroyed the lives and cultures of Indigenous peoples. Few anywhere can look to a past untainted by this crime. Treating genocide as some distant problem, foreign to the societies within which social scientists work, is hardly appropriate or accurate.

Additionally, genocide should be of relevance to most social observers in the modern age since events in one part of the world directly and indirectly impact the global community. As Alain Destexhe reminds us, "the consequence of a genocide always reaches beyond the target group and the country where it took place."[26] Again, to use the United States as an example, American troops serve in Bosnia as part of a multi-national peacekeeping force that emerged from the Dayton Peace Accords, which brought an end to the fighting in Bosnia. The United States military was very nearly deployed in Zaire in the wake of the Rwandan genocide, as the unrest spread to this neighboring country after large numbers of victims and perpetrators moved into refugee camps and undermined the stability of an already fragile society. More recently, the NATO bombing campaign in Kosovo and the subsequent deployment of ground troops provide further examples of the ways in which genocide and genocidal massacres can involve American interests and lives. Domestic and foreign policies pursued by governments everywhere affect the perpetration of genocide around the world. The U.S. government has often had economic interests in and political relations with states engaged in genocidal policies. In its zeal to protect the western hemisphere from communists, the United States has helped train the forces of pro-Western governments and often assisted them in eliminating perceived enemies. The U.S. Army School of the Americas, located in Fort Benning, Georgia, has trained many Central and South American military officers, including Anastasio Somoza; Manuel Noriega; the leader of the Salvadoran death squads, Roberto D'Aubuisson; and General Leopoldo Galtieri, one of the triumvirate during Argentina's "dirty war" against real and imagined enemies. This school taught not only counterinsurgency techniques but also methods of torture, murder, and extortion.[27] In places like Guatemala, American-trained troops have engaged in widespread massacres and human rights abuses that often have genocidal overtones, targeting as they do the Indigenous peoples of the region.[28] In Cambodia, the Khmer Rouge received aid and assistance from the United States after their regime was overthrown by the Vietnamese in the late 1970s. Even though the nature of the genocide perpetrated by the Khmer Rouge was by then well known, the United States saw them as an important check on Vietnamese power in southeast Asia and consequently felt justified in assisting this genocidal state.[29] The current violence against various Native tribes in the Amazon rain forest is being spurred on by many American business interests that, with the collaboration of local governments, regard the Indigenous peoples as an impediment to the economic exploitation of the area. These companies include Bethlehem Steel, Georgia Pacific, Texaco, Gulf Oil, U.S. Steel, Caterpillar, Westinghouse, and many other reputable corporations.[30] Clearly, genocide and related acts of violence are relevant, appropriate, and timely subjects that merit the attention of social scientists and criminologists, as well as the public at large.

Another reason for the academic neglect of genocide is the marginality of state or political crime to the public and scholarly debate on crime. Genocide is typically a formal or informal state policy, carried out by officials and representatives of that state. It is therefore distinct from many other types of crime in terms of the actors involved and the motivating factors. Importantly, state-perpetrated crime has not received the recognition that other crime categories have received. As Kenneth Tunnell points out, political crime "is one of the oldest types of crime but one of the least researched."[31] The majority of criminology and criminal justice texts devote only minimal and superficial attention to political crime, if it is covered at all.[32] The relatively new entrance of this subject into the discourse on crime may explain this lack of attention. Being so new, the concept of state criminality may fall outside of many criminologists' definitional framework for crime.

Because of the peculiar nature of state crime, in that it is perpetrated by a government and sanctified by law, many criminologists may find study of this type of criminality problematic and therefore unattractive as a substantive area of research. Along these lines, R. Wright and David Friedrichs specifically suggest that many criminal justice scholars are ideologically conservative in outlook and are predisposed to give greater weight to predatory street crime than to state criminality.[33] Genocide, falling as it does into this category, clearly suffers from this handicap as a field of study.

Last, at some level it may be that recognition of this issue demands a response that individuals are unwilling to give. As Markusen and Kopf have pointed out,

> Confronting the problem of state-sanctioned mass killing is often tantamount to facing the fact that one's own nation has engaged in it. It also generates the question of when detached scholarship is no longer sufficient and potentially risky political activism may become a moral imperative.[34]

In short, for the reasons discussed above, the study of genocide has remained largely outside of the mainstream of social science and criminological thought, and this book is intended to help remedy this state of affairs.

Genocide in the Context of Murder

This absence of scholarly criminological attention to genocide is somewhat ironic when we consider that killing has been a central concern of criminology, in such contexts as criminal homicide,[35] justifiable homicide,[36] serial killing,[37] and the death penalty.[38] More recently, criminologists have even addressed themselves to political assassinations.[39] This body of work, it should be noted, has contributed substantially to our understanding of the causes and correlates of violent crime, and often guides social policy aimed at ameliorating the individual and structural precipitants of criminal violence. Clearly evident is a primary focus on interpersonal and individualistic killing rather than collective or group murder. Exclusive or near exclusive focus on discrete acts of lethal violence, however, engenders a fairly narrow perception of criminal violence and serves to obscure the criminal nature of much collective killing, especially that perpetrated by government organizations or their representatives. This atomistic emphasis conceals many of the structural and social mechanisms that contribute to group violence and fosters an understanding of killing predicated on unique pathologies and aberrations. In other words, we become predisposed to perceive killers as individual actors who are abnormal psychos, deviants, or, as James Q. Wilson characterizes them, "wicked people."[40] This impression obscures the reality behind much killing. While psychopathic killers do participate in genocide, they are far outnumbered among genocidal killers by people whose psychological processes are normal. The planners and perpetrators of genocide—bureaucrats, professionals, public officials, military and political leaders—number in the thousands, and it is difficult to characterize all these men and women as psychologically abnormal or pathological. Hannah Arendt's reference to the "banality of evil" perfectly captures the uninspired and mundane nature of many genocidal killers.

Killers, then, even mass murderers, may in fact be unremarkable people set apart only by their lethal activities. The traditional criminological emphasis on individual killers obscures both the normality of many who kill and the communal nature of much deadly behavior. The role of organizations, collectives, and governments in the production of mass violence is simply too important an issue to continue to ignore. Markusen and Kopf assert that

> Of all the problems confronting humankind during the remaining years of the twentieth century and into the twenty-first, we believe that none is more urgently in need of solution than the deliberate killing of masses of defenseless people.[41]

Genocide can rightly be considered one of the most devastating crimes facing the world today. No matter how we calculate it, whether in terms of human suffering and misery, or economic dislocation and loss, genocide ranks as the most destructive of modern crimes.

The social science literature, given its insights into governments, organizations, deviance, criminality, and violence, has much to offer the discourse on genocide. More than that, social scientists can also contribute to the analysis of genocide by helping shape popular and legal perceptions of genocide as a significant social problem and crime. By this I do not mean to suggest that most people perceive genocide to be legitimate. Instead, I believe that an interdisciplinary analysis of genocide can bring more urgent attention to genocide as a major problem in the modern age. We must move this crime into the forefront of public consciousness, rather than allow it to be perceived as a foreign problem or a historical memory of no real significance.

In this book, I examine genocide through the lenses of various perspectives that are helpful in explaining the characteristics, processes, and functions of different types of genocide. This approach is informed by a wide variety of social science research from a number of different disciplines, including criminology, sociology, psychology, and political science. Insights from these areas of study allow a new appreciation for the complexity and workings of this type of crime and assist in understanding the ways in which genocide exists at different levels of social organization.

It is helpful to examine genocide with reference to three related spheres of influence. First, genocide is a type of political crime. Therefore, certain elements and qualities of genocide can be explored and clarified through a discussion of the role of the state in perpetrating it. Second, much of genocide is carried out within bureaucratic institutions, which typically serve as its logistical support structure. Because of this, the literature on organizational crime can also help explain certain facets of genocide. Third and last, specific criminological theories about the process of criminality help us understand how individuals come to commit predatory crime. These also allow us to explore how individuals come to participate in genocide. These three levels of examination are closely integrated with one another and are all essential to the explanation of genocide. The state provides the impetus, the ideology, and the resources. This genocidal impulse is in turn disseminated through the various bureaucratic organizations that translate the concept of genocide into specific practice. Last, it is the individual who ultimately acts upon these directives and assignments and turns genocide into a reality. Exploration of genocide at these three distinct yet interconnected levels provides a comprehensive overview of many of its key issues.

The first chapter of this book is designed to provide the framework for the subsequent analysis of genocide. I first discuss the increasing prevalence and lethality of modern genocides and the ways in which they are often simultaneously comparable and distinct. Additionally, the human dimension of genocide is explored through a discussion of victims, perpetrators, and bystanders.

In chapter 2 I briefly review the history of genocide, focusing on its prevalence from the distant past to the modern age. The main focus, however, is on the difficulties of defining genocide. Much of this section involves a critical review of the major contending definitions that have been put forward by various genocide scholars. The chapter culminates in a discussion of the elements common to the various definitions and how they relate to a comparative analysis of genocide.

Chapter 3 focuses on the political nature of genocide. I point out that genocide is a form of state criminality and that it is important to recognize the role of sovereignty and nationalism in facilitating this crime. The chapter considers the role of law in perpetrating genocide and the relationship of genocide to war, and concludes with a discussion of the myths of primitive tribalism so endemic to news coverage of genocide.

In chapter 4 I examine the institutional context within which all genocidal killers operate. Genocide does not take place just in isolated death camps and villages; instead, much of the functioning of genocide is enabled by various institutions and bureaucracies throughout society. This chapter, therefore, comprises an attempt to explain the participation of bureaucrats and functionaries through a discussion of the organizational mechanisms that facilitate such engagement.

Chapter 5 focuses on the internal adjustments made by people who participate in genocide. I examine the ways in which individual attitudes and justifications are created and utilized to enable ordinary men and women to contribute to genocide.

The last chapter provides a summary of the lessons learned and their implications for the future of genocide. Specifically, I review various strategies of detection and intervention. The role of international organizations in preventing and punishing the crime of genocide is also discussed, as well as the international tribunals for the former Yugoslavia and Rwanda.

1 The Age of Genocide

... something happened in the twentieth century that made it morally and psychologically possible to realize dreams of destructiveness that had previously been confined to fantasy.

—Richard L. Rubenstein[1]

Camus called the twentieth century an age of murder, but it is, more precisely, an age of politically sanctioned mass murder, of collective, premeditated death intended to serve the ends of the state.

—Roger Smith[2]

If war is, as Alfred Nobel suggested, "the horror of all horrors, and the greatest of all crimes," then the crime of genocide must surely be its terrible twin. While genocide, or the attempted destruction of a population group, has been a deadly companion to human society for most of recorded history, it has accelerated its locomotive pace and efficiency during this century, especially in the last thirty years. Since 1968 genocides and genocidal massacres have tripled in internal conflicts, and occur so frequently in the present era they may be seen as the norm rather than the exception.[3] More and more, it seems, genocide is the preferred method for destroying perceived enemies. In this century alone, many millions of people have been murdered in genocidal actions across the globe. While some have suggested that the twentieth century should be called the age of total war, it should more properly be referred to as the age of genocide, since the genocides of this century have killed more than four times as many people as all the wars and revolutions of the same time period combined.[4] Even though the twentieth century is often characterized in terms of technological advancement, it is more accurately and appropriately described as an age of increasing lethality for both combatants and noncombatants alike. In short, genocide is a practice in common use today. Omer Bartov puts it this way:

The mechanized, rational, impersonal, and sustained mass destruction of human beings, organized and administered by states, legitimized and set into motion by scientists and jurists, sanctioned and popularized by academics and intellectuals, has become a staple of our civilization, the last, perilous, and often repressed heritage of the millennium.[5]

Specific examples from the modern era abound.

Twentieth-Century Genocide

The first recognizable outbreak of genocide in this century began in 1915 during the First World War, when between six hundred thousand and two million Armenians were killed in Turkey. Long persecuted and politically and socially marginalized, the members of the Armenian minority were vulnerable scapegoats for many of Turkey's ills. After the Ottoman government was overthrown by the Young Turks, the new regime targeted the Armenian population for destruction as enemies and opponents of Turkish nationalism. In an orchestrated series of mass arrests, deportations, and massacres, the three-thousand-year-old Armenian population of Turkey was largely destroyed.[6]

Clearly the most well known example of genocide in the twentieth century is the Nazi government's attempt to "cleanse" the greater German Reich of Jews and other "undesirables" during the 1940s through the deportation and murder of roughly six to eight million Jews, Gypsies, and Slavs in what became widely known as the Holocaust.[7] Less well known is the Nazis' implementation of a covert euthanasia program in the 1930s, known as the T4 project, which killed several thousand mentally and physically handicapped German citizens.[8] This practice of killing those who were defined as *Lebensunwertes Lebens,* or "life unworthy of life," served as a model for the Holocaust. This program, the first to experiment with gassing, was halted after widespread protest by German clergy and citizens.[9] One bishop's letter to Wilhelm Frick, Germany's interior minister, is representative of these remonstrations:

> What conclusions will the younger generation draw when it realizes that human life is no longer sacred to the state? Cannot every outrage be excused on the grounds that the elimination of another was of advantage to the person concerned? There can be no stopping once one starts down this decline. God does not permit people to mock Him. Either the National Socialist State must recognize the limits which God has laid down, or it will favor a moral decline and carry the state down with it.[10]

One wonders whether the subsequent Holocaust could have taken place if concerned citizens and religious leaders had taken a similarly strong stand. However, minimal opposition to the persecution of their Jewish neighbors was forthcoming.

The Holocaust itself remains a horrific example of the deadly efficiency that modern societies can achieve when bureaucratic methods and science are harnessed to ideologies of extermination. It stands apart from other genocides in terms of its organization, scale, and purpose.[11] Importantly, the Nuremberg trials that followed the end of the war provided the legal and philosophical basis for international law regarding crimes against humanity, and for the first time brought the crime of genocide to the forefront of global public consciousness.[12] While it was hoped that the trials would make a reality of the slogan "never again," more recent examples reveal that genocide has instead become a defining feature of the post-Holocaust century.

In the 1970s, for example, the Kampuchean Khmer Rouge regime killed between one and two million of their own citizens in an abortive and disastrous attempt to create a radically new society. In their efforts to purify Cambodian society racially, socially, ideologically, and politically, the Khmer Rouge engineered the destruction of populations from almost every social category, including not only politicians and military leaders of the former government, but also business leaders, journalists, students, and professionals such as doctors, lawyers, and teachers, as well as ethnic Vietnamese, Chinese, and Muslim Chams. Eventually, after running out of enemies, the party turned on itself in a series of deadly internecine purges in which many former perpetrators themselves became victims.

Even as recently as 1994, between five hundred thousand and one million Rwandan Tutsis were slaughtered by their Hutu neighbors in a genocidal spasm featured on the evening news and in news magazines. In some ways the sequel to the earlier and adjacent Burundian genocide of the early 1970s, which also involved Hutus and Tutsis, the Rwandan genocide erupted in the middle of a civil war after the assassination of the country's Hutu president, Habyarimana.[13] Almost immediately after his death widespread massacres were organized in communities throughout Rwanda, sparking a mass exodus into neighboring states as thousands of Rwandan Tutsis struggled to flee the butchery. Ultimately losing the civil war, many Hutu perpetrators subsequently fled into the refugee camps previously occupied by their former victims.[14]

To this list of well-known examples of twentieth-century destruction we can add the Great Terror of Stalin's Soviet Union during the 1930s, which according to some estimates claimed approximately 20 million lives;[15] Iraq's campaigns against the Kurds;[16] the destruction of the Herreros in South West Africa;[17] the extermination of various Indigenous peoples in Central and South America;[18] and Bosnia's ordeal after the disintegration of Yugoslavia. By any account, the twentieth century, this supposedly modern and civilized era, has been notable for extreme brutality. For millions, this century has been a Hobbesian period of "continual fear and danger of violent death."[19] It is rather ironic that in an age when many human beings can expect to live longer and healthier lives through scientific and medical advances, they are also more likely to be killed off before that increased potential life span is attained. Richard Rubenstein summarizes this irony well:

> As fewer men have fallen prey to such natural ills as the plague and epidemic, the technology of human violence has taken up much of the slack. Those whom nature did not kill before their time were often slain by their fellow men.[20]

It will be sad indeed if the twentieth century, for all its advances and achievements, is remembered more for its extreme lethality than for any other accomplishment.

The Similarity of Genocide

All of these examples of genocide are striking, not only for their differences, but for their similarities as well. For example, in August of 1992, when the first photographs of the Bosnian detention centers appeared, it was immediately apparent that concentration camps had been resurrected on European soil. The pictures from Omarska, Manjača, and Trnopolje showed emaciated prisoners, many with shaven heads, peering through barbed-wire fences. These images brought to mind the Nazi concentration and death camps that were such a prevalent feature of the Holocaust. This impression was only heightened when the fact that the Muslim inmates were routinely starved, tortured, and executed by their Serb captors became widely known. While the parallels between the Bosnian and the Nazi camps are powerful, it is important to note that the Bosnian camps were not death camps, like Auschwitz, exclusively designed to kill large numbers of people. The Bosnian detention camps served a multiplicity of goals, and the killing and torture were much more random and haphazard. Nevertheless, the resemblance between the Bosnian camps and the Nazi concentration camps (not extermination camps) is remarkable.

Even though they occurred at different times, in different places, and for different reasons, and had different perpetrators and victims, the Bosnian and Nazi genocides are remarkably alike in some important ways. The propaganda that dehumanizes the enemy, the drunkenness of many of the soldiers and militia members, the involvement of the state, the active participation and complicity of many ordinary citizens are all common features not only of these two examples, but of genocide in general.

Each case also contributes at some level to subsequent genocides. Hitler used the Armenian genocide not only as a model, but as a lesson in the indifference of the world,[21] while Slobodan Milošević repeated the tactics of ethnic cleansing developed in Bosnia to devastating effect in Kosovo. These transcultural and transhistorical elements suggest that a comparative social science–based analysis can be a useful vehicle for developing further understandings of genocide.

While each episode of genocide is certainly unique, differing in scale, ideology, and methodology, most also illustrate commonalities that can be meaningfully related to each other to produce a more generalized understanding of genocide. As Robert Melson writes,

> The point of such comparison is not to diminish the events themselves, certainly not to relativize the crimes of the perpetrators, but rather to try to shed light on the empirical conditions, the underlying pattern of empirical similarity, that led to genocide in the past and may lead to it in the future.[22]

If our objective is to truly understand genocide in order to work toward preventing its recurrence, we must generate understandings that recognize consistent elements of and precursors to this type of crime. Without identifying generalizable characteristics of and antecedents to genocide, the world community can only react to genocidal crimes, rather than develop a more proactive and preventive approach.

This comparative stance is contested by particularists who maintain that the Holocaust is unique and cannot be compared to other examples of genocide. Various scholars of the Holocaust, such as Deborah Lipstadt and Steven Katz, to name two of the more prominent advocates of this position, argue that because of its scale, lethality, and intent, the Holocaust is fundamentally different from all other examples of genocide and cannot be meaningfully compared to other examples of mass killing.[23] As well as asserting its uniqueness, advocates for this position contend that comparisons diminish the suffering experienced by European Jewry and trivialize this singular event in human history. Similar to this position is the viewpoint that the Holocaust can only be understood spiritually or metaphysically, or perhaps not at all.[24] The social sciences, from this viewpoint, can only confuse and detract from any real understanding of the Holocaust. This argument, however, ignores the reality that all genocides, including the Holocaust, share a variety of precursors, ideologies, and structural and behavioral traits, and yet also differ in the specific details of the killing. All genocides are simultaneously unique and analogous. The similarities and dissimilarities can be equally instructive in understanding how genocides arise, how they function, and, perhaps, how they can be prevented.[25]

Explanations of Genocide

Considering the scope and prevalence of genocide, our understanding of this crime is surprisingly limited. The literature that is available on genocide tends to be fragmentary and incomplete, resulting in fragmentary and incomplete knowledge of the causes and correlates of genocide. Research on genocide has often tended to be autobiographical,[26] journalistic, as most of the recent work on Bosnia has been,[27] or purely historical, such as much of the literature on the Holocaust.[28] While this body of work is often extremely descriptive and powerful, it is typically atheoretical and lacks a comparative viewpoint that allows for the identification of consistent elements among different examples of genocide. Recognizing common reference points is a necessary prerequisite for more detailed studies of genocide, especially if one is interested in explaining the prevalence and nature of genocide in this century.

Attempts to study genocide have approached the issue from a variety of disciplines and theoretical stances, and many of these disparate attempts depend on some common elements. Among these can be identified the themes of power, distancing, dehumanization, authorization, and psychological adaptation.[29] Whether overtly or implicitly, genocide scholars usually tend to reference one or more of these concepts in their work.

Power refers to the ability of a government to concentrate force, suppress or neutralize dissent, and perpetrate genocide. Rummel, for example, believes that the primary causative factor in the commission of this crime is power and asserts that genocide is committed almost exclusively by totalitarian states, which, by their very nature, operate without constraints on their exercise of power. He suggests that "as the arbitrary power of a regime increases massively, that is, as we move from democratic through authoritarian to totalitarian regimes, the amount of killing jumps by huge multiples."[30] In short, genocide is a function of power. The more power a state possesses, the more it is able and willing to kill on a large scale. The worst genocides of the twentieth century were all perpetrated by dictatorial states in which the government controlled almost all aspects of social, political, and economic life. Lenin, the architect of the Soviet state, once asserted that "The scientific concept of dictatorship means nothing but this: power without limit, resting directly upon force, restrained by no law, absolutely unrestricted by rules."[31] Democratic states, by contrast, only commit genocide when they act in secrecy and circumvent institutionalized constraints on power. Democracies generally have too many checks and balances to allow the excessive consolidation of authority.

Distancing refers to the physical and psychological separation that is fostered between the participants and their victims. Dave Grossman writes about four different types of distance that facilitate aggressive behavior. These are cultural distance, such as racial and ethnic differences that permit the killer to dehumanize the victim; moral distance, the vengeful or vigilante actions and intense belief in moral superiority associated with many civil wars; social distance, the perception of a particular class as less than human; and mechanical distance, which includes the video-game quality of killing through a computer monitor or some other electronic or optical device that conceals the humanity of the victims.[32]

Various other mechanisms are also utilized to increase the separation between victim and killer. For example, some scholars focus primarily on the bureaucratic aspects of genocide and contend that the efficiency of rational bureaucratic organizations, coupled with the depersonalization and dehumanization they engender, is crucial in facilitating genocide.[33] In other words, the more that functionaries are able to physically and psychologically remove themselves from the reality of mass murder, the easier it is for them to perform their jobs. As the sociologist Max Weber illustrated, by their very nature bureaucracies serve to remove the human element from the equation.[34] Hence the increasing compartmentalization of function, the use of misleading and comforting euphemisms, the diffusion of responsibility, and the reference to authority so common in genocide.

This process can be seen as a form of routinization, in which the details and the process of the work become more important than the meaning and the outcome of the activity.[35] The ordinariness and mundane nature of most of the discrete steps (i.e., paperwork, scheduling trains, etc.) tend to hide the horrible reality of the consequences of genocidal killing. As Fred Katz suggests:

Horrendous deeds may be performed by persons who are addressing themselves to innocuous immediate problems. A person may do horrible things without paying attention to the horror of the deeds, instead focusing only on an aspect of the situation that is relatively benign.[36]

Other genocide scholars focus less on bureaucratic distancing and more on the psychological mechanisms for distancing. For most of those actually involved in the act of killing, the task of mass murder grows easier and easier as they become increasingly inured to it. This distancing process is not a physical one, like the bureaucratic detachment from the actual killing, but a psychological distancing brought about through brutalization, numbing, and the dehumanization of the intended victims. For many, initial revulsion and squeamishness soon change to a calloused indifference to the suffering being inflicted.

The theme of dehumanization concerns the assignation of derogatory labels to a class or group of people, categorizing them as degraded, bestial, or subhuman. Sociologically speaking, this has the effect of removing the people so labeled from the in-group, placing them instead in an out-group.[37] Members of out-groups are generally perceived as inferior, and are more easily stereotyped, scapegoated, and stigmatized. Hostility toward them also serves to strengthen in-group solidarity as members unite against a common enemy. Because this process involves stripping the intended victims of both identity and membership in community, it diminishes or removes any moral or normative opposition to killing them. This process of dehumanization serves to remove people from the "universe of obligation," to use Helen Fein's term.[38]

Another important element that fosters genocide is authorization.[39] This refers to the legitimation of the killing by representatives of the group or state. Regardless of an individual's beliefs or preferences, authorization invariably encourages compliance. As Kelman and Hamilton summarize, "When acts of violence are explicitly ordered, implicitly encouraged, tacitly approved, or at least permitted by legitimate authorities, people's readiness to commit or condone them is enhanced."[40] The theory of authorization is largely derived from the research of Stanley Milgram, who described how ordinary people are willing to behave in overtly cruel and harmful ways when ordered or asked to do so by authority figures.[41] In Milgram's own words:

> The person who, with inner conviction, loathes stealing, killing, and assault may find himself performing these acts with relative ease when commanded by authority. Behavior that is unthinkable in an individual who is acting on his own may be executed without hesitation when carried out under orders.[42]

This theme is consistently cited as an important element for facilitating participation in genocide.[43]

The theme of psychological adaptation is best illustrated by the concept of "doubling" developed by Lifton and Markusen.[44] Doubling refers to a type of psychological dissociation that serves as a "form of adaptation, by means of which people remain sane in the service of social madness."[45] Specifically, it refers to the development of a second self that is not normatively at odds with the genocidal environment. The two selves function somewhat autonomously and allow the participant in genocide to function in two irreconcilable normative worlds: the "normal" and the genocidal. As Lifton and Markusen write,

> The psychological mechanism of doubling is a key to understanding how Nazi doc-tors managed to do the work of killing. Doubling involved the formation of an Auschwitz self, by which one internalized many of the patterns and assumptions of the Auschwitz environment: the reversals of healing and killing, the operative Nazi biomedical vision, the extreme numbing that rendered killing no longer killing, struggles with omnipotence (deciding who would live or die) and impotence (be-ing a cog in a powerful machine), maintaining a medical identity while killing, and somehow finding meaning in the environment.[46]

Arguing that doubling is both a conscious and a subconscious choice that cir-cumvents normative prohibitions to genocide, Lifton and Markusen contend that it is the process of doubling that allows participants to avoid confronting the moral and ethical polarity of their work and their normative self-image.

While other powerful explanations are sometimes discussed, those listed above seem to be among the most widely accepted and influential explanations. Each, however, has its limitations, and our understanding of genocide is there-fore incomplete. While the legal, political, logistical, and human components of genocide have all been explored in great detail, they have usually been studied separately and in isolation from each other. For example, while several studies of genocide explicitly call attention to the role of the state in perpetrating this crime, they tend to ignore or minimize the other levels at which genocide also operates.[47] While it is true that the state provides the impetus for genocide, it is also true that genocide must be operationalized and implemented by various organizations and bureaucracies throughout society that have the structural tools to turn the ideological goals of the state into specific policies and behav-iors. Understanding the role of organizations in the perpetration of this crime is therefore important for understanding the etiology of genocide. It is also nec-essary to recognize that genocide requires the cooperation and participation of individuals who are called upon to carry out the destruction of other human beings. Consequently, an analysis of genocide must also investigate the actions of individuals. Genocide operates in all these spheres, and in the absence of unified and comprehensive explanations of genocide our understanding of this phenomenon will remain distorted and incomplete. We must remember Free-man's words:

> Genocide is a social process, initiated and implemented by various social agents in structured social positions. It consists of many different actions by many different agents located in different positions in the social structure.[48]

Recognizing this fact allows a more integrated and holistic approach to the study of this phenomenon.

The Human Element

Victims

Genocide represents crime, violence, and human suffering on a scale that is truly difficult to comprehend. We are left with raw numbers to describe events because words appear to be wholly inadequate. Words like tragedy, horror, terror, atrocity, and murder do not fully encompass the meaning and experience of genocide. While he is alluding to World War One, Samuel Hynes could also be speaking of genocide when he writes,

> Perhaps "tragic" is the wrong word for such mass-produced carnage; can forty million dead and wounded men be tragic, collectively? Probably not. Nor can they be romantic, individually or collectively. Perhaps there is no adequate vocabulary for suffering on that scale, but only the huge numbers.[49]

Yet even numbers lose their meaning and impact in the face of such overwhelming pain. Stalin's ironic and cynical remark that "one death is a tragedy, while a million are a statistic" certainly applies to genocide.[50] A single victim, or even several, can be personalized, and through this emotional attachment we understand the waste and loss that their death represents. When they are seen in the aggregate, however, it is all too easy to lose sight of their humanity, and, as Tzvetan Todorov says, "the sheer number depersonalizes the victims and as a result desensitizes us to their fate. One death is a cause for sorrow; a million deaths is a news item."[51] A victim, in other words, has a name, a face, a past, hopes and aspirations for the future. In an amorphous mass, however, the victims become nameless and faceless statistics. The humanity of the victims is lost in the vastness of the crime. Yet this is precisely what must be guarded against. We must strive to remember the human dimension of these crimes, and not forget that these numbers, aggregated into sterile and abstract totals, represent human lives brutally and tragically cut short for ideological, economic, and political purposes.

The victims of genocide are killed, not for what they have done, but for who they are. Individuals are murdered simply because they fall into social categories that others have decided to eliminate. Scapegoated, subjected to dehumanizing propaganda, segregated, tortured, and killed, members of targeted groups are members of socially damned categories. Genocide targets identity rather than behavior. A member of the Soviet secret police put it this way:

> We don't make war against any people in particular. We are exterminating the bourgeoisie as a class. In your investigations don't look for documents and pieces of evidence about what the defendant has done, whether in deed or in speaking or acting against Soviet authority. The first question you should ask him is what class he comes from, what are his roots, his education, his training, and his occupation.[52]

Robert Waite points out that Jews were seen in essentially the same terms. "The Jews were killed not because they had *done* anything but merely because they existed—because they had been born. Jews were criminal *by definition*."[53] The same is true for all victims of genocide. Whether Jew, Muslim, Armenian, or Tutsi, the victims' only crime consists of belonging to a stigmatized class of people. This is not to suggest, however, that they are perceived as innocent. In all cases perpetrators portray the victims as deserving their fate because of various imagined crimes. Not only was the mere existence of Jews a crime against the Germans, since they were by definition parasites and subhuman, but they were also alleged to be involved in a worldwide conspiracy to destroy the German race. The Hutus portrayed the Tutsis as seeking to establish a dictatorship of the minority, dedicated to the enslavement of the Hutu majority. In this contested terrain of identity the targeted groups are portrayed as having brought about their own destruction.

In these situations, self-definition is irrelevant. Before the Holocaust, German Jews were among the most secular and assimilated in Europe, perceiving themselves to be German first and foremost, and only "rediscovered" their Jewishness in the crisis of marginalization and extermination.[54] The Tutsi victims of the Rwandan genocide were often identifiable only by a government-issued identity card that specified to which group they ostensibly belonged.[55] For Bosnian Muslims their religion was more a secular national identity than anything else, and often they could be distinguished from Serbs only by name, not by behavior, practice, or belief.[56] In other words, they defined themselves "not as Muslims, but as Bosnians or Yugoslavs or Europeans."[57] One Bosnian Muslim put it this way:

> I never thought of myself as a Muslim. I don't know how to pray, I never went to mosque, I'm European, like you. I do not want the Arab world to help us, I want Europe to help us. But now, I do have to think of myself as a Muslim, not in a religious way, but as a member of a people. Now we are faced with obliteration, I have to understand what it is about me and my people they wish to obliterate.[58]

In other words, victims of genocide are defined not as persons, but as members of a category. This definition is dehumanizing because it disregards individual attributes and characteristics, based as it is on the assumption that all people within a certain category possess specific qualities. There is no such thing as individual worth, since a person is not identified except in terms of perceived group qualities. Divorced from an individual identity in the eyes of the persecutors, they are simply defined as the enemy, and "To be classified as an enemy is enough to be excluded from humanity."[59]

The process of systematically selecting people for murder because of characteristics ascribed to them is all the more abhorrent because it is often performed by friends and neighbors. As Rezak Hukanović, a survivor of the Bosnian camps at Omarska and Manjača, relates, "It was astonishing to witness the chameleonlike transformation of former friends and acquaintances as they turned into crazed servants of the new authority."[60] One Bosnian Muslim survivor of the camp at Manjača found that "there, unbelievably, my former friends were actually beating us. . . . In fact my best friend, Drago Kovač, . . . was a guard at the camp."[61] In the same way that individual criminal homicide is typically perpetrated by assailants who are known to their victims, so too is genocide often committed by people with a connection to their victims.

This dreadful intimacy compounds the horror of the killing because it overthrows the connections that tie us to the social world. At a fundamental level, human beings are social creatures who depend on others to satisfy their physical and emotional needs. Yet during genocide, those bonds of care and support are transformed into networks of destruction. In other words, people who are normally counted upon for help, support, companionship, and sociability (all the things expected from friends, neighbors, and communities), are the ones who become the willing perpetrators of genocide. In Rwanda, "Hutu teachers commonly denounced their Tutsi pupils to the militia or even directly killed them themselves."[62] In former times, these teachers educated, nurtured, comforted, and mentored these children, and yet during the genocide, they helped murder their charges. The journalist Peter Maass writes of events in Bosnia, "They were killed by Serbs who had been their friends, people who had helped harvest their fields the previous autumn, people with whom they shared adolescent adventures and secrets."[63] Similarly, one Serbian commander remarked of the people he was killing, "Before the war we played football with them. Now we throw mortar bombs."[64] During the siege of Sarajevo, Serb soldiers involved in sniper and artillery attacks on that city would call Muslim friends in Sarajevo to see how they were doing and reminisce about old times.[65]

How is this possible? How can the social bonds that are so important to the creation and maintenance of community be subverted to such destructive ends? Are we all capable of committing these outrageous acts against human beings who are often also friends and neighbors, or is there something different about those who carry out such atrocities? In other words, what kind of people become participants in genocide? What is it that allows some people to assist in and carry out the destruction of fellow citizens, neighbors, and even friends?

Perpetrators

While it has been popular to demonize the perpetrators of genocide as monsters and sadists, this is an inaccurate portrayal that is not supported by the facts. It is, however, very understandable. Defining genocidal killers as beasts who are fundamentally different from us is perhaps easier and more comfortable for us to accept. In the face of the seemingly inexplicable human capacity to inflict horror upon fellow human beings, it is profoundly disturbing to recognize that those inflicting the suffering are similar to you. However, as writers such as Bruno Bettelheim suggest, this stigmatized perception is little more than a psychological defense mechanism,[66] and as one scholar says,

we fear discovering that the evil of the camps is not alien to the human race; . . . these evils are not as foreign to us as we might wish, which is precisely why we refuse to admit the fact and instead gravitate so readily to explanations rooted in the notion of monstrousness.[67]

Primo Levi, a survivor of Auschwitz, summarized well the nature of that fear, stating that he felt "guilty at being a man, because men had built Auschwitz," and his recognition that he belonged to the same species that had victimized him and countless other innocents caused him profound distress.[68] In short, the reality of genocide is that it is typically planned and implemented by "normal" people. While some of the participants are clearly sadistic and enjoy the pain and misery they inflict upon their hapless victims, the evidence suggests that these sadists are more the exception than the rule. During the Holocaust, for example, the psychopaths were far outnumbered by the bland bureaucrats and functionaries who quietly and efficiently went about the business of social and political change through the murder of millions. Primo Levi emphasizes that

> We must remember that these faithful followers, among them the diligent execu-
> tors of inhuman orders, were not born torturers, were not (with a few exceptions)
> monsters: they were ordinary men. Monsters exist, but they are too few in number
> to be truly dangerous. More dangerous are the common men, the functionaries
> ready to believe and to act without asking questions.[69]

While the "normality" of most participants is by now fairly well accepted by scholars of genocide, countless popular books and movies continue to perpetu-ate a false image of the perpetrators as fiendish monsters.[70] It is possible, how-ever, to illustrate the "normality" of those who engage in genocidal behavior by pointing out the scale of genocide and some common characteristics of the people who perpetrate it.

Genocide is typically planned and implemented by thousands of people. Daniel Goldhagen, for example, argues that the Holocaust is best understood as a German national project.[71] The deportation and subsequent murder of mil-lions of people was a massive undertaking that strained the resources and lo-gistical abilities of the German Reich. It could not have taken place without the active participation of thousands of Germans and non-Germans, who both di-rectly and indirectly facilitated the process of mass death. Others have pointed out that virtually all strata of German society were involved in the apparatus of the Holocaust.[72] They came from a variety of careers, religious backgrounds, and economic classes, and represented a cross-section of German society. Even the legal, medical, and scientific communities actively aided and abetted the process of extermination.[73] It would be nearly impossible to characterize all of these educated, successful, well-respected people as abnormal or psychopathic. Many became involved in the apparatus of annihilation simply because they held jobs that became necessary for the implementation of the death process. Since participation was such a pervasive phenomenon, it should not be defined as deviant or abnormal. There were simply too many who participated for them to be defined as such.

Similarly, collectivizing Soviet society during the 1930s involved the destruction of the Kulaks, and as James Mace points out,

> Transforming society by force . . . requires the mobilization and motivation of mass constituencies who could be called upon to do the regime's will. . . . In order to expropriate *Kulaks,* enforce collectivization, and take possession of agricultural produce, the authorities mobilized anyone they could.[74]

Trade unions, workers, bureaucrats, activists, peasants, soldiers, police, and many other elements of Soviet society were activated and used in the genocide of the Kulaks. One survivor of the camps stated that the entire society was implicated when he suggested that the guilty ones included "practically the whole country—one part denouncing, one part judging, a third shooting people, a fourth guarding the camps."[75] No matter which genocide we examine, whether the Armenian, Rwandan, or Bosnian, all similarly required widespread cooperation from large segments of society.

The evidence for normality also includes the fact that before and after genocides, most of the perpetrators tend to live unremarkable, law-abiding, family-centered lives. If they were all indeed sociopaths, one would not expect them to live lives so completely devoid of aberration and deviance before and after their genocidal crimes. Many perpetrators of the Holocaust did exceedingly well in post-war German civil society, rising to high positions in business and politics. As Raphael Lemkin wrote,

> The striking fact emerged at Nuremberg and at the subsequent trials that most of the defendants had come from good homes, had had good education and somehow continued to convey the impressions of normal good citizens. They did not look like fiends and they used the words "good" and "bad" as if they had the same meanings for them as for their listeners.[76]

In fact, according to one estimate, of the SS men responsible for daily operations of the Nazi death camps, no more than ten percent could be diagnosed as having gross psychological aberrations.[77] The instigators and perpetrators of the genocide in Bosnia included university professors, lawyers, and medical doctors.[78] Radovan Karadžić, the Bosnian Serb leader who bears a great deal of responsibility for that country's genocide, was a well-educated member of the professional classes. He was not only a psychiatrist, but a poet and writer as well. It is extremely unlikely that all of these successful professionals are abnormal or pathological individuals.

Nor can one claim, although some have argued otherwise, that genocidal behavior is a problem unique to some particular group. For example, Daniel Goldhagen argues that what allowed the Holocaust to take place was a brand of anti-Semitism unique to Germany that he termed eliminationist.[79] It must be remembered, however, that while the Germans were the prime instigators and participants, they were often assisted by members of many other nations who believed in what the Nazis were trying to achieve. The Holocaust was a European phenomenon, aided and abetted by many of the citizens of the occupied countries.[80] So one cannot argue that Germans alone possess some peculiar quality that allowed the Holocaust to take place. The fact that genocide is a global phenomenon, occurring at one time or another on practically every continent, indicates that mass killing is a human problem and is not limited to one racial, ethnic, religious, or national group. It is simply too pervasive and common.

In some cases, instigators of genocide have attempted to make the killings more palatable by excluding those who enjoy it too much. During the Holocaust, for example, the Nazi leadership actually strove to disqualify from participation those who showed too much aptitude for and pleasure in the killing. Bauman notes,

> when . . . members of the Einsatzgruppen and other units similarly close to the scene of actual killings were enlisted, special care was taken to weed out—bar or discharge—all particularly keen, emotionally charged, ideologically over-zealous individuals. We know that individual initiatives were discouraged, and much effort was made to keep the whole task in a businesslike and strictly impersonal framework. Personal gains, and personal motives in general, were censured and penalized. Killings induced by desire or pleasure, unlike those following orders and perpetrated in an organized fashion, could lead (at least in principle) to trial and conviction, like ordinary murder or manslaughter.[81]

In short, the Nazis themselves eliminated those motivated by base and degenerate impulses. Heinrich Himmler specifically condemned those who were not motivated by the lofty ideals of "racial purification."[82] Ironically enough, it seems that, on occasion, participants in the Holocaust were actually executed for the unauthorized killing of Jews for private purposes.[83] While this extreme is almost unique to the Holocaust, it seems likely that perpetrators of other genocides were, similarly, rather ordinary people perpetrating these crimes for reasons other than individual sadism and psychopathy.

Last, it is also clear, after reviewing accounts of various genocides, that many perpetrators find it unpleasant, even traumatic, to exterminate other people. During the Holocaust many of the agents of destruction, such as soldiers of the infamous *Einsatzgruppen,* the mobile death squads operating behind the German front lines, as well as many of the camp guards and functionaries, suffered mental breakdowns, exhibited physical symptoms of stress such as ulcers, were issued alcohol to numb them to the horror and allow them to sleep, and not infrequently committed suicide.[84] One of the leaders of the *Einsatzgruppen,* Artur Nebe, suffered several nervous breakdowns, and his driver shot himself because of his duties.[85] An SS leader once confronted Himmler to complain that the killings were ruining his men, who could not handle their gruesome task.[86] In fact, Himmler himself could not bear to witness the actual killings, and at an *Einsatzgruppen* action had to look away and almost collapsed, so difficult was it for the man in charge of the whole apparatus of annihilation.[87] Similarly, accounts of the Bosnian genocide frequently mention the drunkenness of the Serbs engaged in ethnic cleansing. The Bosnian Serb army supplied its troops with liberal quantities of alcohol, especially plum brandy (*šljivovica*), in order to lower inhibitions and repress the conscience.[88] One survivor of the camp at Omarska described the torture this way: "The beating was constant; they were always completely drunk. They used to laugh or sing while they beat people, and sometimes even pray to their God while they were killing."[89] Similarly, accounts from Rwanda speak of road blocks manned by consistently drunken militia members, who danced and sang in between bouts of killing Tutsis.[90] Alcohol lowers resistance to participation and numbs the senses. Remorseless monsters, incapable of feeling guilt, do not need such aids.

In short, the perpetrators of genocides are not monsters, at least not in a literal sense, even though they perpetrate monstrous crimes. They are relatively ordinary human beings engaged in extraordinary behaviors that they are somehow able to define as acceptable, necessary, and perhaps even praiseworthy. This argument, however, should not be taken to mean that genocidal killers are not brutalized by the killing. Many killers, in fact, may come to enjoy the intoxicating power that being in control and having weapons can bring. One observer notes that "I met lots of young men who loved the ruins, loved the destruction, loved the power that came from the barrels of their guns."[91] Even so, this does not imply mental abnormality. As Rainer Baum asserts, "We should not assume that it takes psychopathology to be engaged in mass murder. Completely normal human beings can do it."[92]

Bystanders

In discussions of the human element of genocide, the role of the bystander must not be neglected or minimized. Genocide is not a crime that happens in dark alleys. It is too massive and all-consuming to be hidden away from public view. In every genocide there are many witnesses to the slaughter. Bystanders have integral roles in the drama of genocide because the consummation of genocide requires not only the active participation of many perpetrators but the willingness of the great bulk of the society to do nothing. One witness to the Rwandan genocide put it this way: "Everybody in the village was an accomplice, by silence or by looting, and it is impossible to divide the responsibility."[93] In other words, governments bent on genocide cannot accomplish their goals without the active complicity of some and the passive acceptance of others. In the prescient words of Edmund Burke, "The only thing necessary for the triumph of evil is for good men to do nothing."

It is important to remember that genocide can be stopped, or at least impeded. The Nazi T4 euthanasia program was brought to an official halt by a public outcry led in part by members of the German clergy.[94] In 1943 a roundup in Berlin netted the Jewish husbands of non-Jewish German women, who spent the next three days demonstrating on the streets of Berlin. The Nazi government, at that point already deeply committed to the "final solution" of the Jewish question, *backed down* and released these men.[95]

Bystanders can impact genocide in many different ways when they choose to take an active part in resisting it. The Jews of Europe were not all equally at risk. While Italy was an ally of Nazi Germany rather than an occupied country, Italians did not support the deportation of Jewish citizens and actively protected them. It was not until the Italian surrender and the subsequent Nazi takeover of northern Italy that Italian Jews began to be deported.[96] Another example of resistance comes from Denmark. According to the United States Holocaust Museum, "Considering the relatively small Jewish population and the steadfast support Danes gave to their fellow Jewish citizens, Germany decided not to make a major issue of the 'Jewish question' in Denmark."[97] Later in the war, Germany did try to round up all the Jews in Denmark for deportation, but was largely unsuccessful because many Danes helped relocate the Jews into neutral Sweden. While some were seized, the vast majority were saved. Of those who were taken by the Germans, most were eventually handed over to the Swedish Red Cross, and "the vigor of Danish protests perhaps prevented their deportation to the killing centers in occupied Poland."[98]

Individuals have also risked much to rescue the persecuted. Rescuers often risk not only their own lives, but those of their entire families. During every genocide exceptional individuals engage in extremely courageous acts to save people who are, in many cases, strangers. These examples of altruism and resistance to genocide are, however, sadly the exception rather than the rule.

Even enlightened and aware people may passively accept what is happening. This is illustrated by Peter Maass, who recounts how he witnessed a Serb accost and prepare to kill a Muslim who had made the mistake of appearing at a local café. Rather than interfering, Maass turned away and later explained,

> We had made the right decision not to intervene, but it didn't feel very good. . . . A man was on the verge of being executed in cold Balkan blood, and we stood aside because it was the prudent thing to do. Was this much different from the Serbs who prudently kept quiet as their Bosnian neighbors were shot or packed off to prison camps?[99]

Similarly, Marguerite Feitlowitz describes how a young woman was kidnapped from a bus in downtown Buenos Aires by soldiers in civilian clothes. None of the other passengers did anything as she was dragged, punched, and kicked off the bus and into a waiting car.[100] Argentina's "dirty war" was in full swing and all of the passengers must have realized that this woman was becoming a *desaparecido*, a disappeared one, yet no one said or did anything.

Those living in countries free of this violence should avoid feeling superior. In the United States, we can remember the case of Kitty Genovese, who was stalked and repeatedly attacked by a knife-wielding assailant for over thirty minutes.[101] Even though she screamed and called for help, not one of the thirty-eight witnesses who saw or heard the assault helped her or even called the police until it was far too late. This did not happen in some far-off foreign country embroiled in a genocidal conflict, but rather in Queens, New York. Evidently, the willingness to sit idly by as violent crimes are perpetrated is not unique to certain genocidal societies, but may instead be found in many communities.

The passivity of bystanders is aided by what may be termed a "willful ignorance" on the part of the social audience, who essentially choose not to know about the distasteful acts being perpetrated. In fact, James Glass argues that what many call indifference is in actuality an unwillingness to recognize the anguish and pain of those being victimized.[102] Many Germans who lived near concentration camps, or whose Jewish neighbors were being deported, ignored the evidence and pretended they didn't know what was going on. They lived as described by Eva Fogelman: with blinders on.[103] The journalist Fergal Keane interviewed the vice-rector of a Rwandan university about the genocide. Even though this man was highly educated and a world traveler, he nonetheless closed his eyes to the killing and professed ignorance. As Keane describes him, "He is a man of such cleverness that he has contrived not to see any of the tens of thousands who have been killed in and around Butare. Nor has he heard any screams of dying people."[104] This willful ignorance is an essential defense mechanism and is found not only among the bystanders, but even among the victims. Many inmates of Auschwitz, for example, living within sight and smell of the crematoria, professed ignorance of the purpose and functions of the camp.[105] If this purposeful not-knowing can be found among the victims, how much easier it must be for those bystanders far removed from the camps to convince themselves that they don't know and don't want to know what is happening around them.

As the latter half of the twentieth century has shown, the world community is also often a bystander to genocidal events. As a Bosnian Serb soldier told a Muslim refugee from Srebrenica, "There was nothing you could do. The world has allowed us to do this. Tomorrow they will allow us to do the same in Žepa."[106]

While we often hope that the lessons of the past have not been lost on the present, recent examples illustrate the continued unwillingness or inability of the global community to actively address itself to the problem of genocide. Take for example the dedication ceremony of the Holocaust Memorial Museum in Washington, D.C., on April 22, 1993. While President Clinton gave a moving speech about the failure of the Allies to prevent or even hinder the Holocaust, the Serb campaign against Bosnian Muslims was in full swing. President Clinton said,

> The nations of the West must live forever with this knowledge: Even as our fragmentary awareness of these crimes grew into indisputable facts, we did far too little. Before the war started, doors to liberty were slammed shut. And even after we attacked Germany, rail lines to the camps, within miles of significant targets, were left undisturbed. Mass deaths were left to occur, enshrouded in our denial. . . . The evil represented in this museum is incontestable. It is absolute. As we are its witness, so we must remain its adversary. We owe that much to the dead, as we owe it to our consciences and our children. So we must stop the fabricators of history

and the bullies as well. Left unchallenged, they would still prey upon the powerless, and we cannot permit that to happen again.[107]

These fine words are reduced to mere hypocrisy by the recognition that at the time of this speech the Clinton administration was fully aware of the scope of the tragedy then engulfing Bosnia. Members of the American government knew that concentration camps were once again operating on European soil. Elie Wiesel, a survivor of the Holocaust, had also been asked to speak, and he took President Clinton to task for the failure of the administration to recognize and act upon the Bosnian tragedy.

At its heart, genocide is a human tragedy, played out between the participants, victims as well as perpetrators, and with an audience who through inaction allow the drama to continue. Genocide is not created by monsters, and its victims are not faceless and anonymous "things." Human beings create these tragedies and also suffer the consequences. With this in mind, let us now turn to an examination of the term "genocide" and the various competing definitions vying for attention and credibility.

2   A Crime by Any Other Name

> Thus says the Lord of hosts, "I will punish what Amalek did to Israel in opposing them on the way, when they came up out of Egypt. Now go and smite Amalek, and utterly destroy all that they have; do not spare them, but kill both man and woman, infant and suckling, ox and sheep, camel and ass."
>
> —1 Samuel 15:2–3

> In fact, social scientists do not appear to understand or acknowledge the historical background or significance of genocide studies. Genocide is certainly not a new topic needing acceptance from the social sciences; it is as old as humanity and hardly an idiosyncratic occurrence in human history.
>
> —Herbert Hirsch[1]

While the term "genocide" has only recently entered the modern lexicon, it must be pointed out that genocide is by no means a new phenomenon. As Leo Kuper points out, "The word is new, the crime is ancient."[2] Appearing in many guises and epochs, genocides have punctuated the historic landscape from time immemorial, although they were not always perceived as crimes. Many societies saw nothing wrong in the wholesale massacre of various peoples. On the contrary, some gloried in their achievements, proudly proclaiming them far and wide and commemorating them in writing and art. A good example of this is the well-known bas-relief on the Column of Marcus Aurelius depicting the beheading of German prisoners. Certainly, this tribute to Roman military prowess does not indicate revulsion or shame; instead it celebrates a proud moment in Roman history. Because of this apparent legitimation and pride, Roger Smith argues that Kuper's statement should be amended to read "The word is new, the phenomenon ancient."[3] Regardless of genocide's perceived criminality or acceptability, the historical literature is rife with examples of this and closely related types of mass killing. A selected review of different cases quickly reveals its prevalence.

Past as Prologue

An arbitrary beginning in the history of genocide can be made with the Roman republic and empire, which were built upon the bodies of countless conquered peoples. After defeating Carthage at the end of the Third Punic War, Rome razed the city, killed most of the inhabitants, and sowed the ground with salt to symbolize that it should forevermore remain barren. Rome's attitude to its famous rival can be summed up with Cato's famous dictum, repeated at the end of every speech he made: *ceterum censeo Carthaginem esse delendam*—"for the rest, it is my opinion that Carthage must be destroyed."[4] In fact, Raphael Lemkin, the originator of the term "genocide," specifically referred to the destruction of Carthage as an early example of this crime. In later times, Julius Caesar's victorious campaigns in Gaul were often achieved through the annihilation of entire Celtic tribes that had either opposed him or rebelled against Roman control.[5] The famous *Pax Romana* was created on the ashes of countless communities.

Further east, on the Asian steppes, the conquests of Chinggis Khan, more commonly known as Genghis Khan, were usually brutal affairs marked by numerous genocidal massacres. The destruction of the Khwarezmian empire, for example, was accomplished through the destruction of numerous cities and the killing of their inhabitants. As Erik Hildinger writes of the exploits of Tolui, one of the Khan's sons and generals,

> Balkh surrendered to him, but he massacred the townspeople and burned the city all the same. Tolui rounded up peasants from near Khurasan and besieged Merve, which surrendered too; but the entire population was slaughtered. Tolui then took by storm Nishapur, where the Mongol general Toquchar had been killed in an assault. Again the entire population was killed.[6]

These feats were by no means unusual, as the widespread massacres perpetrated by the Khan and his successors during other conquests amply illustrate. Similarly, Timur Lenk, also known as Tamerlane, was renowned for his extreme tactics, such as creating mountains of skulls in front of cities he had conquered. While not well known in the west, Timur Lenk is often conceded to be one of the most brutal of early warlords.

The rise of the Zulu nation in southern Africa, under Shaka, was marked by the wholesale extermination of numerous clans and tribes that had offended or posed a threat to his empire.[7] A brilliant military innovator, Shaka revolutionized tribal warfare in southeastern Africa, turning it from a largely bloodless and symbolic contest into a lethal tool of empire building. Pushed inland by the Zulu, who controlled the land from the Indian Ocean to the Drakensberg Mountains, dispossessed clans and tribes embarked on a ten-year orgy of destructiveness that became known as the *Mfecane*, "the crushing," for which some estimates place the dead at between one and two million.[8] Just south of Shaka's kingdom, the Bushmen of southern Africa were decimated by both the European settlers and other African tribes who hunted down and killed these diminutive nomadic pastoralists because they saw them as subhuman and dangerous vermin.[9]

The Christian Crusades were marked by numerous massacres as soldiers of Christ hacked their way to the holy land in the name of Jesus. The most infamous example is probably the sack of Jerusalem, in which Crusaders ran riot through the streets of the newly conquered holy city. Of this event, Robert Payne writes,

The massacre at Jerusalem was carried out deliberately; it was the result of settled policy. Jerusalem was to become a Christian city. The Jews, too, must be destroyed. They had all rushed to the chief synagogue, where they hoped to receive shelter and protection. The Crusaders, hungry for simple solutions, burned down the synagogue with the Jews inside.[10]

Not all the violence was directed at infidels in other lands, however. From 1205 to 1214, Cathar heretics in southern France were exterminated by Christian crusaders under Papal orders in what became known as the Albigensian Crusade.[11] The soldiers of Christ destroyed entire cities and massacred their inhabitants as they ravaged and depopulated the entire Languedoc region during this religious struggle.[12]

In 1649, Oliver Cromwell arrived in Ireland at the head of a British army and proceeded to pacify Ireland through the wholesale destruction of Irish cities, such as Drogheda, and the slaughter of the Irish, both combatants and noncombatants, thus setting the stage for three hundred years of English domination.[13]

The expansion into and colonization of Siberia and Alaska by the Russians was characterized by many attempts to eradicate tribes such as the Kamchadals, Yukaghir, and Koryaks.[14] Similarly, the European conquests of North, South, and Central America were accompanied by wholesale destruction of entire civilizations, cultures, and tribes.[15] As Ian Steele points out, "contact was synonymous with invasion."[16] While the vast majority of Native peoples in the Americas died of disease, many others were systematically hunted, rounded up, and worked to death, or killed outright.

As is evident, genocide was both a military and a political strategy widely used in historic times and these elements are still present in modern examples of this crime. We find, for example, that genocide has frequently been launched under cover of war. Warfare, always brutalizing and degrading, inevitably seems to produce related atrocities and crimes in its wake, and helps create a climate conducive to genocide. This is certainly the case for the Armenian genocide, perpetrated as it was during the First World War, and the Holocaust, in which the systematized killing began only after the German invasion of the Soviet Union. Other times genocides occur in the wake of wars, such as the Cambodian genocide, which began after the war and the overthrow of the Lon Nol government.

Modernity and Genocide

As the preceding discussion indicates, the phenomenon we now identify as genocide has been a frequent, if not prevalent, part of human history. Its perpetration, however, is not limited to the historical past, banished from the modern age by the rationalizing process of science, technology, and "civilization." As evidenced in chapter 1, genocide has, in fact, been increasing in frequency and efficiency. Some scholars have even argued that modern Western culture is inherently genocidal, because it contains several dominant motifs that contribute tremendously to the perpetration of this type of crime.[17] Richard Rubenstein, for example, writes that the Holocaust

> was an expression of some of the most significant political, moral, religious, and demographic tendencies of Western civilization in the twentieth century. The Holocaust cannot be divorced from the very same culture of modernity that produced two world wars and Hitler.[18]

Similarly, Zygmunt Bauman argues that the modern process of separating violence and power from moral and ethical considerations is crucial to understanding genocide in the modern age. As he eloquently summarizes, "In a system where rationality and ethics point in opposite directions, humanity is the main loser."[19] These arguments essentially suggest that genocide is a terrible byproduct of the increasingly rational, bureaucratic, and scientific nature of modern life, in which cold, calculating, amoral cost/benefit analyses take precedence over human considerations. More specifically, Bauman goes on to assert,

> The choice of physical extermination . . . was a product of routine bureaucratic procedures: means-ends, calculus, budget balancing, universal rule application. . . . The "Final Solution" did not clash at any stage with the rational pursuit of efficient, optimal goal-implementation. On the contrary, it arose out of a genuinely rational concern, and it was generated by bureaucracy true to its form and purpose.[20]

In other words, while modern bureaucratic and technological advances have increased the efficiency of modern organizations, they have also removed much of the human element from the organizational equation. As a result, a climate has been created in which qualities of concern and compassion for fellow humans are irrelevant and regarded as an unwanted hindrance to the dispassionate application of rules and policies. Some theorists, in fact, see many of the instances of mass violence in the twentieth century as inextricably linked together in an escalating chain of increasingly impersonal, bureaucratized, and industrialized killing, with each example paving the way for the next. As Omer Bartov suggests,

> If Auschwitz could have neither been imagined nor come into being without the Great War, then by the same token the mechanical slaughter of the Great War could not have come about without the inescapable heritage of the Age of Rationalism and the French Revolution, namely, the "armed nation," made all the more formidable through the rapid industrialization of the Western world and emergence of the modern bureaucratic state.[21]

As each threshold of violence is passed, the previously unimaginable becomes increasingly acceptable. Richard Rubenstein, for example, argues specifically that the First World War set the stage for later genocides, especially the Holocaust. This position is echoed by Paul Fussel, who writes that "the drift of modern history domesticates the fantastic and normalizes the unspeakable.

And the catastrophe that begins it is the Great War."[22] In a similar vein, Yehuda Bauer explains that "Auschwitz cannot be explained without reference to World War I."[23]

In that conflict, for the first time, large numbers of people became expendable and superfluous as battles were fought, not for territory, but simply to kill mass quantities of enemy soldiers. The battle of Verdun, for example, was conceived and implemented by German strategists as a means to lure increasing numbers of French troops onto the killing ground around the forts at Verdun, where artillery and machine guns could destroy them in a battle of attrition.[24] The goal was not territory, but simply a large "body count," to borrow a phrase from a later war; the intent was to bleed the French army white. Unfortunately for the German plan, the battle took on a powerful symbolic value for both sides, so that the Germans were also forced to commit large numbers of troops. When this ten-month battle was finally finished, more than seven hundred thousand French and German soldiers had become casualties.[25]

The First World War was marked by impersonal, large-scale mechanized slaughter and introduced onto the world stage an industrialized mode of killing that, for all intents and purposes, became a model for the later Holocaust. It is revealing that the enduring images of the Great War are machine guns mowing down rank after rank of soldiers in front of barbed-wire defenses, primitive tanks trundling across the scarred landscape, and the serpentine system of trenches that dominated the geography and the lives of the soldiers of that conflict. Scarcely recognizable as human, covered as they were in mud and rags, the soldiers of the troglodyte world of the trenches were impersonally and mechanically slaughtered in such numbers, and with such predictability, that late in the war French troops would go to the front bleating like sheep being led to the slaughter. The First World War truly was a watershed event of the twentieth century.

Supporters of this modernization thesis stand in opposition to those who suggest that increasing modernization has resulted in less violence as values, sensibilities, and cultures have become more refined and less tolerant of individual acts of violence. Norbert Elias, for example, argues that the long-term trend in Western societies has been a "civilizing process." That is, since ancient times normative systems of behavior have evolved and developed toward more humanistic orientations that place greater constraint on violent impulses.[26] In support of this argument, various scholars have pointed to the dramatic and steady decreases in rates of violent crime in most Western societies from the Middle Ages to the present day.[27] Evidently, violence was much more prevalent in European life during the medieval era, not only in the perpetration of crime, but in every sphere of life, including family, leisure, and work.

This perspective has merit, but while rates of individually perpetrated violent crime have certainly decreased in the modern age, collective or mass-perpetrated violence, such as is found in wars and genocides, has substantially increased. Rather than a terrible by-product of modern Western civilization, genocide is something older and more fundamental to human communities. Certainly, some elements of modern life may facilitate the perpetration of genocide, such as bureaucracies that apply impersonal organizational principles to individuals. However, the roots of genocide are grounded in a variety of cultural, structural, and political factors that interact in various ways to create societies willing and able to perpetrate this crime. Modern Western cultures do not have a monopoly on genocide, as events in Africa, Asia, and the Americas illustrate.[28] Genocide is a global phenomenon, and while certain elements of modern Western society can be portrayed as contributing to genocide, a strong argument can also be made that other components of Western society are fundamentally opposed to genocide. Condemnation of murder and praise of charity, compassion, and the human potential are as much a product of modern times as dehumanization, bureaucratization, and impersonal forms of killing. Perhaps Freeman sums it up best when he asserts that while modernity has certainly created the potential for genocide, it has also created values and beliefs antithetical to genocide, and to assert that genocide is caused by the forces of modernity is too simplistic.[29] What modernity has done is reshape genocide into a more efficient and rational endeavor capable of killing on an industrial scale. The modern age has not created genocide; rather, it has altered its nature, application, and efficiency.

Rhetoric, Confusion, and Genocide

As prevalent and historically persistent as genocide has been, it is surprisingly difficult to reach agreement on what exactly is meant by the term "genocide." Widely applied in a variety of contexts with a tremendous range of definitional criteria, the notion of genocide is marked by conceptual confusion, often compounded by its rhetorical use on the part of those seeking to inflame and stigmatize social and political discourse.[30] For example, Michael Ignatieff notes that "'Genocide' is a worn and debased term, casually hurled at every outrage, every violence."[31] The term has been applied to everything from family planning to urban sprawl, and these clear misappropriations of the term, while politically and emotionally potent, add to the conceptual confusion surrounding genocide. The conspicuous lack of definitional clarity is engendered by other factors as well.

In part, the existing delineations vary tremendously in scope and applicability due to the conflicting goals and agendas of those proposing them. Raphael Lemkin, a jurist and activist, for example, wanted to bring both public attention and legal action to bear on the behavior of the Nazi regime in occupied Europe, while R. J. Rummel, a scholar, has been primarily interested in exploring the lethality of modern totalitarian governments.[32] While they share a common revulsion and outrage at genocide, they differ in their orientation and have distinctive agendas that foster divergent definitions. Frank Chalk summarizes this issue well when he writes,

For international lawyers, defining genocide means defining a crime. Like any criminal offense, the definition of genocide must be appropriate for legal prosecution, and it must withstand review by judges and lawyers for the accused. Social scientists have a different set of objectives. When defining genocide, they are outlining the boundaries of a set of cases which they want to study for the purpose of discovering their common elements and analyzing the processes that brought them about.[33]

In addition, Israel Charny has shown that definitions of genocide are subject to "ideological and political pressures from the societal establishments within which thinkers do their work,"[34] and these tensions tend to produce definitions that differ as much as they agree. In other words, definitions of genocide often revolve around particular political agendas of inclusion and condemnation, even of exclusion and outright denial, depending upon the perceived legitimacy of the perpetrator. The Turkish government, in its continuing effort to deny the Armenian genocide, funds an institute in the United States that ostensibly conducts research on Turkish history. Not surprisingly, scholars from this organization not only produce work exonerating the Turkish government of genocide, but also provide advice to Turkish officials as to how they should respond to other writers who do consider the treatment of the Armenians to constitute genocide.[35] David Stannard points to a parallel process when he compares

> the American response to genocide in Cambodia (horror—since the Cambodian government was our enemy, thereby making its victims worthy) with the U.S. reaction to the simultaneous genocide in East Timor (silence—since Indonesia, the perpetrator of the genocide, is our friend, thereby making its victims unworthy).[36]

We can also examine the stance of certain Holocaust scholars, known as Particularists, who maintain that the Holocaust is the only true example of genocide and is fundamentally different from other examples of mass killing.[37] These Particularists not only deny that many instances in which specific populations and groups were targeted for destruction constitute genocide, but also tend to gloss over or ignore the non-Jewish victims of the Nazi-perpetrated Holocaust. While it may be argued that this glossing-over is done in order to reserve for selected victims "a privileged nation status in the moral honor roll,"[38] it may also be that these scholars hope to avoid trivializing comparisons that relativize the killing and diminish the responsibility of the perpetrators. Ward Churchill, on the other hand, goes so far as to suggest that the Particularists are essentially similar to Holocaust deniers in that both subvert the truth and rewrite history in order to forward specific agendas.[39] The point is that definitions of genocide are not always objective and based purely on the dictates of science and scholarship. Clearly, the institutional, cultural, political, and societal settings within which genocide scholars work affect, consciously and unconsciously, their definitions and their research.

Much of the conceptual imprecision found in the literature on genocide is due to the topic's inherent indeterminacy, since the term encompasses such overlapping and related behaviors. Helen Fein writes that "Genocide . . . is intrinsically a 'fuzzy concept': its exact borders are unclear and there are both overlapping and marginal phenomena."[40] Leo Kuper, for example, specifically refers to the bombings of Hiroshima and Nagasaki as genocidal, while Chalk and Jonassohn omit these acts from the realm of genocide.[41] While clear similarities often exist, the context, intent, and scale often vary tremendously, which leaves it unclear whether or not specific examples of mass killing, including massacres and acts of war, should be considered genocide. How does one tell the difference between war crimes and a full-blown act of genocide when both often happen during times of war? The difficulty in distinguishing between and comparing these phenomena makes Helen Fein's point concerning unclear borders particularly forceful.

It is a significant task, therefore, to categorize and distinguish between related yet conceptually distinct types of state-perpetrated killing. A starting point for clarifying some of these issues may be to present some of the proposed definitions, in order to review their criteria for inclusion and reveal commonalities and consistent themes among scholars of genocide.

Raphael Lemkin and the Origins of the Term

The term itself, "genocide," was originally coined by the jurist Raphael Lemkin in 1944 in his book *Axis Rule in Occupied Europe*. The appellation was derived from "the ancient Greek word *genos* (race, tribe) and the Latin *cide* (killing), thus corresponding in its formation to such words as tyrannicide, homicide, infanticide, etc."[42] Lemkin coined the term in order to criminalize Nazi atrocities, and accordingly he defined genocide as follows:

> Generally speaking, genocide does not necessarily mean the immediate destruction of a nation, except when accomplished by mass killing of all the members of a nation. It is intended rather to signify a coordinated plan of different actions aiming at the destruction of essential foundations of the life of national groups, with the aim of annihilating the groups themselves. The objectives of such a plan would be the disintegration of the political and social institutions of culture, language, national feelings, religion, economic existence, of national groups and the destruction of the personal security, liberty, health, dignity, and even the lives of the individuals belonging to such groups.[43]

According to Lemkin, he had to create a new word because traditional terms, such as "mass murder," do not include all the different types of lethal and non-lethal activities involved in genocide. Lemkin's definition is a broad one that explicitly recognizes that this crime may be perpetrated in different ways, include many victim types, and involve numerous related activities apart from killing. In fact, he explicitly states that genocide may or may not include the mass murder of the members of a targeted group when he writes that

> the crime of genocide involves a wide range of actions, including not only the deprivation of life but also the prevention of life (abortions, sterilizations) and also devices considerably endangering life and health (artificial infections, working to

death in special camps, deliberate separation of families for depopulation purposes and so forth).[44]

While Lemkin's original intention was to define the term somewhat broadly, we shall see that subsequent definitions have been considerably narrower. Perhaps the most important aspect of Lemkin's work, aside from his initial development of the concept, is that he was the first to forcefully and persuasively advocate for legal and social condemnation of this and related crimes. His work provided an early impetus to international condemnation of this crime and provided a template for subsequent attempts to define genocide, especially for the United Nations.

The United Nations Genocide Convention

On December 9, 1948, the United Nations General Assembly approved the Genocide Convention, which defined genocide as a crime under international law. Created in the wake of Raphael Lemkin's advocacy and the precedent-setting Nuremberg trials, the United Nations convention created a legal framework for identifying and categorizing genocide. In the Nuremberg war crimes trials that followed the defeat of Germany in the Second World War, members of the Nazi government and military had been tried, convicted, and in some cases executed for acts committed in their official capacities. The Allied powers created a tribunal to try three categories of crimes: crimes against peace, war crimes, and crimes against humanity. The last category included the offenses of the Holocaust. Additionally, the tribunal had the power to declare "(in connection with any act of which the individual may be convicted) that the group or organization of which the individual was a member was a criminal organization."[45] Ultimately the court defined three Nazi organizations as criminal: the infamous SS, the Gestapo-SD, and the "Leadership Corps" of the Nazi Party. The court's ruling that these three agencies of the Nazi government were criminal was, in one sense, a de facto judgment against the Nazi state as a whole. Of the twenty-two officials tried at Nuremberg, nineteen were judged guilty, and twelve were sentenced to death by hanging.[46] In subsequent trials in the ensuing years over a thousand more Germans from a variety of professions were tried and judged for their role in the perpetration of the Holocaust. These lesser trials were based largely upon the jurisprudence established at Nuremberg. Similarly, the war crimes trials of the Japanese (conducted by the International Military Tribunal for the Far East) were also based upon the legal principles instituted at Nuremberg.[47] The Nuremberg trials, therefore, established a clear legal precedent for the prosecution of those responsible for genocide and were instrumental in providing the groundwork for the tribunals of the 1990s against the perpetrators of the genocides in Bosnia-Herzegovina and Rwanda.

Implicit within all of these trials was the assumption that agents of a government, acting on behalf of that government in enforcing policy and law, could be considered criminals, notwithstanding domestic laws to the contrary.

Revolutionary in impact, these trials provided the legal and philosophical framework for the subsequent United Nations convention on genocide.

With the exception of cultural genocide, or ethnocide, as it is more commonly known, Lemkin's earlier definition was in large part adopted by the United Nations Convention on the Prevention and Punishment of the Crime of Genocide, which defined genocide, under Article 2 of the convention document, as consisting of

> any of the following acts committed with intent to destroy, in whole or in part, a national, ethnical, racial or religious group, as such: (a) Killing members of the group; (b) Causing serious bodily or mental harm to members of the group; (c) Deliberately inflicting on the group conditions of life calculated to bring about its physical destruction in whole or in part; (d) Imposing measures intended to prevent births within the group; (e) Forcibly transferring children of the group to another group.[48]

This document also affirmed under Article 1 that

> genocide, whether committed in time of peace or in time of war, is a crime under international law which they [the signatories] undertake to prevent and to punish.[49]

Created in a highly politicized process, the definition agreed upon in 1948 has proven to be limited and overly exclusive, drawing artificial distinctions between examples of mass killing. This often conflictual process is well summarized by Leo Kuper, who writes,

> In the deliberations of the Committees, there were major controversies regarding the groups to be protected, the question of intent, the inclusion of cultural genocide, the problem of enforcement and punishment, the extent of destruction which would constitute genocide, and the essential nature of the crime. Almost every conceivable argument was advanced, and critically tested.[50]

Perhaps the most striking outcome of this process was the decision to exclude political groups from the calculus. Various nations opposed the inclusion of political groups as potential victims of genocide, arguing that these groups were short-lived and inconstant, while others asserted that it would encourage outside intervention into domestic concerns and transform internal political conflicts into international issues.[51] One result of this exclusion is that the U.N. definition recognizes the Turkish treatment of the Armenians as an example of genocide, but not the destruction of the Kulaks in the Soviet Union, even though these examples share many characteristics. Both groups were targeted for destruction, forcibly removed from their homes and land, and murdered in large groups, yet because the Armenians constituted an ethnic and religious minority in Turkey, while the Kulaks were a politically created and defined group,[52] only the Armenians qualify as victims of genocide according to the United Nations definition. The fact that the U.N. definition excludes such cases constitutes a significant weakness of this definition. Similarly, Argentina's "dirty war" of the 1970s illustrates weaknesses in the United Nations definition.

On March 24, 1976, in a coup that is widely recognized as having had widespread support among Argentineans, the military ousted Isabel Perón and took control of the government. Headed by a triumvirate with one member from each of the three branches of the military, the new government almost immediately began a campaign against leftist guerilla organizations. It soon began to include among its targets intellectuals, writers, journalists, union organizers, union sympathizers, psychologists, and social workers, all of whom were defined as threats to the well-being of Argentina.[53] Argentina became a society in which citizens were routinely kidnapped, tortured, and murdered by the thousands. One favored method of killing was to take the victims on an airplane out over the Atlantic. They were sedated, stripped, and then thrown, drugged but alive, into the ocean. These people, from all walks of life, including children and pregnant women, became known as the *desaparecidos,* the disappeared ones. While the government was ostensibly fighting communist insurgency, its real goals were put into words by one political leader who stated that "First we will kill all the subversives, then we will kill their collaborators, then . . . their sympathizers, then . . . those who remain indifferent; and, finally, we will kill the timid."[54] Before the military junta lost power after the debacle of the Falklands war, more than thirty thousand civilians had been "disappeared." Does this constitute an example of genocide? Marguerite Feitlowitz certainly believes so, and uses the term throughout her account of the "dirty war." Recently, Spain filed extradition papers against various Argentine military officers for the crime of genocide, in part because several Spanish nationals were among the *desaparecidos.* The Spanish court referred specifically to the United Nations Convention on the Prevention and Punishment of Genocide, of which Argentina was a signatory. The convention stipulates that there is no statute of limitations for genocide and that the perpetrators may be tried in any country bringing charges.[55] The Argentinean case is still definitionally problematic, however, since most of the victims were not members of any recognizable group. If anything, they were defined by the government as subversives and communists. This would classify them as a political group, and as noted above, the U.N. definition does not include this type of category. Additionally, one may ask if the scale of the killing in Argentina works against its being defined as genocide. According to the U.N. definition, genocide involves the attempted destruction, "in whole or in part," of a collective. Does killing thirty thousand people meet this criterion? This is a relatively small number compared to the millions of victims found in other examples, yet the Argentine military and police certainly intended to eliminate all the subversives and communists in Argentina. Does this number prevent the "dirty war" from being included as an example of genocide? Some scholars certainly imply a minimum numeric threshold for genocide, while others see the numbers as irrelevant and instead focus on intent. These are difficult issues to resolve, and the inability of the U.N. to effectively address these kinds of problems translates directly into a fundamental incapacity to intervene in a meaningful way.

Additionally, other critics have pointed out that the United Nations has not had much apparent success in enforcing the document and it therefore remains a mere abstract exercise in political rhetoric. In spite of these difficulties the U.N. definition has become a widely accepted standard for determining genocide, since it provides a legal context. But while the United Nations has played a role in promoting genocide as an international problem, the organization has been largely impotent in preventing or effectively ameliorating recent genocides in Cambodia, Rwanda, and Bosnia.

The relevance of the United Nations and its definition lies in their potential. If genocide is ever to be prevented and punished, the United Nations will almost certainly need to play a pivotal role in that process and its definition will therefore gain further importance as the legal mechanism within which international legislative policy is implemented. In fact, the potential of the United Nations is slowly and painfully being evidenced. On May 25, 1993, the United Nations created the International Criminal Tribunal for the Former Yugoslavia, with a mandate to prosecute people for four kinds of violations of international law: grave breaches of the 1949 Geneva Convention; violations of the laws or customs of war; genocide; and crimes against humanity.[56] As of August 1999, the tribunal had leveled ninety-one indictments, taken thirty-one accused into custody, conducted three trials, and received one guilty plea.[57] While this is a very small number of cases relative to all the people involved in various acts of genocide and war crimes in the former Yugoslavia, it is a legitimate attempt to live up to the intent of the Genocide Convention and a significant step in the right direction. On July 17, 1998, the United Nations Diplomatic Conference of Plenipotentiaries on the Establishment of an International Criminal Court adopted a resolution establishing a permanent International Criminal Court with jurisdiction over genocide, crimes against humanity, war crimes, and crimes of aggression. This court will have the authority to investigate and prosecute these types of crimes on a permanent and ongoing basis. How effective this court will be remains to be seen, yet it nevertheless represents another step forward in the establishment of effective international legal interventions.

The United Nations definition has been useful for scholarly purposes as well. Avoiding much of the definitional infighting so prevalent in the study of genocide, Leo Kuper grudgingly adopts the United Nations definition for the purposes of his research. He does not "think it helpful to create new definitions of genocide, when there is an internationally recognized definition and a Genocide Convention which might become the basis for some effective action, however limited the underlying conception."[58] His most pressing concern about the United Nations definition is its exclusion of political groups. For Kuper, genocide is first and foremost a crime of the state. In his view, "the major arena for contemporary genocidal conflict and massacre is to be found within the sovereign state."[59] Linking genocide to political forces reflects his goal of forcefully advocating that the United Nations begin to actively work at preventing and punishing genocide. Of note also is his contention that many of the acts of war perpetrated in this century constitute, if not genocide, at least genocidal massacres. Among these he would count the atomic bombings of Hiroshima and

Nagasaki, as well as the fire- and carpet-bombings of Tokyo, Dresden, and Hamburg during the Second World War.

However, in spite of its potential and the work of writers such as Leo Kuper, many scholars have concluded that the U.N. definition is essentially useless to scholars of genocide,[60] and have accordingly developed various definitions more suited to their perspectives and needs.

Dominance and Genocide

In one attempt to provide an alternative to the U.N. definition, Vahakn Dadrian, the well-known scholar of the Armenian genocide, defined genocide as

> the successful attempt by a dominant group, vested with formal authority and/or with preponderant access to the overall resources of power, to reduce by coercion or lethal violence the number of a minority group whose ultimate extermination is held desirable and useful and whose respective vulnerability is a major factor contributing to the decision of genocide.[61]

Implicit within this definition is the recognition that genocides are committed by formal or informal agents of the state or some similar entity with a maximum "dissymmetry of forces" between the vulnerable targeted groups and representatives of the power structure.[62] It is the imbalance of power that enables the perpetration of genocide and that emerges as a common constituent of many definitions that are offered to make sense of the term.

Dadrian expanded his definition by distinguishing between different types of genocide, categorizing them by issues of intent and motivation:

1. Cultural genocide is the destruction of the defining characteristic and qualities of a group and involves forced assimilation and suppression of their ethnic characteristics;
2. Latent genocide is the unintended or unanticipated destruction of a group as a byproduct of war;
3. Retributive genocide is perpetrated in reprisal for real or perceived challenges and threats to the established order on the part of some minority group, and therefore tends to be fairly localized and short-lived;
4. Utilitarian genocide is a form of widespread massacre committed for specific tactical, economic, or political advantage;
5. Optimal genocide intends the complete destruction of a group, and encompasses those genocides perpetrated as part of a systematic and definitive attempt to eradicate all the group's members.[63]

While this typology is helpful in distinguishing between specific examples of genocides, the items are not entirely mutually exclusive and the categorical overlap between differing types of genocide leaves one unclear about which class or classes of genocide specific examples fall into. Additionally, the first two categories do not deal with motivations or reasons for genocide; instead, they describe the process or method by which it occurs. While Dadrian's work has been rec-

ognized as providing one of the first social science–based definitions of genocide, it has been criticized as being too broad and unclear, providing more explanation than clear criteria for purposes of analysis.[64] Additionally, the inclusion of latent genocide as a subcategory can be critiqued since it implies an
equivalency between intended and unintended crimes, and yet in terms of legal
and moral responsibility there is a world of difference between crimes of intent
and accidental crimes. The law on criminal homicide, for example, typically
categorizes intentional killings as murder and unintentional killings as man-
slaughter, with correspondingly more lenient sanctions. Nevertheless, even with
these shortcomings, Dadrian's work is useful for illustrating the diversity of
genocidal crimes and encourages recognition of genocide as a multifaceted phenomenon rather than a unidimensional type of crime.

A Genocidal Continuum

Robert Melson defines genocide as "a public policy mainly carried out
by the state whose intent is the destruction in whole or in part of a social collectivity or category, usually a communal group, a class, or a political faction."[65]
In formulating this definition of genocide, Melson argues that genocides are
linked in a continuum that originates with massacres and pogroms and moves
through partial to total genocides, with the Holocaust as the ultimate example.
Genocides, according to this analysis, differ in terms of their intended lethality
and duration. The Holocaust, for example, is perceived as an absolute attempt
to kill all the Jews and is therefore rather unusual. According to Melson, "The
Holocaust may be distinguished from other instances of total genocide in representing the extreme of physical annihilation, cultural destruction, and global scope."[66] He also differentiates between total genocides and the Holocaust
by pointing out that while in total genocides some members of the targeted
group may save themselves by abandoning their identity, this option was not
open to Jews during the Holocaust. For all this, Melson does not adequately
clarify the differences between total genocides and the Holocaust, since total
genocides typically share much of the intent and lethality of the Holocaust. The
continuum of lethality, however, is a powerful tool that allows comparison of a
wide range of genocidal crimes.

One-Sided Killing and Genocide

In another attempt to create a useful definition, Frank Chalk and Kurt
Jonassohn define genocide as

a form of one-sided killing in which a state or other authority intends to destroy a
group, as that group and membership in it are defined by the perpetrator.[67]

Important for these scholars is the idea that genocide is one-sided and therefore does not include warfare, which by definition has at least two combatants.
Genocide, according to Chalk and Jonassohn, is perpetrated upon a group even

when that group offers no resistance, which echoes Dadrian's recognition of the vulnerability of the targeted group. This distinction between warfare or mutual combat and genocide is an important one that remains somewhat controversial because other scholars have recently begun arguing that modern total warfare is often genocidal in character, or at least contains genocidal components.[68]

Chalk and Jonassohn's view of genocide also stresses that membership in a targeted group is defined by the aggressor, not the victims. Rather than setting somewhat arbitrary criteria for the inclusion of specific groups, they follow a more sociological approach by relying on the perpetrator's definition to designate the group and its membership. This approach allows for the recognition of socially situated meanings inherent in any definition of membership. In other words, the perpetrator's definition is most relevant for analysis since it is that viewpoint that is operational in the perpetration of genocide, regardless of whether it is objectively accurate or fair. While the Nazi definition of Jewishness was based on flawed and faulty concepts, it was nonetheless the template used to differentiate between victims and gentiles. While Helen Fein sees this approach as a weakness, it does allow the situational perception of the perpetrator to be revealed.[69] If an individual is murdered because of perceived membership in a group targeted for destruction, it is somewhat irrelevant if the criteria for membership are ontologically false.

Also significant to Chalk and Jonassohn is the notion of intentionality. They contend that for a crime to be considered genocide, the destruction of the targeted group must be a conscious goal on the part of the perpetrators, and the intent must be the group's complete destruction. This last point distinguishes their definitions from others, such as the U.N.'s, that hold that the entire group does not have to be targeted. The U.N. definition, for example, asserts that genocide is the destruction of a group in whole or *in part*.

Like Dadrian, Chalk and Jonassohn divide genocide into different types, according to its purpose or motive. They distinguish among genocides perpetrated to 1) eliminate a real or potential threat; 2) spread terror among real or potential enemies; 3) acquire economic wealth; or 4) implement a belief, a theory, or an ideology. This is important since the motivation often dictates, constrains, and guides the specific processes and methods employed. The definition of genocide proposed by Chalk and Jonassohn is a noteworthy attempt to grapple with a difficult conceptual topic. It is a broad and inclusive explication that allows exploration of a wide range of genocidal killings and, as we shall see, is similar in many respects to that suggested by Helen Fein.

Destroying Collectives

Helen Fein asserts that genocide is

sustained purposeful action by a perpetrator to physically destroy a collective directly or indirectly, through interdiction of the biological and social reproduction of group members, sustained regardless of the surrender or lack of threat offered by the victim.[70]

Her explicit purpose is to develop a sociological perspective on genocide, and to this end she also develops a paradigm for identifying genocide that includes the following points:

1. There was a sustained attack or continuity of attacks by the perpetrator to physically destroy group members.
2. The perpetrator was a collective or organized actor or commander of organized actors.
3. Victims were selected because they were members of a collectivity.
4. The victims were defenseless or were killed regardless of whether they surrendered or resisted.
5. The destruction of group members was undertaken with intent to kill and murder was sanctioned by the perpetrator.[71]

Fein provides a powerful conceptualization that, while providing for the inclusion of various types of victims, still retains enough definitional rigor to clearly differentiate between genocides and other forms of mass violence and killing. Moreover, the use of the term "sustained purposeful action" indicates that she does not accept the notion of unintentional or accidental genocides. In other words, for genocide to exist there must be intent. Her definition also makes clear that she accepts the notion of one-sidedness suggested by Chalk and Jonassohn, but does not necessarily exclude as victims of genocide those who are able or willing to defend themselves. It is a slightly more refined approach to the issue of resistance and defense. Fein, similarly to Dadrian, recognizes both overt and covert killing. While both are intentional, Helen Fein distinguishes between direct killing and the indirect destruction of the collective through the prevention of births or removal of children from the group. In other words, Fein's definition specifically includes the cultural genocide of a group that leaves the individual member physically alive, but the culture and the individual's cultural identity dead.

Defenseless Victims and Genocide

One of the most impassioned and humanistically oriented of genocide scholars, Israel Charny, has suggested a generic definition of genocide:

the mass killing of substantial numbers of human beings, when not in the course of military action against the military forces of an avowed enemy, under conditions of the essential defenselessness and helplessness of the victims.[72]

These criteria are intentionally extremely broad, since his avowed purpose is to create a general definition of genocide that

does not exclude or commit to indifference any case of mass murder of any human beings, of whatever racial, national, ethnic, biological, cultural, religious, and political definitions, or of totally mixed groupings of any and all of the above.[73]

Charny's definition has been criticized for being much too sweeping and all-encompassing and thus losing its ability to differentiate and categorize.[74] As Irving Horowitz points out, "there is a danger in broadening the concept of genocide so that it becomes symbolically all-embracing and hence meaningless."[75] Nevertheless, Israel Charny's concern that specific groups not be excluded from conceptualizations of genocide remains a valid and important consideration as genocide scholars struggle to comprehend and study this phenomenon. Of what use is a definition if it ignores and discounts the suffering of human beings who are targeted for elimination because of real or perceived membership in some group? As he eloquently states, "The definition of genocide adopted in law and by professional social scientists must match the realities of life, so that there should be no situation in which thousands and even millions of defenseless victims of mass murder do not 'qualify' as victims of genocide."[76] His work, therefore, stands as a powerful reminder not to let theoretical constraints interfere with a recognition of the humanity of those suffering.

Charny proposes a definitional matrix for genocide that contains genocidal massacres, intentional genocides, genocide in the course of colonization or consolidation of power, genocide in the course of aggressive and unjust wars, war crimes against humanity, and genocide as a result of ecological destruction and abuse. He also proposes that accomplices to genocide be held responsible for their ancillary roles in facilitating the perpetration of these genocidal crimes, thus recognizing the importance of the bureaucrats and other professionals who assist in genocide but don't actually kill. Interestingly, he also includes cultural genocide in the matrix but distinguishes between ethnocide, the destruction of a culture, and linguicide, the eradication of the language of a people.[77]

State Bureaucracies

Irving Louis Horowitz defines genocide as "a structural and systematic destruction of innocent people by a state bureaucratic apparatus."[78] His is also a broad, if rather vague, definition that emphasizes the role of the state in perpetrating genocide. Furthermore, Horowitz regards genocide as one end of a continuum that emphasizes the amount of control and tolerance that a particular society has. He categorizes societies into eight types:

1. genocidal societies, in which the state arbitrarily takes the lives of citizens for deviant or dissident behavior;
2. deportation or incarceration societies, in which the state either removes individuals from the larger body politic or in some form prevents their interaction with the commonwealth in general;
3. torture societies, in which people are victimized short of death, returned to the societies from which they came, and left in these societies as living evidence of the high risk of deviance or dissidence;
4. harassment societies, in which deviants are constantly being picked up, searched, seized, or held for violation of laws that are usually remote from the actual crimes the state feels these individuals have committed.

Since laws can be invoked against almost any behavior, the possibility of harassment of individuals through legal channels is infinite;

5. traditional shame societies, where participation in the collective will is enforced through instilling in the individual an awareness of disapproval from outside sources, and insured by the isolation suffered as a result of nonparticipation in the normative system;

6. guilt societies, which are closely akin to shame societies but which internalize a sense of wrongdoing in the individual, causing him to conform to normative standards;

7. tolerant societies, where norms are well articulated and understood, but where deviance and dissidence are permitted to go unpunished; they are not celebrated, but not destroyed either. These can be described as a series of pluralisms operating with a larger monism;

8. permissive societies, in which norms are questioned and community definitions rather than state definition of what constitutes normative behavior emerge in the decision-making process.[79]

Horowitz, as is evident, clearly links genocide to specific types of societies, with particular emphasis on the mechanisms of social control utilized by governments to either control or tolerate deviance. For Horowitz, genocide is perpetrated by repressive totalitarian regimes. One weakness of this theorization is that he does not address how we should conceptualize a tolerant or permissive society that provides support and assistance to more repressive societies engaged in genocides. The United States, for example, has often done so. Nevertheless, Horowitz's work is extremely helpful for identifying the types of government that are prone to engage in genocide and allows comparisons across the political spectrum. This politicized perception of genocide is also reflected in the work of R. J. Rummel.

Democide

Because of all the definitional inconsistencies and shortcomings surrounding the term "genocide," R. J. Rummel suggests the broader concept of democide, which includes any governmental action intended to kill a group of people because of their membership in a demographic group, or because of real or specious opposition to the government.[80] Specifically, Rummel writes,

a death constitutes democide if it is the intentional killing of an unarmed or disarmed person by government agents acting in their authoritative capacity and pursuant to government policy or high command. . . . It is also democide if the death was the result of such authoritative government actions carried out with reckless and wanton disregard for the lives of those affected. . . . It is democide if government promoted or turned a blind eye to the death even though it was murder carried out "unofficially" or by private groups. . . . And the death also may be democide if high government officials purposely allowed conditions to continue that were causing mass deaths and issued no public warning. . . . All extrajudicial or

summary executions comprise democide. Even judicial executions may be democide. . . . Judicial executions for "crime" internationally considered trivial or non-
capital . . . are also democide.[81]

Democide, then, is a wide-ranging conceptualization in which genocides are
merely one specific subtype of democide, along with politicides, mass murders
and massacres, and terror campaigns. His is an addition to the literature since
it explicitly relates genocide to other governmentally induced forms of mass
killing. It thus contextualizes genocide within a larger, more comprehensive
theoretical framework that reconciles similar, yet distinct, types of mass killing.
Like Horowitz, Rummel sees genocide largely as a creation of totalitarian governments, and his research supports this assertion. Rummel points out that, according to his calculations, of the many millions of victims of democide in
the twentieth century, only a small percent were killed by democratic governments.[82] But while Rummel's analysis provides a powerful reminder of the dangers of authoritarian governments, he does not recognize the role that democratic governments also play in creating genocides around the world. Many of
the Argentine kidnappers, torturers, and assassins were trained by American
and French experts in counterinsurgency tactics that included kidnapping, torture, and assassination.[83] Additionally, businesses, American ones among them,
are largely responsible for the exploitation of the Amazon rain forest and the
accompanying expulsion and destruction of its inhabitants. Democratic governments, in other words, have assisted and exploited the genocidal policies of
other states. Rummel's analysis does not adequately address this fact. While
democratic governments are certainly not as overtly lethal and oppressive as totalitarian ones, they are also not the shining exemplars of moral purity implied
in Rummel's discussion. Nevertheless, that criticism aside, Rummel's ability to
distinguish among different types of politicized mass killing and the types of
states most likely to perpetrate them has certainly contributed to our understanding of the dynamics of this type of crime.

Politicides

In work similar to Rummel's, Barbara Harff and Tedd Gurr developed
the idea of politicide, which they define as the killing of political groups. According to their definition, politicides are distinct from genocides, which involve the destruction of groups defined in terms of their communal characteristics, such as race or ethnicity.[84] It is an idea that mirrors Rummel's conception
of democide. They also seek to categorize the different forms of genocide and
politicide by expanding upon previous typologies. Specifically, they distinguish
among

hegemonial genocides: mass murders that occur when distinct ethnic, religious, or
national groups are being forced to submit to central authority, for example during
the consolidation of power by a new state or in the course of national expansion;

xenophobic genocides: mass murders of ethnically, religiously, or nationally distinct groups in the service of doctrines of national protection or social purification, which define the victims as alien and threatening;

retributive politicides: mass murders that target previously dominant or influential groups out of resentment for their past privileges or abuses;

repressive politicides: mass murders that target political parties, factions, and movements because they are engaged in some form of oppositional activity;

revolutionary politicides: mass murders of class or political enemies in the service of new revolutionary ideologies;

repressive/hegemonic politicides: mass murders that target ethnically or nationally distinct groups because they are engaged in some form of oppositional activity.[85]

Harff and Gurr's conceptualization emphasizes two important ideas. First, they argue that both genocide and politicide are perpetrated by the state; in this recognition, their work mirrors Rummel's focus on government. Second, they assert that both types of mass killing must be intentional to qualify for inclusion. As we shall see, intent is an element common to many definitions.

Definitional Commonalities

While other conceptualizations of genocide have been developed, the definitions reviewed above constitute the bulk of the extant literature and are sufficient to allow a discussion of the common themes revealed in this assessment. As illustrated, there is a decided lack of agreement as to what specifically constitutes genocide. Debate rages around the inclusion or exclusion of various groups, the types of killing that should or should not be included, and whether or not cultural genocide is a genuine form of genocide.[86] Regardless of the particular definition forwarded and its unique characteristics, common threads run through most of the definitions, and these conceptual intersections can help produce a more concrete understanding of behaviors generally considered genocidal.

The first pervasive element is the recognition that genocide is committed by the state or a similar authority structure. Whether explicitly or implicitly, the various definitions agree that genocides are overwhelmingly carried out by agents or representatives of the state acting in their official capacities, using the power derived from their office or position, or at the very least that those perpetrating genocide act with the complicity and tacit approval of the state. Examples of this latter type include unofficial death squads with links to the power structure of the state. In El Salvador, for example, the notorious death squads of the 1980s were funded by a wealthy oligarchy and controlled by members of ARENA, the right-wing and extremely conservative party of El Salvador's elites.[87] This latter category also includes the militias that were such a pervasive and lethal element of the Serbian and Rwandan genocides. The official instruments of genocide are most commonly found in the government, the military, and the police. In short, genocide is committed by state entities and their minions. A genocide does not begin spontaneously, nor is it caused by old hatreds and tribal enmities, as is so often claimed. In that sense at least, genocide is a rational and instrumental tool to certain political, economic, or ideological ends. In the next chapter, genocide will be explored at length as a form of state crime.

A second common feature of genocides is that they are planned, systematic, and ongoing attempts to eliminate a group of people. Spontaneous events are typically massacres, which may in fact have genocidal overtones, but are not genocide per se. They simply do not have the sustained and routinized character of genocides. In the previously discussed definitions, several scholars use the term "genocidal massacre" to refer to isolated examples of governmental mass killing. It should be noted, however, that massacres may take place during genocides, and in fact may be part of a larger campaign against a group. For example, the Armenian genocide was perpetrated by means of a series of massacres, first of the intelligentsia, soldiers, and all able-bodied men, after which the women and children were subjected to a succession of attacks as they were forcibly removed to the Syrian desert. Similarly, prior to the industrialized extermination of the death camps, the Nazis began their genocide with massacres perpetrated by roving death squads who followed the advancing German army and killed large numbers of Jews and Soviets in places such as Babi Yar, a ravine near Kiev. Here, in the space of two days, over thirty-three thousand Jews were murdered.[88] The genocide as a whole, however, can last years. The killing in the Nazi-perpetrated Holocaust began with the invasion of the Soviet Union on June 22, 1941, as mobile killing squads, the infamous *Einsatzgruppen,* followed behind the rapidly advancing German army and began killing Soviet commissars and Jews.[89] Ultimately formalized into the more lethally effective organization of the death camps, the murders lasted until the defeat of the German Reich in 1945. Similarly, the Cambodian genocide lasted nearly four years, from the time that the Khmer Rouge took power in 1975 and emptied the cities until their defeat by the invading Vietnamese army in 1979. On the other hand, genocide can also occur quickly. The bulk of the killing during the Rwandan genocide occurred over the course of several months.

The third common principle is that victims are chosen because of real or imagined membership in a group targeted for destruction. As Markusen states, "the individual identity of the victims is in general irrelevant, as are distinctions among sex and age. What concerns the state is that the individual belongs to the group targeted for destruction."[90] Recognizing this point as well, Raphael Lemkin similarly wrote that "Genocide is directed against the national group as an entity, and the actions involved are directed against individuals, not in their individual capacity, but as members of the national group."[91] Genocide constitutes a type of depersonalized victimization, since the individual characteristics of the victims are not taken into account. Victims are merely inhabitants of categories. If they are given an identity, it is usually a derogatory and dehumanized one applied to all members of the group. To the German perpetrators, all Jews were a subhuman form of animal life or, alternatively, were equated with disease and sickness.[92] To the Hutu perpetrators in Rwanda, the Tutsis were *inyenzi*, or insects.[93] Defining a person as a lesser form of life makes it easier to discriminate against, torture, and kill that person. Killing an insect or an animal does not call forth the same emotional reaction and empathy that killing a fellow human being would.

A fourth commonality is the vulnerability of the targeted group. The collectives victimized in genocide are chosen, in part, because they are relatively powerless. The victims are typically members of minority groups that have been socially and politically marginalized, historically so in many cases. Often they are members of what have been termed "middleman minority groups," or groups that serve as intermediaries between producers and consumers in a society, and these roles often set them apart from the communities they serve.[94] These groups are often composed of immigrant populations who fill economic niches that are left vacant by the original or native inhabitants. Both needed and utilized, yet also disdained, envied, and hated, middleman minority groups have long been the targets of racial and ethnic violence fostered by their marginalized status. For example, because they were legally prohibited from owning land and limited to only a few trades, Jews in medieval Europe often survived as moneylenders. Since Christians were prohibited from lending money by canonical restrictions on usury, Jews performed a necessary role in providing loans and capital to Christian businessmen and nobles. At the same time, they were also despised and hated as "bloodsuckers" and nonbelievers by the very people who utilized their services. During times of crisis and upheaval this population was relatively vulnerable to persecution.[95]

If the members of the targeted group are relatively well entrenched within the genocidally inclined society, the regime must take steps to remove their power prior to any genocide. In fact, the very success of a group is often taken as a sign that they are "trying to take over" or that they must have had help and are conspiring to secretly assume political or economic power.[96]

The Turkish Armenian intelligentsia and leadership were among the first arrested and sent to the interior, where they were presumably killed; none were ever seen again. Armenians in the military were also removed from their positions and placed in penal battalions, where most were killed, while other ablebodied males were summarily gathered together, arrested, and then murdered.[97] Thus, the Turkish government was able to eliminate the most likely sources of resistance to the genocide. Similarly, prominent Bosnian Muslims were often the first targeted for arrest or execution in order to deprive the Muslims of possible leaders.[98]

The German government systematically stripped Jews of all political, legal, and economic power. As Rubenstein writes, "Once defined as a Jew, by the German state bureaucracy, a person was progressively deprived of all personal property and citizenship rights."[99] Thus, step by painful step, law by law, and edict by edict, one of the most assimilated, educated, and economically well-off Jewish communities in Europe was deprived of rights, wealth, and power, and this process helped enable the subsequent Holocaust. The ability of the modern state to marginalize specific collectives, and to impose its will upon those groups, is unparalleled and has contributed to the increased frequency and efficiency of this crime.

Fifth, many of the definitions point out that genocide appears in various forms and guises, each characterized by different goals and motivations, and these different goals shape the various strategies and tactics of the individual genocides. For example, the genocide perpetrated against the Indians of the South American rain forest is occurring because of economic forces that seek to open up and exploit the Amazon basin. The Indians present a hindrance to the exploitation of the land that they live on and so they are being removed.[100] While the killing is often masked by justifying ideologies, the motivation for these genocides is almost exclusively economic. They are examples of what Dadrian termed "utilitarian genocide" and fall into Chalk and Jonassohn's third category of genocide, that perpetrated to acquire economic wealth. These genocides are, consequently, conceptually distinct from more ideological genocides such as the Holocaust, motivated as it was by pseudo-scientific beliefs about racial superiority and buttressed by a long tradition of anti-Semitism. The Nazis believed that they were protecting the noble Aryan race from the depredations of the subhuman Jews, Gypsies, and Slavs. The Cambodian genocide was also ideological; the Khmer Rouge wanted to return the country to a mythic past by eliminating all foreign and, in their view, corrupting influences and return the nation to a pure and agrarian society. It was in the course of implementing this vision that the genocide was committed.

To Yehuda Bauer, genocides may best be perceived as falling on a continuum that ranges from cases of mass murder through various types of genocide, with its ultimate extreme being the Holocaust.[101] Melson similarly uses the concept of a continuum of destruction to illustrate that genocides are manifested in numerous guises, each with its own methods, motives, and victim groups. Each genocide, in that sense, exhibits certain unique characteristics that differentiate it from others.

Sixth, genocide includes many different types of activities, only one of which is the blatant or immediate murder of a population. All activities, however, are organized toward the eradication of a people, involving either the physical or cultural destruction of a population. For example, some have pointed out that the Serbs not only tried to expel or kill their Muslim neighbors, but also engaged in a systematic campaign to destroy all artifacts of the Bosnian Muslim culture, including bridges, mosques, libraries, and museums.[102] The physical eradication of a people was accompanied by an attempt to remove all traces of their unique culture. While there is disagreement over the concept of cultural genocide, all concur that the essence of genocide involves the annihilation of the members of a group in order to eliminate that group. Genocide, in other words, employs a number of tactics to achieve a variety of ends, all of which involve the physical or cultural destruction of a group of people. The individual methods may vary tremendously but the intended result is always the same. Genocidal killing ranges from the efficient, dispassionate, and impersonal gassings of the Holocaust, to the up-close, bloody murders of the Rwandan genocide, which were carried out largely with clubs and machetes. Often several methods of killing compete for dominance within a genocidal state, but regardless of the means and methods of extermination, fundamentally genocide is a way to kill. Even ethnocide, all controversy aside, involves the assassination of culture and of identity. It is the murder of the ties that bind a group of people together and make them unique.

Seventh, another component common to many definitions is intent. Intent is one of the most basic doctrines within most criminal law systems and relates to a person's basic culpability for any given offense. To be guilty of an offense in most Western legal systems, a person must have deliberately perpetrated the act. If the act was accidental, the person is generally believed to be not as responsible as if it had been deliberate. As Supreme Court Justice Oliver Wendell Holmes once remarked, "Even a dog distinguishes between being stumbled over and being kicked." Important to the issue of intent is *mens rea*, a Latin term that literally means "guilty or evil mind" and is captured by the precept *actus non facit reum nisi mens sit rea* ("an act is not bad without an evil mind").[103] According to this principle, a person is not criminally culpable for his or her behavior if that guilty mind is absent.

Among genocide scholars intent has been an important, albeit contentious, issue. Some have argued that the issue of intent simply be removed from the criteria for genocide, while others suggest the development of a hierarchical scale for intent such as is found in the law on criminal homicide (i.e., first-degree murder, second-degree murder, etc.).[104] For example, the United Nations Genocide Convention asserts that a crime is only genocide if the listed behaviors are committed with the "intent to destroy, in whole or in part." Critics of the United Nations definition see this as a weakness because of the difficulty of proving intent, especially since the Convention provided no criteria for identifying or proving intent. Herbert Hirsch points out that

> If one adheres to a strict interpretation of the language of intent, then the Serbs are, for example, able to argue that their intent is not to commit genocide but to acquire territory, or as perpetrators often argue, to protect themselves from the threat raised by the Bosnian Muslims or Croatians. The concept of "intent" is ambiguous.[105]

However, it must be noted that this problem of ambiguity is not unique to genocide. Generally speaking, intent is very difficult to prove in a court of law, since the only explicit evidence of a guilty state of mind is a confession. When the crime involves a form of collective intent, or the intent of an organization or bureaucracy, the issue becomes even more problematic. Of this problem, Isidor Wallimann and Michael N. Dobkowski note that "In the modern age, the issue of intentionality on the societal level is harder to locate because of the anonymous and amorphous structural forces that dictate the character of our world."[106]

Intent is usually illustrated through indirect evidence, such as behavior. In other words, *mens rea* is inferred from the actions of the perpetrator.[107] The problem of intent is therefore not any more problematic for genocide than it is for other types of crime. Additionally, the debate among genocide scholars concerning intent is often not informed by a clear understanding of the varied nature of the legal definition of intent. Many genocide scholars seem to assume that there exists only one form of intent. Legally speaking, however, there are four types: general intent, specific intent, transferred intent, and constructive intent. General intent encompasses most people's understanding of intent, containing as it does the principle of *actus reas*. That is, a person must consciously and knowingly perpetrate the criminal act. According to Samaha,

> the required act in burglary is breaking and entering, in larceny the taking and carrying away of another's property, and in rape sexual penetration. General intent refers to the intent to commit those acts.[108]

The problem, according to many genocide scholars who perceive only general intent, is that it is very difficult to prove this type of intent in genocide. While the concepts of specific and transferred intent are not particularly relevant to this discussion, constructive intent is very helpful. Constructive intent includes cases in which the perpetrators did not intend to harm others but should have realized or known that their behavior made the harm likely.[109] Constructive intent, therefore, resolves the dilemma seen by those who suggest that the unintentional destruction of a people does not constitute genocide. The destruction of the Aché, for example, was condemned by various sources as a crime of genocide. The defense minister of Paraguay replied to these accusations by asserting that

> Although there are victims and victimizer, there is not the third element necessary to establish the crime of genocide—that is "intent." Therefore, as there is no "intent," one cannot speak of "genocide."[110]

This is clearly a narrow and self-serving interpretation of intent. Systematically hunting down and killing members of a group, forcibly removing other members to reservations and then withholding food and medicine, and kidnapping many of their children to raise as slaves outside of the group's culture clearly results in the destruction of that group of people, even if that result is neither intended nor desired. In a similar vein, Franz Stangl, the former commandant of the Treblinka death camp, said, "the only way I could live was by compartmentalizing my thinking. By doing this I could apply it to my own situation; if the 'subject' was the government, the 'object' the Jews, and the 'action' the gassings, then I could tell myself that for me the fourth element, 'intent' was missing."[111] Again, this is an example of a very narrow and limited definition of intent. A German court did not agree with Stangl's definition of intent, and after his extradition from Brazil he was sentenced to life imprisonment in 1970; he eventually died in prison.[112] Unquestionably, constructive intent frames the actions of the Paraguayan government as acts of genocide, as well as those of Franz Stangl.

Eighth and last is the implicit recognition among scholars that genocide is a crime, a crime that must be prevented and punished. While genocide is generally condemned, its recognition as a form of crime often depends upon the particular perspective of the social audience. The Turkish government, for example, continues to deny that a genocide was perpetrated against its Armenian population. Because genocide is perpetrated by an official authority structure, typically with legal sanction, it is easy to accept the official version of events and not question the legitimacy of a government's actions. To counter this type of influence, it must be stressed and emphasized that genocide is intrinsically criminal, even though it is perpetrated under the auspices of the state. While this emphasis is somewhat symbolic, its importance should not be underestimated. As Gregg Barak and others have pointed out, popular attitudes and behaviors are affected by how behavior is defined.[113] Therefore clear and unambiguous perceptions of genocide as a crime must be fostered.

To sum up, even though no one clear, universal, and unambiguous definition of genocide exists, enough elements are common to most definitions to allow a working understanding of the crime of genocide. Most of the examples of genocide discussed in this book clearly qualify for inclusion according to the criteria discussed above. The most problematic of the cases discussed in this book is that of Bosnia. It is worth exploring this particular example in greater detail.

When discussing the issue of genocide in the former Yugoslavia during the 1990s, one must first recognize that many types of violence occurred at different times throughout the numerous conflicts in the region. The first significant violence took place after the Slovenian and Croatian declarations of independence on June 2, 1991. The next day, elements of the Serb-dominated Yugoslav National Army (JNA) moved into Slovenia. However, after several days of fighting a truce was declared and Slovenia managed to avoid much of the destruction that began to engulf Croatia and Bosnia. In contrast, the fighting in Croatia involved many atrocities and war crimes and resulted in over 200,000 refugees, 20,000 people killed, and over 350,000 displaced.[114] Large parts of Croatia, such as the Krajina region, were taken over by Serb forces and the Croatians living there were terrorized, forced to leave, or killed. As horrible and tragic as that violence was, however, it did not constitute genocide. That was saved for Bosnia.

When Bosnia declared independence in March of 1992, Serb forces in large parts of Bosnia immediately orchestrated a campaign of violence against non-Serbs. Recognizing the drift toward independence, Bosnian Serbs had earlier that year begun to train and arm paramilitary militia groups and had also declared a Serbian Republic of Bosnia-Herzegovina.[115] After the fighting broke out, Croatian forces also took the opportunity to try and increase their territorial holdings and fought against the Muslim forces in several parts of Bosnia.[116]

The fighting essentially took place on two levels. First, the Serb and Croat forces sought to acquire new territory by wresting it from the Bosnian Muslims, and second, they sought to "ethnically cleanse" the land under their dominion. For the Serbs, by 1994 this amounted to the vast bulk of Bosnian territory. While atrocities and war crimes were perpetrated by all sides during the fighting, evidence indicates that the vast majority of them were committed by the Serbs, largely against the Bosnian Muslims.[117]

The violence in the Serb-occupied territories was characterized by four related types of acts: executions and mass murder; forcible dispossession and displacement; mass rapes; and arrest and detention. These acts were often accompanied by various other cruelties and tortures. While these atrocities are horrific, do they constitute genocide? Ethnic cleansing, it is important to note, is not genocide.[118] Do the actions in Bosnia constitute more than just a terrible series of ethnic outrages—do they sink to the level of genocide? While there is some debate about this, I believe that the answer is yes, for the following reasons.

The intent of the Serbs was to destroy the Bosnian Muslim population. The killing and ethnic cleansing were not unforeseen and unfortunate byproducts of the military campaigns, they were their central aim. The destruction of the Bosnian Muslim people was not incidental to the territorial aspirations, rather it was a principal part of it. Most of the victims of the fighting were civilians, not soldiers. Serb forces targeted Muslim civilians specifically because of their identity, regardless of their ability or inability to resist, because the avowed purpose of the Serb forces was to create an ethnically pure greater Serbian nation.[119] The available evidence also clearly indicates that Serbian and Bosnian Serb political and military leaders were instrumental in planning and directing the campaigns against the Muslims, which also gives credence to the notion of intentionality.[120]

It is also important to keep in mind that the destruction of a population does not necessarily entail murdering all members of that group. Some have argued that the release of some inmates from the detention camps, and the fact that most of the victims of the killing were boys and men rather than women, signal a lack of genocidal intent. This view, however, is not consistent with the criteria for genocide. According to most of the definitions discussed above, genocide may take many different forms, not all of them physically lethal. Forcibly removing a people from their homes and communities; destroying all visible symbols of their culture, such as mosques, libraries and the like; murdering many thousands of men, women, and children; and subjecting thousands of women to mass rapes with the intent of impregnating them with Serb babies are clear attempts to destroy their culture and communal identity. The violence in Bosnia was about destroying the Bosnian Muslims as a people, which, in my opinion, certainly qualifies as genocide. One might even argue that the mass murder of many thousands of men and boys fits the U.N. criterion of destroying, "in whole or in part, a national, ethnical, racial or religious group." The phrase "in part" does not mandate a minimum numerical threshold.

For all of these reasons, I will be referring to the Bosnian case throughout this book as an example of genocide, along with the Holocaust, the Armenian genocide, and those which occurred in Rwanda and Cambodia.

With these definitional guidelines in place we can begin to specifically review the different levels at which genocide operates. This discussion begins at the primary level of responsibility and involves a review of the role of the state in the creation and perpetration of this crime.

3   Deadly Regimes

The twentieth century is an age of genocide in which sixty million men, women, and children, coming from many different races, religions, ethnic groups, nationalities, and social classes, and living in many different countries, on most of the continents of the earth, have had their lives taken because the state thought it desirable.

—Roger Smith[1]

The more power a government has, the more it can act arbitrarily according to the whims and desires of the elite, and the more it will make war on others and murder its foreign and domestic subjects.

—R. J. Rummel[2]

In an interview just months before his death, Pol Pot, former Khmer Rouge leader and the architect of the Cambodian genocide, denied being responsible for the genocide committed against his people during the 1970s. Asserting that "I came to carry out the struggle, not to kill people," Pol Pot portrayed himself as a misunderstood and unfairly vilified figure, instead of the leader of a movement considered one of the most brutal of the twentieth century. Incredibly, he also declared, "Am I a savage person? My conscience is clear."[3] What do we make of these statements? Did he truly believe in his innocence, or was this just a self-serving attempt to manipulate public opinion? Perhaps he was truly unaware of the effects of his policies on the Cambodian people. Never leaving the capital, and surrounded by subservient minions who would not dare imply that his policies were destroying an entire society, he may not have known, or cared to know, the harsh realities of Khmer Rouge rule.[4] But if Pol Pot was not responsible for the killings, who was? While Pol Pot denied culpability for the death of more than a million of his fellow Cambodians, his disavowal was rejected by many, including his former followers. Ousted by rivals within the party, the former leader was recently put on trial by the organization he helped create. It is rather ironic that the Khmer Rouge could hold their former leader accountable and hang banners that read "Down with Pol Pot and his genocidal clique" and "Cambodians do not kill Cambodians."[5] Memory seems to have been selectively applied among the Khmer Rouge.

The simple reality is that Pol Pot was responsible for the genocide and the Khmer Rouge were the instrument of his will. The mass murder of large segments of the Cambodian population was carried out at the behest of *Angkar Loeu*, the leadership clique of the Khmer Rouge state, of which Pol Pot was the head, hence his nickname of *bong ti muoy,* "Brother Number One." In fact, the ideology of Cambodian genocide can be traced directly to him and members of his inner circle, who developed it when they were students together in France.[6] Pol Pot and the state he created bear complete responsibility for the murder of several million human beings. His disavowal of accountability simply does not withstand scrutiny.

Responsibility for genocide invariably rests with the leadership of the government in power, since the crime of genocide is largely planned and perpetrated by both formal and informal agents of the state. While genocides may vary in their amount of direct state oversight, planning, and control, it is nonetheless true that public officials are the prime movers of genocide in the twentieth century. Participants do not act individually, but carry out mass murder as part of a larger movement. Their motivation for the act does not lie in individual pathology, but is grounded in institutional and societal goals and strategies; it is a means to a political end. In this sense, genocide can be perceived as an "advanced form of state terrorism,"[7] and given that "most of the world's landmass today is divided into states, and most of the world's population falls under the jurisdiction of political organizations that rightly can be called states,"[8] this constitutes a significant problem in the modern era. The state is one of the most persistent and pervasive elements of modern communal life, and since this century has also seen a tremendous increase in state power and control,[9] any discussion of genocide must first recognize that it is a form of state criminality.[10]

The State

The state can be defined as "a centralized, institutionalized, authoritative system of political rule."[11] It comprises the governmental and administrative institutions of a society and the ideologies that support the legitimacy of those institutions,[12] as well as a geographically bounded territory over which that state has a perceived legitimacy of control and authority known as sovereignty.[13] In short, the state is a concentrated and bureaucratized system of control and management that provides a powerful and relatively efficient means of organizing the people in a given region or territory.

A fairly recent creation, the state is generally conceded to have first come to prominence after the Peace of Westphalia in 1648.[14] Ending the Thirty Years' War in Europe, the peace marked the end of decentralized feudal governments dominated by allegiance to the church, and legitimated the substitution of centralized political units that recognized no higher authority than their individual sovereignty. To understand the origins of the centralized political structure known as the state and its relationship to genocide, one must first look at the particular European context within which it developed.

The collapse of the Roman empire and the transition to feudalism marked the descent of Europe into anarchy and continuous warfare for five hundred years. The constant struggles and conflicts served ultimately to destroy the feudal system, characterized by local nodes of power and control, in favor of more centralized arrangements of political power. The continual pressures of warfare assured that weaker rulers either were destroyed and replaced or developed alliances with other leaders for mutual protection. Thus began a long process by which local political structures were consolidated into larger, more unified, and more powerful mechanisms of control. Eventually, the strongest of these evolved into politically defined units with centralized forms of rule and governance.

The interminable warfare necessitated that political structures mobilize tremendous resources, subdue any internal dissent, and develop unifying ideologies that appealed to citizens being asked or forced to wage the wars. In this environment, the state logically arose as the mechanism by which those needs could be met. As Bruce Porter puts it, "States make war, but war also makes states. The origins of the modern state, its rise and development, are therefore inextricably linked with violent conflict and military power."[15] This argument is by no means unique to Porter. Anthony Giddens defined the state as "a political organization whose rule is territorially ordered and which is able to mobilize the means of violence to sustain that rule,"[16] while Pierre van den Berghe contends that the state "has been the prime killer in human history. Killing is, in fact, in the very nature of the state. States are killing machines controlled by the few to steal from the many."[17] The demands of war provided an irresistible impulse toward a more centralized and bureaucratic form of administration better able to harness the technological and logistical resources needed to wage war. Bruce Porter outlines this process of state creation in five steps:

1. *An internal power struggle* between the center and the periphery of a given geographic area;
2. *A shift in favor of the center* due to developments in military technology and organization that increased the cost and administrative complexity of waging warfare;
3. *A revolution in taxation* as the rising fiscal demands of warfare, both internal and external, caused the government to intensify efforts to extract revenue;
4. *The rise of central bureaucracy* in response to the fiscal and administrative challenges of warfare;
5. *A feedback cycle* in which the increasing fiscal and bureaucratic power of states enabled them to field larger and more powerful armies, which meant larger and more destructive wars, which drove the whole process in a circular spiral upward.[18]

This developmental sequence illustrates how the dictates of political and military survival transformed feudal holdings, with their relatively small, isolated, and dispersed system of rule, into larger and ever more powerful states with the ability to more effectively control the greater amounts of resources needed to endure the endless conflicts. This process, it should be noted, lasted hundreds of years, culminating with the Peace of Westphalia.

The process did not happen uniformly, but involved many local variations influenced by purely regional issues and processes. But while the individual stories vary, the end result was always the same; a centralized system of political organization capable of defending itself from various threats. The ubiquity of the state around the world today is evidence of its singular ability to unite and protect populations. The state was successful, at least in part, because in its evolution it developed two ideologies that transformed it from merely an effective form of governance and protection into an autonomous force capable of commanding widespread belief in and subservience to the political power structure. These two constructs of belief are sovereignty and nationalism.

Sovereignty

Sovereignty refers to the political independence and autonomy enjoyed by modern states. It connotes the belief that the state is accountable to no higher authority. While states are increasingly vulnerable to international pressures and sanctions, they have historically acted without outside interference as far as their own society and citizens were concerned. Since individual states have resisted outside interference in internal matters, they have been extremely reluctant to interfere in the domestic actions of other states. Genocides are often greeted with a blind eye or limited censure by other states that, because of sovereign self-interest, are reluctant to intrude in the internal affairs of other sovereign entities. The world community has usually been silent while the worst genocides of the twentieth century were perpetrated, or has only perfunctorily condemned the killing. The Armenian genocide, the Holocaust, Stalin's Great Terror, and the Cambodian genocide were largely ignored by the international community. While this silence is often made easier by the control many nations have over the information that filters out through their borders, ignorance has never been a plausible excuse for noninterference. In each case of genocide, credible evidence established what was taking place, yet no forceful or effective protest was raised. Sovereignty appears to promote a quiet acceptance of genocide.

Amazingly enough, issues of sovereignty sometimes even promote international support for genocidal regimes. For example, Vietnam invaded Cambodia in 1979 after a series of border confrontations and quickly took control of the vast majority of the country, sending the Khmer Rouge forces back into the forests. While it was not Vietnam's primary intent, the invasion quickly ended the genocidal policies of the Khmer Rouge. The international reaction, however, was overwhelmingly negative. As Henry Kamm writes,

> The Western world, led by the United States, supported the Pol Pot regime's claim to legitimacy because it had been overthrown by a foreign invasion, a clear violation of sovereignty and international rules of conduct. Faced with a choice between upholding the most tyrannical and bloodthirsty regime since the days of Hitler and Stalin, or a puppet regime put in place by an invader, it backed the tyrant's claim to legitimacy. The elevation of sovereignty to the pinnacle of interna-

tional virtue is a damning comment on the sincerity of the Western democracies' constantly proclaimed advocacy of human rights.[19]

It is rather ironic that, because of issues of sovereignty combined with American antipathy toward Vietnam, the United States publicly supported a genocidal regime. It is doubly ironic since the Khmer Rouge were not only genocidal, but communist as well, a grave sin by the standards of the Cold War.

The importance of the relationship between sovereignty and genocide can also be illustrated by the refusal of the United States to ratify the United Nations Convention on the Prevention and Punishment of the Crime of Genocide, which passed the General Assembly of the United Nations on December 9, 1948. Even though enough countries had endorsed the Genocide Convention by 1951 for it to become binding under international law, the United States refused to sanction it. It was not until 1988, a full forty years after it was created, that the United States finally ratified the Genocide Convention. Approval, however, was contingent upon two reservations and five understandings.[20] The "sovereignty package," as these clauses were known, stipulates that the United States does not recognize the jurisdiction of international courts over it, that the American constitution has primacy over international law, and that no Americans can be extradited for violations of the Genocide Convention; lastly, it excludes discriminatory domestic policies and military actions from being classified as genocide except where genocide was the explicit and stated goal.[21] It essentially nullified the Genocide Convention's effect on the United States, and thus voided the American ratification. Many countries have objected to and refuse to recognize the U.S. acceptance of the Genocide Convention, specifically because of these stipulations.[22] It is ironic that the United States, a nation instrumental in the development of international law on crimes against humanity and genocide as well as a vocal proponent of human rights around the world, should insist on qualifying the declaration before signing it. As these points illustrate, the United States has been obsessed with allowing no constraints on its sovereignty. Its unwillingness to relinquish sovereign power is by no means unique, but rather is common to most states, which perceive that relinquishing their sovereignty diminishes their authority and makes the leadership and citizenry vulnerable to international sanctions for domestic actions.

In the former Yugoslavia, sovereignty was a fundamental catalyst for the violence and killing. Created from the ruins of the Austro-Hungarian empire in the aftermath of the First World War, Yugoslavia was a multiethnic nation composed of various republics and territories that did not achieve any real stability until Tito attained power after successfully fighting the Nazis in the Second World War. During his years in power, Tito worked hard to suppress nationalistic distinctions in favor of a common Yugoslav identity. With his death in 1980, and the waning of Cold War tensions a few years later, long-suppressed nationalistic sentiments were awakened by self-serving politicians like Croatia's Franjo Tudjman and Serbia's Slobodan Milošević. who both sought to maintain and broaden power in a rapidly changing world. Their nationalistic rhetoric and actions served to alienate other ethnic groups and fostered hostility and divisiveness. Ultimately, the outbreak of war was sparked by declarations of Croatian and Slovenian independence in 1991 and Bosnian independence in 1992. These newly proclaimed states, in asserting their freedom, directly challenged the sovereign primacy of the Yugoslav state, which was unacceptable to Serb politicians like Milošević who had a vested interest in retaining control over the breakaway republics.

Alija Izetbegović, the future president of Bosnia, stressed the importance of sovereignty when, in 1991, he said, "I would sacrifice peace for a sovereign Bosnia-Herzegovina, but for that peace in Bosnia-Herzegovina I would not sacrifice sovereignty."[23] Clearly, he recognized not only the importance of sovereignty, but the dangers of declaring it. Sovereignty assumes that a state has the sole and exclusive right to control a population and territory. Serbian politicians asserted their exclusive dominion over peoples throughout the Yugoslav republics, especially over Serb populations in predominantly Muslim, Croat, Slovenian, or Albanian republics. The pretext for much of the violence was the idea that Serb minorities were being dominated and oppressed by other Slavic groups. The violence was consequently portrayed as a necessary measure intended to save and protect Serbian lives and interests. Similarly, Franjo Tudjman portrayed Bosnia as Croatian territory and argued that the Croatian state had exclusive dominion over the Croats throughout the Yugoslav territory. Tudjman, an ardent Croatian nationalist, once told American ambassador Warren Zimmermann that "Bosnia has historically been a part of Croatia and has always been in Croatia's geopolitical sphere. Not only do Croats live in Bosnia, but most Muslims consider themselves Croats."[24]

The Serbs also used sovereignty as a pretext in their attempt to legitimize their actions in Bosnia. In September 1991, "Serb Autonomous Regions" were established in Bosnia, and on December 21, 1991, a "Serb Republic of Bosnia-Herzegovina," or *Republika Srpska*, was proclaimed under the leadership of Radovan Karadžić.[25] Three primary intentions appear to underlie these machinations.

First, they allowed the Bosnian Serbs to prepare the mechanisms by which the impending declaration of Bosnian independence could be contested, violently if necessary. Arms and munitions were brought in from Serbia, paramilitary groups were created, and a campaign of television and radio propaganda begun, all under the auspices of this new republic. Their goal was to prepare the Serb population, militarily and psychologically, for the impending conflict.

Second, creation of the Bosnian Serb state was intended to establish the legitimacy of the Serb cause and the violence they would ultimately employ. By definition, the actions of a state seem legitimate. Individuals and groups acting on behalf of that state are much more likely to have their actions condoned and accepted than if they are perceived to be acting out of naked self-interest. The Bosnian Serb army and the militias enjoyed the legal protection, as tenuous as that may have been, that derives from statehood.

Third, the establishment of this Bosnian Serb political entity concealed the involvement of Serbian puppeteers in Belgrade. Much evidence exists that the Serbian regime in Belgrade oversaw and directed, in large part, much of the conflict in Bosnia. Their role in the conflict, however, was disguised behind the legal fiction of the *Republika Srpska*. While portrayed by its advocates as an independent and sovereign state, the *Republika Srpska* was anything but. The real power resided in Belgrade, and it was there that the campaigns of ethnic cleansing in Bosnia were dictated.

On March 1, 1992, 64 percent of Bosnian citizens participated in a referendum, and over 99 percent of them voted for Bosnian independence and sovereignty.[26] Even though boycotted by Serbs, this referendum indicated strong support for a multinational Bosnian-Herzegovinian state. Almost immediately violence broke out as the Bosnian Serbs began their campaign to destroy the fledgling state. From the Serb perspective, their actions were protected, sheltered, and legitimized by the concept of the Bosnian Serb Republic. After all, they were merely protecting their sovereign rights as citizens of the Serb Republic. At the same time, moreover, Croatian nationalists attacked Bosnian territory in order to expand their own.[27]

Nationalism

Nationalism is the other bedrock of state ideology that has been a powerful influence on the crime of genocide. The state, in the course of its development, needed the unifying power of nationalism in order to survive and prosper; in Bruce Porter's words, "Nationalism did not create the modern state: rather the modern state stimulated the rise of nationalism."[28] As states evolved from the preceding feudal system, a mechanism was needed to assure loyalty to and belief in the state. Medieval society, decentralized as it was, emphasized loyalty to family, church, local community, and local lords, not to some distant political entity.[29] It was imperative, therefore, that the state create a sense of allegiance among the people it controlled in order to mobilize loyalty and commitment to a centralized government, rather than to diverse and local people and institutions. In essence, nationalism provided a new frame of reference that allowed collectives to define themselves. This process has been so successful that according to some, "nationalism has become an ersatz religion."[30] Indeed, looking at the militant rhetoric so common to many emerging or reemerging nationalistic movements, one perceives a fervency, militancy, and self-righteousness that is more often associated with religious fanaticism than with secular notions of community.

Nationalism operates at several different levels, as illustrated by Michael Ignatieff, who defines it this way:

> As a political doctrine, nationalism is the belief that the world's peoples are divided into nations, and that each of these nations has the right of self-determination, either as self-governing units within existing nation-states or as nation-states of their own.

As a cultural ideal, nationalism is the claim that while men and women have many identities, it is the nation that provides them with their primary form of belonging.

As a moral ideal, nationalism is an ethic of heroic sacrifice, justifying the use of violence in the defense of one's nation against enemies, internal or external.[31]

In short, nationalism is the embodiment of an ideology that supports and strengthens the perceived legitimacy of the state as the representative of a unified group of people. In a similar vein, John Rourke suggests that nationalism is

a matter of mutual perceptions of cultural kinship. . . . nation is a cultural term. It refers to a group of people who identify with one another politically because of common characteristics such as a common heritage, language, culture, religion, and race.[32]

Nationalism, then, is the perception that a group of people are somehow united because they share common attributes that bind them together and distinguish them from other peoples. These ties, however, are not inherent or even always obvious. Nationalism is as much a state of mind as anything else, since it is often based on perceived connections rather than any truly objective linkages. In other words, nationalism is, to borrow Benedict Anderson's oft-quoted term, a manifestation of "imagined communities."[33] Nationalistic identity is created rather than innate. Individuals identify themselves with strangers because of some believed or imagined fraternity. If certain distinctions have political utility, they are amplified; if not, they are discarded.

Ernest Gellner once wrote that "Nationalism is not the awakening of nations to self-consciousness; it invents nations where they do not exist,"[34] by which he also suggests that nationalism involves a manufactured system of belief. This is not to say that nationalists recognize the fabricated nature of their communal identity. Ethnic nationalism, for example, assumes a collective identity based on inherited traits, yet ethnicity, like race, is more a social construct than a biological or physiological one; as one scholar puts it, "ethnicity is a mode of thought, not a category in nature."[35] We assume difference where little or no real difference exists. It is what Sigmund Freud once termed the "narcissism of minor difference," in which small differences between peoples are amplified to assume a disproportionate significance.[36] In the former Yugoslavia, for example, much has been made of the differences between the various ethnic nationalities in nationalist rhetoric, yet Ignatieff points out that they come from the same racial stock and speak the same language.[37] While regional dialects exist for the Serbo-Croatian language, "Serbs *and* Croats, and Muslims for that matter, of a given region tend to speak the same dialect."[38] In other words, ethnic nationalism in the Balkans exacerbates perceived differences among people, and transforms those divisions into all-important definitions of identity.

The case of the Hutus and Tutsis in Rwanda also illustrates this "narcissism of minor difference." Historically the two groups were able to change identity through intermarriage and patronage to such an extent that scholars of ethnicity today agree they are not distinct and separate ethnic groups.[39] Small differences of appearance, class, even milk consumption have been exaggerated to create difference between the groups. These methods, however, were so imprecise that often the killers selected those to die only by personal knowledge of a person's category or by checking a government-issued identity card. "Hutu who looked like Tutsi were very often killed, their denials and proffered cards with the 'right' ethnic mention being seen as a typical Tutsi deception."[40] With such artificial distinctions mistakes are unavoidable and sometimes grimly ironic. During the Holocaust, Solomon Perel, a Jew hiding in disguise in a school for Hitler Youth, of all places, was held up for the class to see as an example of a typical Baltic Aryan.[41]

In short, nationalism exacerbates differences, sometimes to an extreme degree. Some forms of nationalism, for example, preach a spirit of elitism and exclusiveness that teaches that one's own people are not only different, but superior to other groups as well. In these situations national identity becomes conflated with ethnic and racial hatreds. These antipathies often verge on the xenophobic. The Nazis, for example, believed not only that the German *Volk* were superior to other "races," but that many other minority groups, most notably the Jews and Slavs, were subhuman.[42] These dehumanizing attitudes undoubtedly contributed to the willingness and ability of the Nazis and other Germans to carry out their genocidal policies. The Cambodian Khmer Rouge were also extremely xenophobic. Many of the targets of the genocide were non-Khmer minorities living in Cambodia, such as the Vietnamese and Chinese populations, who were believed to be racially inferior to the native Khmer. In the past, the Khmer kingdom had been a powerful empire and controlled much of Southeast Asia.[43] The Khmer Rouge saw themselves as working to restore this ethnic Khmer greatness by destroying minority groups. Serbian nationalism also has overtones of a chosen and special people in contrast to the demonized "Turks," "Ustasha" (Croatian nationalists), and "Islamic fundamentalists" so pervasive in Serb propaganda. In fact, some Serbs have characterized themselves as a "celestial people," which certainly connotes feelings of superiority and distinction.[44] In each of these examples, it can be argued that the impact of nationalistic sentiments has been to create sentiments of superiority among an in-group and intolerance for the out-group.

While race, ethnicity, religion, and language are some of the more pervasive bonds that tie members of a state together, they are not the only ones. As Catherine Samary points out, nationalism also needs "A political and socioeconomic cement,"[45] which is often provided by a sense of collective history and experience. Through the cultivation of shared memories, legends, and stories of a common heritage, a consciousness is developed that is used to define a people. This sense of a shared history is often a prominent feature of the cultural landscape of a society and allows a people to distinguish itself from other groups. And this process is time and again exploited by genocidally inclined states that motivate and inspire participants in genocide through reference to real or mythic events in the national history. Hirsch explicitly argues that the way to "motivate people to commit such acts is to manipulate their historical memories by creating myths designed to stimulate racial, ethnic, or national hatreds that feed on violence."[46] These images often center on notions of past wrongs or past glories, notions that Vamik Volkan describes as a "Chosen Trauma."[47] The history of the Serb peoples, for example, has created a population vulnerable to politicians who use nationalistic ideas of past victimization as a powerful force for shaping popular consciousness and arousing popular hatred. For Serbs, "Faith and nation merged in a mystical way, at once compelling and dangerous."[48] Nationalism, then, for the Serb people, has taken on a powerful reality that distinguishes Serb identity through references to history rather than to contemporary and distinct qualities and characteristics. This identity is based largely on perceptions of an idealized victimization that begins with the battle of Kosovo Polje in 1389. In this battle Serb armies under the legendary Prince Lazar and other Serb nobles fought an Ottoman army in an attempt to prevent further Turkish depredations and advances in the Balkans. In nationalistic mythology, this battle was transformed from a fairly bloody but inconclusive clash to a heroic defeat. In fact, early accounts of the battle hailed a great Christian victory, and a Serbian state survived for the next seventy years.[49] But these facts conflict with the stylized imagery of noble victimization, so they have been conveniently ignored. This Serb notion of a victimized national identity was only reinforced by the massacres Serbs suffered during the Second World War at the hands of Nazi and Croat fascists. Political figures have since been able to revive nationalistic Serbian sentiments through repeated references to these historic wrongs inflicted on the Serb people. This concerted appeal to history was designed to sharpen nationalistic loyalties and predispose Serbs to accept the policies of ethnic cleansing that would serve to right this ancient injustice.[50] Individuals are not usually too concerned about their group identity until it is perceived to be threatened. Although historically inaccurate and misleading, these images served their purpose by reminding Serbs of a common past full of victimization and injustice, and provided an identifiable enemy and the motivation to act in the present.

Nationalism does not require historical accuracy and objectivity, it merely requires a unifying message or lesson, and in fact E. J. Hobsbawm writes that "nationalism requires too much belief in what is patently not so."[51] Nationalism provided the Serb political leadership with the ammunition it needed to change neighbors into enemies and intoxicate ordinary people with crude, yet powerful, images of victimization and retribution. As Hirsch summarizes well, "All cultures and nation-states construct political myths that involve glorification and romanticization of the nation-state. Whether in war or in peace, the state is correct, and the enemies of the state . . . are wrong."[52]

The Serbs' status as a victimized people transformed their violence from aggression to self-defense, from attacks and assaults to protective and reactive force. As described by Cohen, "The Serb, as perennial victim, could not see himself as executioner; the Serb, as eternal liberator, could not see himself as enslaver; the Serb, as concentration camp survivor, could not see the concentration camps he built."[53] Even the siege of Sarajevo was portrayed, not as an aggressive military act, but as a circular defensive maneuver to protect Serbs outside the city from attacks from within it.[54] From this perspective, the sniping and bombardment of Sarajevo were justified and acceptable strategies. The fact that the Serbs were portrayed around the world as the aggressors did not deter them. On the contrary, their sense of victimization was increased by the unanimous condemnation they faced. In other words, everyone was out to get them.

In similar fashion, the Khmer Rouge often referred to the ancient Khmer civilization that had built the famous temple at Angkor Wat. Pol Pot and the leadership of the Khmer Rouge were captivated by the idea of recapturing the former economic, military, and political greatness of the Angkorean empire.[55] Any outside influence, such as from the ethnic Vietnamese and Chinese in Cambodia, was seen as harmful and destructive, and an obstacle to a new and pure Khmer greatness. The virtues of the ancient Khmer people were extolled in idealistic imagery that orchestrated past glories for present-day politics. In fact the Khmer Rouge ideology had much the same "mixture of self-pity and delusions of grandeur," to borrow Margolin's phrase, as the Serb.[56]

Nationalism may also become problematic when the fit between state and nation is inexact. In such societies, known as multinational states, one state has jurisdiction over numerous nationalities.[57] This is not to suggest that all multinational states are prone to genocide; only 9 percent of all states can truly be called nation-states, in which the ethnic and political boundaries are the same, and most of the other 91 percent have never perpetrated genocide.[58] In these heterogenous states various types of competition and antagonism between the various groups normally exist, but, as Helen Fein points out, "although ethnic competition and conflict is a normal phenomenon in multi-ethnic states, it in itself does not usually prompt genocide."[59] However, the multiethnic state can become unstable when members of specific nationalities are in relatively weak positions and vulnerable to scapegoating, or when members of national groups seek to break away and establish their own nation-state. This latter situation, for example, contributed to the genocidal massacres against the Kurds perpetrated by the Iraqi state under Saddam Hussein. The Kurds form a distinctive ethnic group in a region that encompasses parts of western Turkey and northern Iran and Iraq. They have often been in conflict with the three governments of the region, seeking at various times either greater autonomy within these existing countries, or, alternatively, a separate and independent Kurdish state. In response to Kurdish nationalistic aspirations, Iraq began a genocidal campaign against the Kurds in 1988 that included the use of mustard gas and nerve agents and resulted in the complete destruction of over two thousand villages and settlements.[60] This Anfal campaign, as it was known, is a clear result of the disjunction between states and nationalities.

The situation in Bosnia-Herzegovina also reflects many of these realities. The Cold War, with its East/West divisions, ended with the breakup of the Soviet Union, and nationalistic impulses, long suppressed by the polarizing forces of the conflict, were resurrected by Balkan politicians seeking to protect or enhance their power. While violence occurred throughout the region, Bosnia was most vulnerable to destabilization, for several reasons. First, Croatia was more prepared than the other new Balkan states to defend its independence militarily. Second, Bosnia moved for statehood after Slovenia and Croatia, which meant that those who opposed the breakup of the Yugoslav state and Bosnian independence had had more experience and more time to prepare. Third, both Croatia and Serbia hoped to expand into Bosnian territory. And fourth, Bosnia was more ethnically mixed than the other republics, and its large Serbian and Croatian population meant that its declaration of independence was more easily contested. The Slovenian declaration of independence, on the other hand, coming as it did from a largely homogenous republic that was almost 90 percent Slovenian, did not offer the same opportunities for those wishing to contest Slovenian sovereignty from within. Any opposition had to come from outside in the form of military aggression. In short, the genocide was caused by politicians who wanted to "build ethnically based countries on ethnically mixed land." [61]

Both nationalism and sovereignty are found in every state, yet not all states perpetrate genocide, and the historic evolution of the state does not make genocide inevitable. As the former American ambassador to Yugoslavia writes,

> The challenge to the world community is not to break up multiethnic states, but to make them more civil. It's the borders in the mind—the borders of prejudice, supremacy, and hate—rather than the borders on the map that are most in need of changing. [62]

However, it is a sad fact that while the development of the modern state has revolutionized the structural, economic, and social organization of human communities, for the citizens of many societies the state has also been a deadly form of social organization. While scholars have long recognized the importance of nationalism to the state, the destructive characteristics of nationalistic sentiment run counter to many popular perceptions that define the state as that which protects and serves, and view public officials as concerned with the needs and safety of the citizenry. This "common good" image of the state is especially pronounced in Western democracies, but exists to varying degrees in other types of society as well.

This vision of the state contends that governments are created by human communities in order to serve the community members' needs and protect their rights. Philosophically based on the progressive ideas of social and political theorists such as Thomas Hobbes, John Locke, Jeremy Bentham, and James Mill, it depicts benevolent states as protecting citizens from each other and allowing individuals to realize their potential as human beings free from unnecessary governmental interference. [63] As we have seen, however, the reality is often far different from this benign ideal.

In the twentieth century the state has posed the greatest threat to life, both the lives of its own citizens and those of other populations. According to Rummel, more than 203 million people have been killed in this century by state-perpetrated wars and democides.[64] The genocides committed in countries such as the Soviet Union, Kampuchea, Nazi Germany, and Rwanda clearly illustrate that ordinary people often have far more to fear from fellow law-abiding citizens acting in their capacity as officials or followers of the state than from the most predatory and opportunistic criminals and street gangs. In the words of one observer, "those who enforce the law are more dangerous than those who break it."[65]

Genocide, as an example of what is often termed governmental mass killing,[66] may also be understood in relationship to another example of state violence, namely war. Practically every example of genocide in the twentieth century occurred either during a war or subsequent to one. The Armenian genocide occurred during the First World War, while the Holocaust was perpetrated during the Second World War. The Cambodian, Bosnian, and Rwandan genocides all originated either during or after regional conflicts. This is no coincidence. Genocide and warfare are intimately linked together as twin manifestations of the extreme destructiveness of modern states. A closer examination of this relationship reveals some important correlations between the two.

Genocide and War

Genocide is a frequent and, in some cases, obvious outcome of war. The state, evolving as it did within the crucible of endless rounds of combat, served initially as a more efficient apparatus to fight wars. Warfare, as noted by many, is an inherently brutalizing process, not only for the soldiers involved, but also for the civilian populations in combatant nations.[67] Violence and death become facts of life, striking down not just soldiers at the front but civilians at home as well. The industrialized form of war so common to the twentieth century has ushered in an era in which civilian populations are perceived as legitimate targets of mass destruction. The firebombings of cities and other nonmilitary targets in Germany and Japan during the Second World War, when the Allied powers consciously decided to force enemy civilian populations into submission, stand as eloquent testimony to this fact.[68] The Russian attack on Grozny, the capital of Chechnya, in the fall of 1999 is an example of the tactic's continuing prevalence. In fact, during the twentieth century civilians seem to be more at risk than soldiers. Sixty-six percent of the victims of the Second World War were civilians, and from the 1970s till the present, civilian casualties of war accounted for over 80 percent of the dead.[69]

War exaggerates nationalistic impulses as populations come together under outside threats. During peaceful times, national affiliations are only marginal to a person's self-image. However, during conflict group identities are strengthened as the gap between "us" and "them" is magnified, and individuals increasingly emphasize their solidarity with the threatened group. War forces constant reaffirmation of nationalist identities since people are forced to choose sides and loyalties. Porter sums this process up when he writes,

War is a powerful catalyst of nationalism. It infuses the collective consciousness of peoples with a sense of their national identity, while simultaneously linking that identity closely with the fate of the state itself. Nationalism in turn magnifies the unifying effect of wars, promotes a sense of shared destiny, and strengthens political bonds that might otherwise suffer centrifugal failure.[70]

In addition, the effects of war linger for a long time, not just on the physical landscape, but on the cultural and psychological terrain as well. The endless cycle of killings, atrocities, massacres, and reprisals so common to modern wars leaves an indelible mark on the people it touches. It becomes part of the historical memory of a people and can be resurrected by manipulative politicians seeking to inflame and incite. Nationalist Serb leaders reaped a fertile crop of animosity from the ashes of the Second World War in Yugoslavia.[71] The images of past atrocities committed against Serb populations by Nazis and Ustasha were a potent force for mobilizing Serb support against Croats and Bosnian Muslims during the recent conflict.

In addition to the brutalizing effects of war and its impact on collective memory, war also facilitates genocide in several other ways. Eric Markusen argues that five specific mechanisms facilitate genocide.

First, war "produces widespread psychological and social disequilibrium."[72] This anomic condition may inflame hostilities and tensions between different groups within society, some of whom may be targeted as scapegoats. War causes tremendous psychological and spatial dislocation as entire populations are uprooted and set adrift. During modern wars and genocides, refugee populations spread out from the violence like ripples in a pond, placing neighboring communities under tremendous stress as their social and physical infrastructures and resources are severely strained or broken. While some communities may pull together and strengthen their communal ties during these times of crisis, others are unable to withstand the pressure. Communities where traditional formal and informal social controls are weakened or removed are much more prone to deviance and crime.[73] The inability of such disorganized communities to regulate themselves allows for the development and transmission of deviant values and criminal behavior. Order and restraint break down as people struggle to survive under very difficult circumstances. In such a situation, minority groups and other vulnerable communities may be scapegoated and attacked as a consequence of the weakened sense of community and diminished social control.

Second, during times of war, states tend to become more secretive and defensive, and actively amass more power.[74] State organizations develop characteristics that make genocide possible, and reduce the ability of others to perceive and oppose any genocidal intentions. R. J. Rummel, for example, perceives genocide as a problem of totalitarian regimes that consolidate and exercise power without democratic constraints.[75] In fact, these kinds of governments perpetually emphasize conflict and war, since combat serves to mobilize their populations and increases the flow of power toward the state.[76] Genocide, in this view, is a result of power, and this certainly is an era in which states have consolidated and centralized tremendous amounts of power, surveillance, and administration. Since the turn of the century, we have seen the creation of totalitarian state systems unparalleled in their ability to control and dominate the public and private lives of their citizens. The Soviet Union and Nazi Germany, for example, created Orwellian societies able and willing to direct and monitor virtually all areas of Soviet and German life. All too often that near-absolute power has been used for destructive and genocidal purposes. The more concentrated and total the power wielded, the greater the possibility of genocide,[77] thus proving the validity of Lord Acton's famous dictum that "Power tends to corrupt and absolute power corrupts absolutely." R. J. Rummel's research leads him to amend this famous axiom and assert that "Power kills; absolute Power kills absolutely."[78]

Threats from outside may also increase the likelihood that the state will try to eliminate any possible internal threat, which contributes to its willingness to perpetrate genocide. Suspect ethnic groups may be perceived as a "fifth column" and steps taken to eliminate them. In short, war exacerbates states' tendency to consolidate power and operate without internal or external constraints on their exercise of that power. All of these trends facilitate the perpetration of genocide.

Third, during times of war, the state can rely on an effective instrument of force to carry out genocide. In other words, military and police forces are equipped and practiced in mass violence during wartime and have the necessary resources, organization, logistics, and personnel to carry out genocide. It is a relatively easy matter to shift the application of these forces from one target to another. It is also important to note that during war, military and police personnel are frequently inured to violence, having experienced its brutality firsthand, and are also more heavily indoctrinated to conform to the ideals and obey the commands of the state. Therefore, they are less likely to question orders. Additionally, Staub argues that wars create individuals who suffer from post-traumatic stress disorder, and these individuals will be attracted to "a movement and leader offering them a sense of significance as well as scapegoats and enemies."[79]

Fourth, minority groups become increasingly vulnerable during times of war because they are more easily isolated and marginalized by the increasingly powerful bureaucracies of the state. Groups disconnected from the mainstream of social and political power are more easily stigmatized, fragmented, and alienated from possible sources of support. When this is combined with the greater compartmentalization within society and the institutionalized secrecy so common to states during times of war, greater latitude exists for managing, controlling, or eliminating different populations.

Fifth and last, warfare brutalizes populations and desensitizes them to violence, making it more likely that individuals will support, or at least not contest, genocide. Human life becomes much less sacred or valuable. Instead it is seen to be cheap and expendable. It becomes much easier, therefore, to target a specific group for extermination during wartime, because the moral imperatives protecting individual human life are tremendously weakened, especially if that group has been stigmatized and blamed for many of the problems associated with the war. Archer and Gartner write,

> Wars provide concrete evidence that homicide under some conditions is acceptable in the eyes of a nation's leaders. This wartime reversal of the customary peacetime prohibition against killing may somehow influence the threshold for using homicide as a means of settling conflict in everyday life.[80]

In other words, the traditional injunctions against killing are relaxed. Killing becomes a service to the nation and is rewarded rather than punished. War, in short, acts as a catalyst to genocide because it creates a climate in which brutality flourishes, and states increase their power and their ability to first marginalize and then victimize targeted populations. Central to this process is the consolidation of power in the state. The state, as noted earlier, is an effective instrument of power. Most of the organs of the modern state—the central government, the military, police agencies, the judiciary—are designed to apply force to protect the state and maintain order. In some countries that power is overtly manifested; in others it is concealed and limited by democratic constraints. In all cases, however, the state is able to draw upon tremendous amounts of power in order to achieve specific goals.

But how exactly is that power manifested or translated into genocide? The answer to this question is that the power of the state is inherent in the control of the law. The legal system conveys tremendous resources to the group or state that controls it. It provides not only concrete assets, but legitimacy as well. The law, by its very nature, defines right and wrong. Control of the legal system is a tremendous enabler for genocide since, in many cases, control of the law is synonymous with the state. Each is inextricably intertwined with and inseparable from the other.

Law as a Set of Resources

Contrary to those who simply see law as a tool of conflict resolution,[81] Austin Turk argued that law often creates conflicts as different groups struggle to have their voices heard and use the law as a vehicle to further their own agendas. Specifically, he asserted that law is "a set of resources for which people contend and with which they are better able to promote their own ideas and interests against others."[82] According to Turk, groups that control the legal mechanisms of a society or are in a position to create or hinder the creation of laws control five legal resources. These are

1. control of the means of direct physical violence, i.e., *war* or *police* power;
2. control of the production, allocation, and/or use of material resources, i.e., *economic* power;
3. control of decision-making processes, i.e., *political* power;
4. control of definitions of and access to knowledge, beliefs, values, i.e., *ideological* power; and
5. control of human attention and living-time, i.e., *diversionary* power.[83]

Law, then, becomes a servant to those who have gained power, and can be mobilized to serve their needs and protect their interests. Respect for the law is generally synonymous with respect for the state.

In order for an organization or clique to perpetrate genocide, it must first ascend to political power through force of arms, appointment, or election. For example, it was only after Adolf Hitler came to power in 1933 that the Nazi party was able to begin the legal marginalization of German Jews in a process that eventually culminated in the "Final Solution." Prior to the legal takeover, the Nazis were largely limited to hate rhetoric and street brawls. Only after Hitler was appointed chancellor could the Nazis act more decisively. As chancellor, he quickly changed the process of government to suit his ideological agenda. Within a week of his appointment he was able to pass an emergency decree closing down and confiscating all Communist Party buildings and printing presses, and three weeks after that he used the burning of the Reichstag as a justification for laws allowing the police to arrest and imprison anybody without the benefit of due process.[84] Thus, he used the law to suppress dissent and resistance and moved the country a significant distance toward totalitarianism. From there, the Nazis began to systematically change the laws in order to legally marginalize the German Jewish community. Of this process Karl Schleuner writes,

> The framework for discriminatory legislation had been provided by passage of the Enabling Act of March 24. The Reichstag's action had given the government formal power to govern and legislate by decree, thereby providing the Nazis a cloak of legality with which to cover their official actions. Most importantly, the act enabled the Nazi regime to set aside those provisions of the Weimar constitution which stood in its way, especially those guaranteeing legal equality to all citizens.[85]

As chancellor, Hitler controlled the law, and this enabled him to profoundly change the political process in Germany. Ultimately creating a dictatorship, Hitler set Germany on a path that ended at the gates of Auschwitz.

In similar fashion, the Cambodian genocide did not begin until after the Khmer Rouge took power and ousted the Lon Nol government. In this case, however, they did not modify the political process, but instead completely replaced the old government structure with one centered on the Central Committee of the Communist Party of Kampuchea (CPK), known as *Angkar Loeu* (high organization).[86] Having spent years in the jungle fighting the government, the Khmer Rouge were thoroughly indoctrinated in the belief that Cambodian society was contaminated with Western ideas, the only answer to which was the complete elimination of foreign influences and the return to a pure agrarian past. Only then, they believed, could Cambodia return to greatness. From the national to the local level, political leaders of the ousted regime were removed and killed, and replaced by Khmer Rouge officials. The entire political structure of the country was wiped clean and replaced with one dictated by Pol Pot and his ideologues.

A comparable process was implemented in the Serb-controlled regions of Bosnia during the initial stages of ethnic cleansing. In some communities, non-Serbs were barred from all management and senior positions in large businesses.[87] In the town of Čelinac, non-Serbs had a curfew of 4:00 P.M. and were forbidden to gather in public places, make contact with relatives who didn't live in the town, drive or travel by car, sell real estate without going through Serb authorities, or leave without permission.[88] In this legalistic way, the Muslim population was pressured into leaving Serb-controlled territory. These legal decrees had the effect of socially and economically marginalizing the non-Serb population, making it more vulnerable to more extreme measures. It remains a truism for genocide that only after political power is achieved can a group begin the process of implementing genocide, since without the power to manipulate the political process the necessary resources are not controlled. Horowitz puts it this way:

> A central tendency in all genocidal societies is to initially create juridical-legal separations between citizens and aliens, elites and masses, dominant and backward races, and so forth. This serves as a pretext for genocide and also as a precondition to the implementation of genocidal policies.[89]

Austin Turk also referred to control of the means of direct physical violence, which he termed war or police power. Genocide, as we have discussed, is typically sanctioned by law, and the violence that is used to carry it out is therefore protected and officially, if not morally, legitimate. Police officers and soldiers are often the active perpetrators of genocide, the ones who actually carry out the killing. While private citizens are sometimes invited or forced to participate in genocidal massacres, they typically do not cause the majority of deaths. It is members of institutionalized organizations who do the bulk of the killing. During the Holocaust, members of the infamous *Einsatzgruppen*, the mobile killing squads, were drawn from the Security Police, the Security Service, the Gestapo, the Criminal Police, the regular uniformed police, the Order Police, and the Waffen SS, as well as from among soldiers who were unfit for duty at the front.[90] The concentration and death camps were organized and run by a branch of the SS known as the *Totenkopfverbände SS*.[91] These were the infamous Death's Head SS, who carried the skull-and-crossbones emblem on their uniforms. Pol Pot and his cohorts relied on Khmer Rouge soldiers to murder the victims of the killing fields, and in Rwanda the perpetrators were civil officials, soldiers, police officers, and irregular militia forces such as the *Interahamwe* ("those who stand together" or "those who attack together"). These groups not only engaged in much violence, they also served to organize and control the participation of ordinary citizens. The paramilitary groups who were in the forefront of the killing in Bosnia were often funded and supplied by the security forces of the Serb Interior Ministry.[92] Similarly, the camps that gained such notoriety in the West were organized and controlled by Bosnian Serb police forces,[93] while much other violence, such as the massacres that occurred after the fall of Srebrenica, was perpetrated by the embryonic Bosnian Serb army under General Ratko Mladić.[94]

Genocide, in short, is not perpetrated by mobs acting spontaneously and independently of any organizing authority. Soldiers and police are often the only groups in a given society legally empowered to use violence. Modern states enjoy a monopoly on the legitimate use of coercive force. Although private violence was once quite common, violence has generally been taken out of the hands of the populace and placed in the hands of state-appointed guardians of the social order. Prior to the development of the state, private justice relied on ordinary members of society to ensure that the law was upheld. But the state, as a means of consolidating power, has usurped the authority and legitimacy of force so that private citizens cannot resort to it except in extreme situations, such as self-defense. This means that those who control the legal process also command those organizations that are given the legal authority to use force.

Members of military and police organizations are trained and armed for violent acts, and are thus prepared to commit them and highly capable of doing so on command. Additionally, such organizations are often the only ones in a state that give their members such training. Through control of the law, then, the state gains control of the legitimate agents of violence, who are people rehearsed, adept, and comfortable in its application.

Another element of the law, according to Turk's thesis, is control of economic power. Genocide is a resource-intensive enterprise, especially on a large scale such as the Holocaust or the Armenian genocide, and requires a tremendous economic investment. For example, Daniel Goldhagen calls the Holocaust a "German national project."[95] Genocide is also enormously costly to the economy of the society, disrupting as it does the very fabric of the economic infrastructure. Killing large numbers of people is expensive, and only governments and large corporations have the capital necessary to engage in such monstrous projects. Corporations, however, don't usually have the necessary legitimacy that states possess, nor the ideologies that provide the impetus to genocide. The ability to mobilize countless bureaucracies; appropriate supplies; schedule and run trains; build camps; train, arm, and pay soldiers and militia members; and change laws represents an incredible investment in time, personnel, and money. Very few private organizations have the resources necessary to engage in such an all-consuming activity.

To some extent these costs are offset by the opportunity to exploit genocide for profit. Economic power also confers upon its holder the ability to garner greater wealth from those targeted. Many of the laws passed by the Nazis stripped Jews of their property and possessions and transferred ownership to the state. Not only were German Jews forced to give up their belongings, those who wanted to immigrate had to pay a flight tax and atonement payment, which together yielded the German government 841,000,000 reichsmarks in 1938.[96] Many reputable German companies used concentration-camp inmates as free slave labor and profited immensely from their partnership with the state.[97] Even in death the Jews funded the Reich, as their bodies were searched for gold teeth, fillings, and other concealed valuables.

In Bosnia-Herzegovina, the Serbs used the violence and the killing for personal gain so often that, for many, "'defending Serbdom' was indistinguishable from making money."[98] Muslim refugees were routinely searched and deprived of anything of value. One Bosnian Muslim describes an example of this legalized robbery:

> One night two policemen came to my door. They were squabbling over my house, right in front of me, it was incredible. One of them wanted it, and another said, No, he wanted it. It's a nice house, I put a lot of work into it. Then they came to some sort of agreement and told me that I had two days to leave, or else I'd be executed.[99]

Material gain was a powerful incentive for many who, steeped as they were in a mentality of perpetual victimization, suddenly understood that they had the ability to take from those they saw as privileged and better off. In some cases, when ethnic cleansers arrived in a town, the Muslim inhabitants were told they had forty-eight hours to leave and that they should sell their possessions in order to pay for transport.[100] One journalist reported seeing Serb army trucks packed with furniture and appliances looted from Muslim homes, while the Serbian officers drove around in expensive luxury cars confiscated from the victims of ethnic cleansing.[101] These depredations were so profitable that Arkan's Tiger militia, which was originally funded by Serbia's Interior Ministry, became self-financing.[102] Serbs working in the camps also extorted money from the Muslim inmates and their families for their release, for food, or to avoid torture.[103] Reportedly, some people were even paid for killing. One Serb bragged to Muslim prisoners that he was being paid three hundred dollars for every Muslim he killed.[104] In Rwanda, one politician offered fifty Rwandan francs for each Tutsi head collected; collecting the bounty was euphemistically termed "selling cabbages."[105] Additionally, in Rwanda the genocide offered opportunities for much looting of cattle and other belongings as well as the possibility of obtaining the victims' land.[106]

This economic incentive is a common factor in many other examples of genocide as well. During the Armenian genocide, many Turks "prospered by liquidating Armenians' businesses, stealing their stocks, and seizing Armenian farms and real estate."[107] Argentinean police and military officers took advantage of the "dirty war" to steal houses, cars, furniture, and even children from their victims, and sometimes the victims were ransomed to their families for significant sums.[108] As Turk writes, "economic power is enhanced or eroded by law."[109] The victimized group's economic power is diminished through legal processes while the victimizer's is strengthened.

Austin Turk also asserts that control of the law helps create ideological power. Simply put, the law is a tool of propaganda, lending credibility to certain groups, actions, and behaviors, and delegitimizing others. To define certain people as criminal is to take away not only their rights, but also their identity as citizens. Criminals are generally perceived as different from and alien to the "law-abiding" and "decent" citizens of a society. The perpetrators of genocide, protected as they are by the state and its laws, are defined as model citizens engaged in a patriotic civic service. The victims of genocide, on the other hand, are portrayed as devious and scheming enemies who pose a threat to those being asked to kill them. In this Orwellian universe, roles are reversed and victims are portrayed as perpetrators while the perpetrators see themselves as victims. In other words, the killers are provided with ideologies that alter perceptions of reality in order to justify their lethal behavior.

Ideological power encompasses the ability to shape awareness and belief through manipulation of the dominant images and messages transmitted throughout a society. As Jeff Ferrell reminds us, "Authority operates not only through prison cells and poverty, but by constructing and defending epistemologies of universality and truth."[110] The state creates popular perceptions of right and wrong, good and evil, and works vigorously to reinforce and defend them. Ideological power is a formidable instrument in the creation of public support or condemnation. It provides a patina of legitimacy that serves to deflect much criticism. "Evil," as Frank Hagan warns, "often gilds itself with an ideological gloss."[111] This power is especially potent in totalitarian governments, where the mass media are dependant organs of the state and there is no alternative to them.

Popular conceptions of reality are largely shaped by the media, along with personal experience, significant others, and social groups. In other words, an individual's understanding of the world is created not only by personal experience and the opinions of family and friends, but also by the messages and images received in print, television, radio, and film.[112] Therefore, the importance of ideological control cannot be overstated. Neil Kressel summarizes this powerful effect well when he writes,

> The success of many modern dictatorships comes from an ability to mix threats, manipulation, persuasion, and bribes to change a person politically and psychologically, without that person ever grasping why he or she has changed. Direct control or indirect influence over the media, schools, police, military, and other institutions, over time, can result in the wearying and transformation of many formerly decent souls.[113]

We must not forget that prior to the recent Rwandan genocide, government-controlled radio stations spent several months priming the well of hatred by broadcasting messages designed to increase the Hutus' fear and hatred of, and paranoia about, the Tutsis.[114] Similarly, Serb-controlled radio and television stations spewed hate propaganda in the months preceding the beginning of the Bosnian war and consequent ethnic cleansing. Slobodan Milošević's control of television was extremely important, because most of the population watched the nightly news.[115] As Milan Milošević asserts, "nationalism would be the means and television the instrument."[116] These constant broadcasts in both Rwanda and Bosnia helped lay the groundwork for genocide. This power to shape reality is still greater in technologically illiterate societies. As one African minister explained to journalist Robert Kaplan,

> the greatest magic is the radio. This box, it talks to you, in your own language. Yet it has no wires connecting it to anything. Now, that's magic! Therefore, whatever comes out of this box must be true.[117]

It is no surprise, therefore, that Albert Kiruhura, a twenty-nine-year-old Rwandan Hutu participant in that country's genocide, could say,

> I did not believe the Tutsis were coming to kill us, but when the government radio continued to broadcast that they were coming to take our land, were coming to kill the Hutus—when this was repeated over and over—I began to feel some kind of fear. . . . We believed what the government told us.[118]

Echoing this theme, the journalist Peter Maass recounts a conversation he held with two Bosnian Serb women, a mother and daughter:

> I asked, out of politeness, whether the fighting in the village was heavy.
> "Why, no, there was no fighting between Muslims and Serbs in the village," she said.
> "Then why were the Muslims arrested?"
> "Because they were planning to take over the village. They had already drawn up lists. The names of the Serb women had been split into harems for the Muslim men."
> "Harems?"
> "Yes, harems. Their Bible says men can have harems, and that's what they were planning to do once they killed our men. Thank God they were arrested first."
> "How do you know they were planning to kill the Serb men and create harems for themselves?"
> "It was on the radio. Our military had uncovered their plans. It was announced on the radio."
> "How do you know the radio was telling the truth?" I asked.
> "Why," she demanded to know, "would the radio lie?"[119]

Examples like these show that the radio has the power to influence people's perceptions of reality, even in the face of personal experience. As Maass discovered, these two women had had excellent relations with their Muslim neighbors. However, this personal experience counted for naught against the power of the radio to shape attitudes. Lest one believe that such media are effective only in nontechnological societies, it might be prudent to think of the words of one

Serbian journalist who remarked, "You must imagine a United States with every little TV station everywhere taking exactly the same editorial line—a line dictated by David Duke. You too would have war in five years."[120]

Austin Turk's conception of the law as a set of resources is a powerful theoretical tool for analyzing why genocide is exclusively perpetrated by the state. Simply put, nothing else has the power, the will, or the resources to engage in genocide. Control of the law gives the state the ability to tether the forces of government to genocidal impulses and make this crime a reality.

Governmental mass killing is distinct from most other types of crime because it typically enjoys the protection of the legal system. It constitutes what Hannah Arendt terms "legal crime": actions that, while reprehensible in a moral sense, are protected by law.[121] Similarly, Kelman and Hamilton write about "crimes of obedience," defining such a crime as an "act performed in response to orders from authority that is considered illegal or immoral by the larger community." [122] In other words, whereas crime is generally perceived to be behavior that violates the law, genocidal activities and policies are typically protected by validly enacted laws, perpetrated by agents of the state acting on behalf of the state. Gourevitch's comment on Rwanda is true for every other example of genocide as well: "During the genocide, the work of the killers was not regarded as a crime in Rwanda; it was effectively the law of the land, and every citizen was responsible for its administration."[123] What sets genocide apart from many other forms of crime is that it is perpetrated by individuals and groups who have the authority and legitimacy of the government backing them up. As Archer and Gartner explain, "The private acts of destructive individuals are treated as illegal violence, while official acts of violence are granted the mantle of state authority, and thus shielded from criticism and criminal sanctions."[124] Others are therefore predisposed to accept and validate the violence. The umbrella of state authority, as well as the collective nature of genocide, also serves to relieve the perpetrator of many of the feelings of guilt and responsibility that ordinary criminals may be prone to.

A Matter of Policy

It is often popular to portray genocide as a spontaneous phenomenon. In this view, the killing is typically seen as resulting from ancient hatreds and conflicts that periodically erupt into genocide. Popular news accounts of genocide often stress that the groups involved are traditional antagonists. For example, a *Time* magazine article on Bosnia was titled "O Nationalism! Yugoslavia Shows How Ancient Tensions Can Suddenly Boil Over."[125] The title implies that the violence simply erupted because of historical tensions and hatreds. Similarly, a *Newsweek* magazine article asserted that "Religion and nationality make the Balkans more a flash point than a melting pot. The unstable region provided the spark that set off World War I and produced some of the worst atrocities of World War II."[126] Explicit within this text is the notion that the causes of genocide lie in the past, not in the present. This argument also conveys an implicit sense that nothing can be done; that the violence is inevitable and unavoidable. How can one prevent something that has roots in the distant past? About the genocide in Bosnia, Ali and Lifschultz write,

> the war was characterized as the product of centuries-old enmities between the Serbs, Croats, and Muslims—a tribal blood-feud, a "typical" Balkan convulsion which could not be understood much less mediated by any intervention by the civilized world.[127]

Even scholars sometimes fall into the trap of this argument. Frank Hagan, in his discussion of the genocide in Rwanda, writes that "Four centuries of tribal hatred exploded in a blood lust, civil war between Hutu and Tutsi tribes."[128] Again, characterizing the recent genocide in this way suggests that it was produced by a decades-long buildup of hostility that sooner or later was bound to detonate.

The problem with this argument is that it is inaccurate and diverts attention from the true culprit: the state. The argument is harmful because it hides contemporary political manipulations that utilize genocide as a rational means to some political, ideological, or economic goal. Genocides do not suddenly happen, nor are they precipitated by age-old animosity between groups. Rather, they are the result of conscious choices made by political and military leaders. This is not to say that ancient resentments and antipathies do not play some role in genocide or that they are not powerful. They can be powerful weapons. They are the cloak under which the state disguises its actions; they provide the excuses and apparent motives, but they are not the cause of genocide. As Michael Ignatieff summarizes, "it is not how the past dictates to the present but how the present manipulates the past that is decisive."[129] While Hutu and Tutsi, and Bosnian Muslim and Serb, have experienced historical conflict and antagonism, in recent times many believed that the hostility had faded. Serb and Muslim lived together, worked together, and frequently intermarried. The same is true for Rwandan Hutus and Tutsis. The Nazis, Serbs, and Rwandan Hutus truly came to hate their enemies. But it was a resurrected hatred, one that had rested quiescent in those populations until politicians awoke its demons. Nationalist leaders are masters at fanning the flames of hatred, resentment, and jealousy that exist in all societies. Social life is always potentially divisive and conflictual. But the potential does not always manifest itself. In other words, the killing was and is not inevitable. Old hostilities were revitalized in modern times by politicians who had clear reasons for doing so. History, as one scholar notes, has been used as "an ideological club" and as a "potential mobilization vehicle for political objectives."[130] In the pursuit of modern political objectives, political leaders manipulate feelings, rework history, and revive antagonisms, or, as one ambassador said, "The manipulators condoned and even provoked local ethnic violence in order to engender animosities that could then be magnified by the press, leading to further violence."[131] Examining specific examples of genocide more closely makes this process much more evident.

For example, many have suggested that the violence in the former Yugoslavia was an inevitable result of the traditional divisions among Serbs, Croats, and Bosnian Muslims. This argument usually suggests that the Balkan peoples have been fighting each other for hundreds of years and that the violence of the 1990s was only the latest example of a recurring pattern of ethnic hostility. With the death of Tito and the collapse of socialism, the traditional antagonisms once again emerged as these ancient enemies began to settle old scores. Warren Christopher, the U.S. secretary of state, described the situation as "terrifying, and it's centuries old. That really is a problem from hell."[132] Lawrence Eagleburger, the former secretary of state, said, "They have been killing each other with a certain amount of glee in that part of the world for some time now."[133] In like fashion, another American politician spoke of "ancient and complicated roots."[134] The truth, however, is far removed from this portrayal. The ethnic cleansing that came to symbolize the killing in Bosnia should not be perceived as an unavoidable flare-up of old tribal hatreds. Instead, one must look at the political and nationalistic aspirations of the various factions in the post-Yugoslavian landscape.

With the end of the Yugoslavian state, Slobodan Milošević, for example, recognized that he needed a way to preserve a power base that was in danger of disappearing with the end of communism. Creating a myth of a resurgent Islamic Bosnian state preying upon, victimizing, and enslaving Bosnian Serbs, Milošević garnered widespread support by portraying himself as the savior of those threatened Serbs and was able to gain political power in Serbia with his nationalistic rhetoric.[135] In Radovan Karadžić, leader of the Serb Democratic Party, a Serbian nationalist political party in Bosnia-Herzegovina, Milošević found an ally who became his willing proxy in implementing the plans for a greater Serbia and preventing the establishment of an independent Bosnian state.

The genocide in Bosnia was perpetrated for modern political goals and ambitions, though it was disguised as the righting of a historical wrong. Its perpetrators intended to prevent the establishment of a sovereign Bosnian state, to retain a political power base for politicians in Belgrade, and to create a greater Serbian nation with access to the Adriatic Sea. In part, the genocide was the result of a modern attempt at the expansionist nation building so prevalent during the last century. This recent incarnation of territorialism was disguised as a crusade to protect ethnic Serbs living in Bosnia who were allegedly being persecuted and discriminated against by Bosnian Muslims.[136] According to Peter Maass,

> Milošević and his followers used the specter of Islamic persecution as a smoke screen. The reason they started the war and pursued it with a brutality unseen in Europe since Nazi times is that they wanted to enlarge the borders of Serbia to include parts of Bosnia (and Croatia), thereby creating a "Greater Serbia." For Milošević, an apparatchik without a future in a democracy, it was a matter of staying in power by playing the nationalist card. For hard-core nationalists, it was a matter of achieving a historical dream. And for the Bosnians, it was a nightmare.[137]

Maass is not alone in making this assessment. Norman Cigar writes of the geno-cide in Bosnia,

> it was a rational policy, the direct and planned consequence of conscious policy de-cisions taken by the Serbian establishment in Serbia and Bosnia-Herzegovina. This policy was implemented in a deliberate and systematic manner as part of a broader strategy intended to achieve a well-defined, concrete, political objective, namely the creation of an expanded, ethnically pure Greater Serbia.[138]

Most scholars of the conflict in Bosnia now recognize these underlying motives as the real reasons for the recent genocide, rather than the oft-repeated refrain of primitive ethnic hatreds. The events in Bosnia, therefore, constitute a clear and unequivocal example of state crime. Even Slobodan Milošević himself dis-counted the historical argument in a speech he gave on the six hundredth an-niversary of the Battle of Kosovo, a potent rallying point for nationalist sympa-thy:

> Today, it is difficult to say what is true and what is legend about the Battle of Kosovo. Today, that is not even important. Hearkening back to history, in fact, is not the basis upon which to carry out our mobilization. To be sure, history pro-vides an obligation to us to mobilize. However, the main incentive for the mobiliza-tion of all the Yugoslav peoples and minorities is their present condition and espe-cially the future.[139]

This cynical admission reveals that to Milošević himself, one of the prime mov-ers of the subsequent genocide, history is less important than present needs. History, to people like Milošević, is there to be manipulated and to arouse na-tionalistic and chauvinistic sentiments that can be relied upon to incite a popu-lation to hatred. Obviously, Milošević is a subscriber to the old saw that history is nothing more than an agreed-upon myth and believes that past events can become tools in shaping popular consciousness and motivating people to take genocidal action.

The responsibility of the state is evidenced in the manner in which the geno-cide was carried out. While sometimes portrayed as the work of renegades or overzealous nationalists, the massacres, rapes, torture, and forced relocations that constituted the violence were in actuality part of a coordinated strategy overseen by the head of the Bosnian Serbs, Radovan Karadžić, who in turn fol-lowed the dictates of Slobodan Milošević. Members of Karadžić's staff were documented as having planned and carried out genocidal policies in towns such as Fŏca. These policies included setting up detention camps and conducting mass rapes of Muslim women.[140] Several hundred camps, dispersed throughout Bosnian Serb territory, were dedicated to destroying the Bosnian Muslim popu-lation through detention, deportation, intimidation, and murder. The camps were usually under the control of police or army authority and, as one camp commander related, "There is no question that orders came from the highest level. Our army had a strict chain of command from the outset."[141] Wiretapped conversations between Milošević and Karadžić reveal the role Belgrade had in directing, funding, and supplying the genocide in Bosnia.[142] One conversation reveals Milošević telling Karadžić that he could get weapons and help from a general in the Yugoslav national army.[143] Since the Serbian Department of State Security was deeply involved in underwriting the ethnic violence, both formal and informal Serb militia groups responded with alacrity to the policy dictates of Milošević and Karadžić.[144] These militias, with names such as the White Eagles and the Tigers, were often responsible for the worst massacres, and while they were portrayed as autonomous, the evidence indicates strongly that they were under the direction of Serbian authorities.[145] One paramilitary leader, Vojislav Seselj, told journalists that

> Milosevic organized everything. We gathered the volunteers and he gave us special barracks at Bubanj Potok, all our uniforms, arms, military technology and buses. All our units were always under the command of . . . the Yugoslav army.[146]

Supporting this contention, the executive secretary for Serbia's defense minister wrote,

> Arkan operated within the Territorial Defense system. He had his own group which acted under his command, but all actions were cleared and coordinated with the Yugoslav army.[147]

Clear evidence also indicates that the mechanisms and tools for the campaign of terror were put in place months before the violence began, which also indicates that the genocide was a planned and controlled event.[148] When the word was given, the Bosnian Serbs were able to respond very quickly in implementing their genocidal policies. In short, everything indicates that, contrary to the prevailing imagery of historical and therefore inevitable ethnic enmity, the recent genocide was an example of the leadership of a state coldly and calculatingly manipulating popular understandings to create the illusion of a threat from the Bosnian Muslims. This allowed for the mobilization of various Serbian forces to carry out the leadership's genocidal policies and justified its subsequent aggressions.

A close examination of the Rwandan genocide similarly reveals a pattern of misleading imagery and state culpability. Initial accounts portrayed the killing as an inevitable reversion to primitive African tribalism. Stories in *Time*, for example, referred to "tribal bloodlust" and "tribal slaughter," as if this explained the outbreak of genocide.[149] The *New York Times* reported on "the age-old animosity between the Tutsi and Hutu ethnic groups."[150] Upon his return to the United States, then-ambassador David Rawson also portrayed the violence as tribal in origin, rather than as a directed campaign of genocide.[151] The Hutu government itself fostered this image of spontaneous mob violence in an effort to allay international concern.[152] But when the facts are examined, it quickly becomes clear that the Rwandan genocide is another example of a planned and deliberate attempt to exterminate a population in the service of current political needs and goals. In the words of Fergal Keane:

Rwanda's genocide was not a simple matter of mutual hatred between tribes erupting into irrational violence. Neither were the mass killings the result of a huge and sudden outpouring of rage on the part of Hutus following the murder of their president. The killings—and there is ample documentary evidence to prove this—were planned long in advance.[153]

Lemarchand echoes this position when he asserts,

Contrary to the image conveyed by the media, there is nothing in the historical record to suggest a kind of tribal meltdown rooted in "deep seated antagonisms" or "longstanding atavistic hatreds." Nor is there any evidence in support of the "spontaneous action from below" thesis. . . . However widespread, both views are travesties of reality.[154]

The genocide in Rwanda has its roots not in the pre-existing animosities between Hutus and Tutsis, but in the precarious political condition of the ruling Hutu government. The spark that set the killing in motion was the assassination of Hutu president Juvenal Habyarimana. In 1990, the Tutsi-dominated Rwandan Patriotic Front (RPF) launched a military campaign against the government with the intent of ousting the ruling Mouvement Révolutionnaire National pour le Développement (MRND). The Hutu-dominated MRND portrayed the conflict as an attempt by extremists to impose a Tutsi dictatorship and began a series of pogroms against the Tutsis in order to maintain their grasp on power by providing an easily targeted scapegoat. It was an attempt to unite the nation behind the MRND so that "Privilege would be maintained albeit at the expense of fomenting ethnic hatred."[155] Unfortunately for the MRND, military reverses in the field against the RPF, as well as international pressure, forced President Habyarimana to the negotiating table, where he agreed to share power and give up absolute control of the state. Not surprisingly, many of his followers felt betrayed and saw that their privileged way of life was in danger of disappearing. On April 6, 1994, the president's plane was shot down by anti-aircraft missiles on his return from peace talks to the capital in Kigali. While the perpetrators are officially unknown, ample evidence suggests that members of his own ruling clique orchestrated the assassination in order to reverse the trend toward accommodation.[156] Within hours after the president's murder, the killing began in Kigali, and within days it had spread throughout Rwanda. However, before the killing began one Hutu informant told the second-in-command of the U.N. Assistance Mission in Rwanda, Colonel Luc Marchal, that "his mission was now to prepare the killings of civilian and Tutsi people . . . to make lists of Tutsi people, where they lived, to be able, at a certain code name, to kill them."[157] Because of this planning and the previous pogroms, much of the propaganda and organization were already in place. For example, after the initial RPF onslaught, a massive campaign was begun to recruit and train Hutu militias such as the *Interahamwe*. Officially formed to protect civilians from the RPF, they actually served as a paramilitary force supporting the police and military.[158] Upon the outbreak of genocide after Habyarimana's death, the *Interahamwe* were ready to accelerate their victimization of the Tutsis.

The tools were in place and the genocide relatively easy to implement. Its purpose was to retain power by rallying the large Hutu population against a demonized enemy embodied in the Tutsis. The Hutu hardliners hoped to discredit the RPF and ensure allegiance to their dictatorship. The Rwandan genocide is an example of a rationally enacted policy for specific political goals. Anti-Tutsi feelings of hostility, resentment, and fear were fanned and manipulated in order to create support for the fight against a common enemy and mobilize the Hutu population behind the existing government. It was not an example of unbridled tribalism run amok.

The Holocaust demonstrates the same rationality. For example, the infamous Wannsee conference is a clear indication of the role the Nazi state played in the perpetration of genocide. Held on January 20, 1942, in the exclusive Berlin suburb of Wannsee, the meeting was chaired by Reinhard Heydrich, the number two SS officer under Himmler and head of the *Sicherheitsdienst*, the security service of the SS, which in turn controlled the Gestapo.[159] Invited to the meeting were representatives from various governmental bureaucracies, including the Interior and Justice Ministries, the Ministry for the Eastern Occupied Territories, the chancellory of the Nazi Party, the chancellory of the Reich, and representatives from the various branches of the Reich's Security Main Office (RSHA), which included most of the police, security, and intelligence services, all incidentally under the auspices of the SS, as well as other functionaries.[160] The minutes of this meeting record that

> At the beginning of the discussion Chief of the Security Police and of the SD, SS-Obergruppenführer Heydrich, reported that the Reich Marshal had appointed him delegate for the preparations for the final solution of the Jewish question in Europe.[161]

Here we have an example of officials and representatives of various branches of the Nazi state meeting together for the explicit purpose of perpetrating genocide.

The Holocaust, clearly, was implemented under the direction of the German government. The purpose of the conference was not to begin to kill the Jews; rather, it was to centralize control and rationalize implementation of the destruction of European Jewry. As Martin Gilbert writes,

> What had hitherto been tentative, fragmentary, and spasmodic was to become formal, comprehensive and efficient. The technical services such as the railways, the bureaucracy, and the diplomats would work in harmony towards a single goal.[162]

It was at this meeting that the phrase "the final solution of the Jewish question" (*Endlösung der Judenfrage*) was first used. The RSHA would be the implementing body of genocide, while the other organs of government, as well as various governmental and private bureaucracies, would cooperate with the implementation of the "Final Solution." The participants at the meeting dealt not only with the logistics of deportation, but also with the specific methods of killing that should be employed to exterminate European Jewry. For example, the minutes of the meeting record that

> Under proper guidance, in the course of the final solution the Jews are to be allocated for appropriate labor in the East. Able-bodied Jews, separated according to sex, will be taken in large work columns to these areas for work on roads, in the course of which action doubtless a large portion will be eliminated by natural causes. The possible final remnant will, since it will undoubtedly consist of the most resistant portion, have to be treated accordingly, because it is the product of natural selection and would, if released, act as the seed of a new Jewish revival.[163]

The important point here is that the participants explicitly point out that they expect most of the Jews to be worked to death, or "eliminated by natural causes," as they put it; those who survive will have to be "treated accordingly." These lines make it very clear what the fate of the European Jews was to be. In this way, during a cold-blooded abstract discussion during which the participants were served tea and snacks and sat in comfortable chairs, the groundwork for the murder of millions of human beings was laid.

One of those present at this conference was Adolf Eichmann, an SS bureaucrat from the Reich Main Security Office. It was he who coordinated this massive continent-wide endeavor and, years later during his famous trial in Israel, became an infamous symbol of the *Schreibtischtäter*, the desk murderer. This conference is but one revealing example of the role of the state in perpetrating the Holocaust.

In this chapter I examined the role of the state as the instigator of genocide. Rather than an atavistic example of communal violence, as it is all too often portrayed, genocide is the end result of a series of rational steps undertaken by a government in order to achieve some specific goal. It is the state that provides the motive, the impetus, the legitimation, and the ideology for the genocide. However, genocidal drives must be implemented in concrete policies and strategies designed to achieve those political goals. This is the level at which the institutions, structures, and bureaucracies become important.

4 Lethal Cogs

It is ironic that the virtues of loyalty, discipline, and self-sacrifice that we
value so highly in the individual are the very properties that create destructive organizational engines of war and bind men to malevolent systems of
authority.

—Stanley Milgram[1]

The Holocaust was murder, to be sure. But it was thorough, comprehensive,
and exhaustive murder. To commit a Holocaust, bureaucracy must replace the
mob; routinized behavior must supplant rage.

—Gerald Markle[2]

When you think of the long and gloomy history of man, you will find more
hideous crimes have been committed in the name of obedience than have
ever been committed in the name of rebellion.

—C. P. Snow[3]

On the night of May 11, 1960, in a run-down suburb of Buenos Aires, Argentina, a man was kidnapped just steps away from his house. As he walked
home from work in the dark, two men approached from the opposite direction,
grabbed him, and threw him into a waiting car that quickly sped away. The kidnappers were Israeli security agents, and the abductee was Adolf Eichmann, one
of the most wanted of Nazi war criminals.[4] During the war, Eichmann, an
officer in the Reich's Security Main Office (RSHA), had been responsible for
deporting Poles and Jews. Through his office the policies of first deporting the
Jews, then concentrating them in ghettos, and ultimately transporting them to
the extermination camps were coordinated.

After his capture, Eichmann was secretly held in a safe house for several days,
and then smuggled back to Israel on an El Al flight, where he stood trial for his
role in the perpetration of the Holocaust. He was indicted on four counts of
crimes against the Jewish people, seven counts of crimes against humanity, one
count of war crimes, and three counts of serving in criminal organizations: the
SS, the SD, and the Gestapo.[5]

In his defense at his trial, Eichmann argued that he had no responsibility for
the execution of the Jews since he personally had never killed a Jew, nor did he
give any orders to kill anybody.[6] He asserted that the department he ran was
responsible only for relocating people and organizing the trains and other transport for those relocations. As for the death camps that were the destination of

many of those trains, according to Eichmann, those were someone else's responsibility. This defense illustrates well the bureaucratic mentality that allows ordinary people to participate in extraordinary crimes. By focusing only on their actions in a narrow sense, and avoiding explicit awareness that their efforts contributed to the larger scheme of extermination, bureaucrats performed their jobs without considering the true consequences of their actions.

Eichmann's argument, however, was not accepted by the court and eventually he was found guilty and executed by hanging on May 31, 1962. In his final plea to the court Eichmann stated that he was innocent of the charges brought against him because

> I never had the power and the responsibility of a giver of orders. I never carried out killings, as Höss did. If I had received the order to carry out these killings, I would not have escaped by using a trumped up pretext; during my interrogation I already stated: Since because of the compulsion exerted by an order there was no way out, I would have put a bullet through my brain in order to solve the conflict between conscience and duty.[7]

Eichmann was unable or unwilling to acknowledge his personal responsibility for the Holocaust. In fact, he claimed that he would have killed himself rather than participate and kill Jews: truly an amazing claim from a man who conscientiously implemented genocidal ideologies in practices designed to murder millions. In point of fact, Eichmann was a skillful bureaucrat who overcame with initiative and resourcefulness many obstacles to carrying out the Holocaust. While at one level he was a committed racist and Nazi, at another Adolf Eichmann exemplifies the archetypical bureaucratic participant in genocide who, while far removed from the actual act of murder, is nonetheless complicit in the crime of genocide. The evidence indicates that Eichmann was motivated as much by careerist opportunism as by his ideological beliefs.[8] Eichmann's role was critical in mobilizing the resources of the Reich to assist in the Holocaust. In this sense the Holocaust is not unique, since in all examples of genocide organizations and bureaucracies play essential roles in planning and carrying out the mass murder of populations. All participants act as members of organizations that provide powerful structural inducements to participation. Speaking of the men who sent her to the camps of the Soviet gulag system, one survivor said that they were "merely functionaries earning their pay,"[9] while another said of the same regime, "The new state did not require holy apostles, fanatic, inspired builders, faithful, devout disciples. The new state did not even require servants—just clerks."[10] To a lesser or greater degree, all genocides require the participation of bureaucrats who enable the mass killing to be accomplished. As Lord Russell wrote about Eichmann and others like him,

> He bore the same, if not a greater responsibility, than those who actually carried out the extermination. He is just as guilty, if not more so, than those who with their own hands knotted the hangman's noose, who beat the victims into the gas-chambers, who shot them in the back and pushed them into open graves.[11]

This perception, however, is not always shared. Generally speaking, we do not give bureaucrats the same attention that we give to those actually on the front lines of extermination, even though it is they who provide the logistical and technical support for any mass killing. Moreover, we do not examine the organizations themselves, even though they provide the context within which all genocidal killing takes place. Typically, it is the people whose hands are literally soiled by the blood of their victims who are considered to bear the greatest responsibility.

The killing fields of Cambodia and the death camps of the Nazi Holocaust are often the predominant images associated with genocide. We tend to focus on the actual murders, the beatings, shootings, and gassings, since these are the most visceral and emotionally powerful aspects of genocide. They are real, immediate, and clear. Most of us have seen old newsreel footage of emaciated bodies being thrown or bulldozed into mass graves after the liberation of various concentration camps following the defeat of the Third Reich. For many people, the reality of genocide is captured in the images of countless bodies, most scarcely recognizable as human, strewn about in a welter of limbs and blank staring faces. While this type of mass anonymous death is the fundamental reality of genocide, it must be understood that genocide encompasses many activities in numerous locations, some of which are far removed from the slaughter.

In order to fully understand genocide, as much as that is possible, it is necessary to appreciate that the killing sites where the murders are carried out only represent the end point of a long sequence of steps involving many institutions, agencies, and actors. Genocide is a process, not just an event. The conveyor belts of killing are backed up by entire assembly lines and factories devoted in whole or in part to the production of mass death. The image of the factory is an apt one, especially for the Holocaust. Feingold, for example, writes,

Auschwitz was also a mundane extension of the modern factory system. Rather than producing goods, the raw material was human beings and the end-product was death, so many units per day marked carefully on the manager's production charts. The chimneys, the very symbol of the modern factory system, poured forth acrid smoke produced by burning human flesh. The brilliantly organized railroad grid of modern Europe carried a new kind of raw material to the factories. It did so in the same manner as with other cargo. In the gas chambers the victims inhaled noxious gas generated by prussic acid pellets, which were produced by the advanced chemical industry of Germany. Engineers designed the crematoria; managers designed the system of bureaucracy that worked with a zest and efficiency more backward nations would envy.[12]

Genocidal killing, in other words, is planned, engineered, and manufactured. It requires the acquiescence and cooperation of large segments of the political, economic, and professional sectors of a society, which Raul Hilberg has termed the "machinery of destruction."[13] The Holocaust was created and carried out by thousands of people who both directly and indirectly performed duties that made genocide feasible. This complicity involved practically all segments of German society, since the apparatus of genocide was set up to take advantage of existing bureaucracies and institutions.[14] Raul Hilberg writes,

> Any member of the Order Police could be a guard at a ghetto or on a train. Every lawyer in the Reich Security Main Office was presumed to be suitable for leadership in the mobile killing units; every finance expert to the Economic Administrative Main Office was considered a natural choice for service in a death camp.[15]

In the same way, the Armenian genocide was accomplished through the participation of not only the police and the military, but also journalists, lawmakers, politicians, and others who assisted in various direct and indirect ways.[16] Transportation and communication agencies organized and facilitated the removal of the Armenians to the deserts.[17] Because of this mass complicity, Rouben P. Adalian writes, "Although the decision to proceed with genocide was taken by the CUP, the entire Ottoman state became implicated in its implementation."[18] To this can be added that not only was the entire government apparatus involved, but many other elements of Turkish society as well. Large numbers of ordinary Turkish citizens participated in the brutalization, robbery, and massacres of the Armenians.[19] In Rwanda, the perpetrators ranged from national and local community leaders and professionals to ordinary citizens in every community throughout the country. Guided, armed, and inspired by public officials, militias, and military groups, countless Rwandan Hutus took to the bloody business of killing their Tutsi neighbors. Genocide occurs on such a large scale that it requires the skills provided by institutions and agencies throughout society to control, direct, and coordinate it.

Organizations and Genocide

Genocide is an example of crime committed within an organizational context. While individual genocides may vary tremendously in their level of organization and in the number and types of institutions that participate in coordinating the killing, all share a common denominator of institutional support. While it is the state that provides the motivation, it is the agencies, companies, and institutions of a society that direct the implementation. If the state provides the seed from which genocide grows, it is the organizations that provide the soil in which that seed sprouts. In order to turn policy initiatives, laws, and ideologies of death into reality, organizational structures of all sorts must translate the genocidal impulses of the state into concrete actions and policies. These structures stand between the state, with its genocidal plans, and the individual who is called upon to actually perform the killing in the service of that state. In reference to the Holocaust, Fred Katz writes,

> For Hitler, a multitude of administrative bureaucrats and highly educated professionals—engineers, architects, economists, physicians and lawyers—worked to transform his vision of a racially pure Germany into a reality, donating their expertise and professional skills.[20]

This comment holds true for other examples of genocide as well.

The structural milieu within which participants work is an important aspect of genocide, since participants do not usually kill primarily or solely for personal reasons. While individuals may agree with the reasons given, and even come to enjoy and affirm their participation, those who contribute to genocide do so because they are members of organizations. In this light, it is the institution, not the individual, that is typically called upon to assist in facilitating mass death. Participants in genocide become murderers because they work in a job that requires them to assist in exterminating a group of people. While some enter certain organizations, such as paramilitary groups, with the explicit purpose of partaking in a genocide, many other participants kill because it is a task that they have been assigned. To put it another way, they kill because it is expected of the role they inhabit, not because of any personal desires, qualities, or characteristics they may possess.

Because of this, most participants in genocide differ from predatory street criminals in that the motives for their behavior often have nothing to do with the classic inducements to criminality, such as passion, individual pathology, and addiction. On the contrary, participants collaborate with the process of death because the state requires it. The motivations for participation, then, are essentially similar to those of bureaucrats and executives who perpetrate various types of organizational crime, and, as Katherine Jamieson asserts, "in order to understand why these offenses occur, one must consider what is known about complex organizations, focusing on relevant questions of cause and control of deviant behavior in these settings."[21]

Eichmann once asserted that "It was my misfortune to become entangled in these atrocities. But these misdeeds did not happen according to my wishes. It was not my wish to slay people."[22] In other words, Eichmann simply did what his position required him to do, even though, he asserted, he really didn't want to participate. This claim is somewhat misleading, since Eichmann became involved with the "Jewish Question" because he saw great opportunities for professional advancement.[23] Nevertheless, he was not motivated primarily by hatred of the Jews. It is extremely unlikely that Eichmann would have continued to participate in the "Final Solution" if he had felt it was hurting his career. Similar sentiments were expressed by Dr. Otto Bradfisch, a member of an *Einsatzgruppe* responsible for killing over fifteen thousand people. He claimed that although he did participate, he had always been "inwardly opposed" to the executions. Likewise, a Nazi official named Arthur Greiser claimed that only his "official soul" had perpetrated the atrocities; his "private soul," on the other hand, had always opposed participation.[24] In Rwanda, one perpetrator claimed that "I had to do it or I'd be killed. So I feel a bit innocent. Killing didn't come from my heart."[25] Essentially, these arguments contend that these individuals participated in genocide because their positions required it, not because of any personal motivation, and that they were personally opposed to assisting in genocide. Regardless of the hypocrisy and self-exculpating nature of these protestations, they do reveal that membership in organizations was crucial to initiating and facilitating individual participation.

Participation can also be required because of membership in a racial or ethnic group. When the perpetrators of the Rwandan genocide came to local villages to organize massacres, they called upon local Hutus to help identify and massacre Tutsis. It was assumed that since they were Hutu, and their victims Tutsi, they would willingly engage in genocide. The role they inhabited as Hutus made their individual and personal relationships with Tutsi neighbors irrelevant. Similarly, many Bosnian Serbs were expected to assist and participate in the violence because of their common ethnic identity and shared heritage. Any Serb who hesitated in accepting that exclusionist perception was in danger of being labeled a traitor and one of "Alija's servants," a reference to the Muslim president of Bosnia and Herzegovina, Alija Izetbegović.[26] They also risked death. One Serb who balked at participating was purportedly told, "if you are sorry for them, stand up, line up with them, and we will kill you too."[27] Others were killed. For example, one Serb officer was killed for objecting to anti-Muslim atrocities, and an old Serb man was beaten to death because he didn't want to be separated from his Muslim friends. A seventeen-year-old Serb woman had her throat slit by a militiaman for opposing the execution of Muslims.[28] The example set by this type of brutality ensured that most Bosnian Serbs would acquiesce to the persecution. This threat to life also existed in the Rwandan genocide, as recounted by one Hutu member of the *Interahamwe* militia: "we had to do it or be killed ourselves as traitors or sympathizers with Tutsi."[29] Another Hutu leader of a roadblock also asserted, "You were told you had the duty to do this or you'd be imprisoned or killed. We were just pawns in this. We were just tools."[30]

To understand the nature and functioning of genocide, it is important to recognize the collective or institutional context of participation. But what types of organizations participate in genocide? Generally speaking, there are many institutional settings within which perpetrators operate; some directly involve their membership in acts of killing, while others keep members far removed. Participating organizations can, however, be broadly divided into state agencies and nongovernmental organizations, and, most importantly, into militaristic and nonmilitaristic institutions. The distinct organizational structures of these latter two types mean that they facilitate genocide differently and illustrate the ways in which organizational context influences and shapes participation.

Military and Paramilitary Organizations

Often the most visible perpetrators of genocide are members of various military and paramilitary forces. These groups are the ones on the front lines of the genocidal massacres and include members of a state's armed forces, police organizations, and militia groups. The most well-known killers of the Holocaust were the SS soldiers, who, with their distinctive black uniforms and skull-

and-crossbones insignias, became forever associated with the worst excesses of the Nazi regime. Created in 1922 as the personal bodyguard of Adolf Hitler, the SS (*Schutzstaffel*, or security echelon) eventually grew into a powerful military and political force in its own right with many hundreds of thousands of members.[31] It was associated with numerous war crimes; the *Totenkopfverbände*, or Death's Head units, which were usually in charge of the concentration and death camps, were especially infamous.

In Cambodia, the Khmer Rouge cadres carried out most of the executions.[32] Isolated in the jungles and under attack for many years, the Khmer Rouge were a thoroughly brutalized and indoctrinated fighting force that had no compunction about killing their fellow citizens. Many of them were very young people for whom the Khmer Rouge and its ideologies were, for all practical purposes, the only reality they knew. Believing in nothing but their movement, these young soldiers proved to be among the most ruthless of genocidal killers. Elizabeth Becker writes,

> These were the soldiers who left their families and villages when they were as young as twelve years old and never returned. They were raised and indoctrinated by the party. And they took on the one-dimensional cruelty of adolescents outside civility that was best described in William Golding's *Lord of the Flies*. Many Cambodians compared the young cadre or soldiers to trained guard dogs. A word of command would send them off to commit violent crimes or to run straight into machine-gun fire without a second thought, or so it appeared. They were the vanguard, the young elite who devoted their energies and talent to the narrow ideology of the Khmer Rouge.[33]

During the Rwandan genocide, it was the Rwandan army, the presidential guard, and members of two militia groups, the *Interahamwe* ("those who stand together" or "those who attack together") and the *Impuzamugambe* ("those who have a single aim"), who were responsible for much of the killing.[34] The *Interahamwe* came from soccer fan clubs financed and supported by the ruling party and were recruited primarily from among young unemployed Hutu males, a group highly susceptible to the regime's messages of hatred.[35] Drunk on power and alcohol, the militias spent their time dancing and killing in an orgy of excess. The combination of roadblocks, alcohol, and machetes proved fearsome in the hands of these militia groups.

In Bosnia, the worst perpetrators of the violence were the members of the Bosnian Serb army and several of the infamous militia groups, such as that headed by Želkjo Ražnatović, also known as Arkan, whose Tiger militia was implicated in some of the worst massacres. In fact, it perpetrated the first case of ethnic cleansing in Bosnia, in the town of Bijeljina, where in April 1992 a militia gang dressed in black ski masks and military fatigues and armed with assault rifles rampaged through the town. After routing a local Muslim militia, the militia went house to house killing and stealing. Influential Muslims and young men of military age were dragged out into the streets and executed. Želkjo Ražnatović was a Belgrade gangster with ties to the Serbian secret police; fans of Belgrade's popular Red Star soccer team formed the nucleus of his irregular forces.[36] As in Rwanda, these young male sports fans proved to be among the most enthusiastic killers. Ražnatović reappeared in 1999 during the conflict in Kosovo and began giving interviews to the press after he was indicted as a war criminal by the International Criminal Tribunal for the Former Yugoslavia.

No different from other genocidally inclined governments, the Turkish government also created a special organization for the Armenian genocide, whose membership was composed of murderers and other criminals released from jail. These *Chété* units, as they were called, were led by officers from the War Academy and specialized in plundering the caravans of Armenians on their forced exodus.[37]

These military and paramilitary organizations share certain characteristics that contribute to their ability to commit genocide. First and foremost, they are expert at enforcing ideological and behavioral conformity to the goals of the group. All military establishments have an initiation process, usually known as boot camp or basic training. It is intentionally difficult, brutal, and often debasing, since its purpose is to transform civilians into soldiers capable of killing on command. After the recruits have been degraded both psychologically and physically, they are transformed into soldiers in a sometimes lengthy process that often involves destroying personal identity and replacing it with one that defines them as cogs in the military machine. Unquestioning loyalty, pride, and obedience are inculcated in the new recruits. Basic training is intended not only to teach basic military skills, but also to "inculcate the military ethos in recruits, and to ensure that the individual values which prevail in most civilian societies are replaced by the group spirit and group loyalties."[38] In short, their training is geared toward providing recruits with the technical skills of violence and socializing them into a value system that supports fierceness, aggression, and solidarity with their comrades.

Even informal military organizations employ similar training patterns. Militia members often endure a type of basic training that, while not as thorough as the professional version, serves much the same purpose. Serb militias trained at a large camp near Mount Tara, on the Serb border with Bosnia.[39] Arkan's Tigers were trained in camps by regular army officers. The *Interahamwe* militia in Rwanda used mass rallies complete with alcohol and speeches, along with paramilitary drill maneuvers, to inculcate their members with the appropriate attitudes and behaviors. Recruits also underwent three-week indoctrination sessions at a training camp in Mutara.[40]

This type of indoctrination has several benefits for the organization utilizing it. One is that it closely bonds the members of a group. In fact, according to some, the connection between soldiers is often stronger than that between husband and wife.[41] Undergoing the trials and tribulations of training, depending upon each other during combat and in other traumatic situations, soldiers can come to view their comrades in arms as closer to them than brothers. A great deal of research indicates that most soldiers fight not for glory, country, or patriotism, but rather for each other, and as Grossman notes, "Among men who are bonded together so intensely, there is a powerful process of peer pressure in which the individual cares so deeply about his comrades and what they think about him that he would rather die than let them down."[42] Military organizations work to strengthen these ties through ritualized initiation ceremonies and oaths, unique and distinctive clothing and accessories, and a culture that stresses the primacy of the group. Many Serb militia members sported long beards and old-style hats with the royal double-headed eagle insignia, in conscious imitation of the old Chetnik style. It was an attempt to portray themselves as the modern heirs to traditional Serb patriotism and nationalism.[43] Some Serbs had four S's tattooed on their hands, which stood for "Only Solidarity Saves the Serbs."[44] The SS, on the other hand, considered itself an elite vanguard of the Nazi movement. One SS concentration camp commander put it this way:

> We were Germany's best and hardest. Every single one of us dedicated himself to the others. What held us together was an alliance of comradeship. Not even the bond of marriage can be stronger. Comradeship is everything. It gave us the mental and physical strength to do what others were too weak to do.[45]

Powerful pressure is exerted to make members conform to the expectations of the group and not let their comrades down. Browning's study of the men of Reserve Police Battalion 101 in Poland clearly illustrates its effects. Ordered to participate in the roundup and shooting of the Jews of the village of Jósefów, many of the policemen found the massacre horrible, yet by and large they carried out their terrible duty, even though they had been explicitly told by their commanding officer that anyone who was not up to the task could be excused. Browning argues that most of the men participated because they did not want to let their fellow officers down by making them shoulder an unfair burden and because they did not want to risk being shunned and isolated by their comrades.[46] As Staub notes,

> The more a person's life is centered in a group, the more a person derives identity, self-concept and self-esteem, rewards and satisfactions, conceptions of the right way of life, and ideals from membership, the more difficult it is to deviate and to defy the group.[47]

The group, therefore, acts as a powerful force for compliance even if the duties are difficult. Whether for fear of letting comrades down or of earning their disapproval, individuals act out of a sense of obligation to the group. One SS member put it this way:

> I did not ask Leideritz to be released from certain duties and be given guard duties instead. The reason I did not say to Leideritz that I could not take part in these things was that I was afraid that Leideritz and others would think I was a coward. I was worried that I would be affected adversely in some way in the future if I allowed myself to be seen as being too weak. I did not want Leideritz or other people to get the impression that I was not as hard as an SS-Mann ought to have been.[48]

Militaristic organizations are also highly authoritarian and hierarchical. This stratification is reinforced by the training and indoctrination undergone by members of these groups. In fact, one primary purpose of basic training regimens is to instill into recruits the habits and patterns of obedience. They are taught to obey orders without thinking about the implications or morality of their actions. Todorov's statement that "The goal of the system was to transform everyone into a cog in a vast machine and thus to deprive them of their will"[49] is an appropriate summation of this process. Stanley Milgram's famous experiments indicate that ordinary people are predisposed to act in patently harmful ways if that behavior is explicitly sanctioned by someone in authority.[50] All societies emphasize obedience to the institutions, authority figures, and values of the community. Military and paramilitary organizations simply reinforce and strengthen this natural tendency for individuals to conform to the behaviors and ideals of the group.

These institutions also create a sense of individual absolution. As anonymous members of a group, soldiers defer responsibility for their actions to the group. This process is exacerbated by the collective and official nature of genocide.[51] As one military recruit stated, "When I raised my right hand and took that oath, I freed myself of the consequences for what I do. I'll do what they tell me and nobody can blame me."[52] This is a common reaction to membership in any group. Individuals in groups, especially those not in decision-making positions, often relinquish their moral selves to the morality of the group and defer to the group and its leaders for guidance and direction. As Stanley Milgram explained,

> Each individual possesses a conscience which to a greater or lesser degree serves to restrain the unimpeded flow of impulses destructive to others. But when he merges his person in an organizational structure, a new creature replaces autonomous man, unhindered by the limitations of individual morality, freed of humane inhibition, mindful only of the sanctions of authority.[53]

This process is fostered by the authoritarian and hierarchical structure of military and paramilitary organizations. Heinrich Himmler, head of the SS, told his minions that he and the Führer, Adolf Hitler, assumed all responsibility for their actions, while the military junta in Argentina signed orders for the kidnappings, which not only created an aura of legitimacy around the violence but also served to relieve the officers involved of their sense of personal responsibility. At his trial after the war, Otto Ohlendorf, the leader of one of the *Einsatzgruppen*, was asked,

> "Did you have no scruples in regard to the execution of these orders?"
> "Yes, of course," Ohlendorf replied.
> "And how is it they were carried out regardless of these scruples?"
> "Because to me it is inconceivable that a subordinate leader should not carry out orders given by the leaders of the state," Ohlendorf answered.[54]

Adolf Eichmann, speaking about the notorious Wannsee conference, said, "Here now, during this conference, the most prominent people had spoken, the Popes of the third Reich. Not only Hitler, not only Heydrich, or Müller, or the SS, or the Party, but the elite of the Civil Service had registered their support. . . . At that moment, I sensed a kind of Pontius Pilate feeling, for I was free of all guilt."[55] The perpetrators, in situations like these, can avoid feelings of individual responsibility and defer their capacity for moral choice to the amorality of the group.

Soldiers, militia members, and police officers are conditioned, not only to obey superior officers, but also to use violence. Much emphasis is placed on training recruits in the mechanics of killing, by such means as having them fire weapons at targets shaped like human beings. The *Interahamwe* familiarized their members with the use of grenades and the burning of houses, and had them practice machete skills on hacked-up human-shaped dummies, all skills which were later wielded with lethal effectiveness in the Rwandan genocide.[56] This type of training makes the act of killing easier, since eventually no thought is required. The physical act of killing simply becomes a habit or reflex.

Conditioning recruits also involves desensitizing them to violence. Human beings are infinitely adaptable and can get used to a great many things that are initially repugnant. For example, Serb soldiers were taken to farms and taught to wrestle pigs down, pull their heads back, and then slit their throats.[57] It's no accident that for many Serbs a preferred method of killing Muslims was to slit their throats.[58] Members of these groups were also desensitized through an incremental process of immersion. Members of Serb genocide groups were made to first watch, then participate in, the torture, rape, and murder of Bosnian Muslims.[59] To refuse was to risk injury or death; to participate was to gain acceptance, to become an accomplice, and to ritually cross a threshold of behavior that made subsequent participation easier. This indoctrination was buttressed by belief systems that enabled and justified the violence. SS members were taught that Jews and Slavs were a threat to the superior Aryan peoples. Killing them was a hard but necessary duty that they owed not only to their country, but to their people as well. To remind himself and others of the need to be hard, one SS officer had a sign hung over his desk at Auschwitz upon which was written "Sympathy is a Weakness."[60] The Serb militias were taught that true Serbian patriots exhibited no mercy to their enemies, including women and children.[61] Rwandan *Interahamwe* militia members were taught that they had to kill the Tutsis to protect their nation; this protection included killing women and children in order to prevent the next generation of Tutsis from seeking revenge.[62]

Once engaged in genocide, the perpetrators become increasingly brutalized and used to the killing. What may have been initially quite difficult becomes progressively easier. As Staub points out,

> When our emotions are overwhelmingly unpleasant or painful, we anesthetize ourselves; soldiers become able to tolerate mangled bodies, and the capacity for horror becomes blunted. While this diminishes suffering, it also makes us insensitive to the suffering of others, especially when the other is defined as different, the member of an outgroup, or an enemy bent on our destruction.[63]

What Staub describes is a process whereby individuals protect themselves from unpleasant, stressful situations. This process of desensitization and brutalization is prevalent among all who are repeatedly exposed to acts of violence. Some genocidal killers, however, never become brutalized because they are not directly exposed to the violent activities. Unlike militaristic organizations, non-militaristic ones participate in genocide for a wide variety of motivations, the most prominent of which are bureaucratic.

Role of Bureaucracy

By their very nature, bureaucracies lend themselves to the perpetration of certain crimes, including genocide. That is, bureaucracy's structure and methods of operation foster certain conditions that facilitate criminal acts. Bureaucracies, and the bureaucrats who work in them, help make genocide possible because the settings contribute to attitudes and modes of thinking conducive to criminality and harmful behavior. The nature and functioning of bureaucratic organizations were first explored by the German sociologist Max Weber, who in his analysis pointed to specific components of bureaucracies that make them the most efficient and effective type of social construct. Bureaucracies, according to Weber, are social patterns organized around impersonal regulations and procedures designed to be applied uniformly according to specific guidelines. They are formalized institutions in which roles are clearly laid out and duties pertain to positions rather than to the individuals who happen to be filling those positions at any given time.[64] Individuals may come and go, but the organization continues. Bureaucracies, according to Weber, are the most productive type of administration because of their

> purely *technical* superiority over any other form of organization. The fully developed bureaucratic apparatus compares with other organizations exactly as does the machine with the non-mechanical modes of production. Precision, speed, unambiguity, knowledge of the files, continuity, discretion, unity, strict subordination, reduction of friction and of material and personal costs—these are raised to the optimum point in the strictly bureaucratic administration.[65]

This increased effectiveness, however, comes at a cost. One of Weber's main points was that the efficiency of modern bureaucracies derives from the impersonal application of policies that remove the human element from the equation. Bureaucratic duties are bounded and constrained by formalized rules of conduct that are intended to be applied in clearly prescribed circumstances. The human element, which includes the personal characteristics of the bureaucrat and the client, is irrelevant, and is in fact detrimental to smooth efficiency. As Weber wrote,

> Bureaucracy develops the more perfectly, the more it is "dehumanized," the more completely it succeeds in eliminating from official business love, hatred, and all purely personal, irrational, and emotional elements which escape calculation.[66]

While discarding human elements increases the ability of a bureaucracy to function impartially and effectively, it makes it possible for people to engage in extremely harmful and destructive behavior in the interests of their organization. The impersonal application of formalized directives allows bureaucracies to function more efficiently and mechanically, since they perform on the basis of routines and rules applied uniformly, rather than tailoring procedures to individuals. Of this process, Hummel writes,

> Bureaucracy replaces ordinary *social interaction,* in which individuals act by mutually orienting themselves to each other, by *rationally organized action,* in which individuals orient themselves to goals and meanings defined from the top down.[67]

In other words, human relationships are replaced by bureaucratic objectives. This means that qualities of compassion, humanity, and concern are removed from consideration. Bureaucrats do not take into account the human cost of their performance and the ways in which their actions personally affect people, since these are, for bureaucratic purposes, largely irrelevant. The job of the bureaucrat is simply to complete assigned tasks, rather than to attend to their human consequences or to render decisions based on issues of morality. Human beings are reduced to numbers, cases, or clients, thus becoming neutral "things" to be processed, instead of human beings who must be understood and cared for. Care and the subjective understanding of individual needs and issues are replaced by an objective application of impersonal rules. Fred Katz points out that

> In such a system of control there are explicit rules for guiding the behavior of the bureaucracy's officials in response to problems that might arise; the career of officials is geared to carrying out these rules; success in a bureaucratic career depends on how well the bureaucrat performs tasks, as judged by those higher in the bureaucratic hierarchy; there is clear separation between the official's work and personal life; and, within the bureaucratic organization, there are clearly defined objectives for the organization, and clearly stipulated steps for reaching the objectives. In short, there is a system of control geared to efficient administration. It uses human beings (and machines) to maximize efficiency.[68]

The literature on genocide indicates that Katz's description characterizes many bureaucratic participants, who focused exclusively on performing their jobs while ignoring the ramifications of their activities. It is not surprising that various scholars have linked these characteristics of bureaucracy to genocide. For example, both Raul Hilberg and Richard Rubenstein argue that what enabled the annihilation of the Jews, Gypsies, and other victims to be planned and attempted, especially on such an awesome scale, were modern bureaucratic organizations.[69] Essentially, they argue that the efficiency of such organizations, coupled with the depersonalization and dehumanization engendered by them, facilitated the Holocaust. This contention is supported by bureaucrats such as Walter Stier, a member of the Nazi party and head of Reich Railways Department 33, who, when interviewed by Claude Lanzmann, claimed that he did not know that his "special trains" were bringing people to execution.

> Lanzmann: "Did you know that Treblinka meant extermination?"
> Stier: "Of course not!"
> Lanzmann: "You didn't know?"
> Stier: "Good God, no! How could we know? I never went to Treblinka. I stayed in Krakow, in Warsaw, glued to my desk."
> Lanzmann: "You were a . . . "
> Stier: "I was strictly a bureaucrat."[70]

For Stier, the process had replaced the meaning. While it is debatable whether his ignorance was willful or genuine, this passage does reveal the bureaucrat's ability to ignore the consequences of actions. Kelman and Hamilton describe this bureaucratic fixation on procedure as a form of routinization, in which the details and the process of the work become more important than the results of their actions.[71] The bureaucrats, according to Bartov, "preferred to concentrate on their specific tasks and claim ignorance of, and no responsibility for, anything that happened beyond their individual area of activity."[72] It helps that the familiar and innocuous nature of most of the discrete steps tends to hide the horrible reality of genocidal killing. Filling out forms and shuffling papers can appear meaningful in and of itself. These deceptively harmless steps leading up to annihilation allow bureaucrats to avoid the potentially devastating recognition that they are *Schreibtischtäter* (desk-murderers). This focus on the mundane and apparently harmless procedures of daily bureaucratic routine is aided by the fact that there is a large physical distance, occupied by intermediaries, between the bureaucrats and the genocidal consequences of their actions. This "mediation of action" means that they do not directly experience the consequences of their behaviors and thus find themselves operating in a moral vacuum.[73] Ensconced in comfortable offices, dressed in proper suits, bureaucrats in the Third Reich made decisions that deprived Jews of citizenship and legal rights, took away their possessions, deported them and consolidated them in ghettos, and ultimately sent them to the gas chambers to be murdered.

Bureaucratic organizations assist and enable the perpetration of genocide because they immunize their minions against feelings of compassion and caring. While not all genocides rely upon bureaucracies to the extent that Nazi Germany did, understanding the organizational context remains important for understanding genocide. Not only the Nazis, but also groups such as the Young Turks and the Khmer Rouge, relied upon bureaucrats and bureaucratic procedures to organize genocide. So too did the Serbs. After the initial takeover of power in the Bosnian Serb Republic, Muslims became subject to new rules and edicts, one of which required Muslims wishing to flee Serb-controlled territory to apply to Serb authorities for official permission. Peter Maass describes his visit to the "Bureau for the Removal of Populations and Exchange of Material Goods" this way:

I politely pushed my way inside, up a dark staircase lined with the eyes of the fearful, and went to the office where Miloš Bojinović, the bureau's director, held court. Bojinović was a skinny man in his forties with a wispy goatee that looked straggly, perhaps in sympathy with the pale face it was attached to. The only sturdy thing about him was the pistol strapped to his waist. He was the man, I had been told, who decided who got out and who didn't. In the universe of Banja Luka, he was a god of sorts, playing with people's lives. This one stays, that one goes, this one lives, that one dies. I didn't quite know what to expect out of an ethnic cleanser, but surely it wasn't a nervous, underweight man who could be wrestled to the ground by a fish. His was the face of evil that I had been seeking out, yet I felt a bit like Dorothy when she finally reaches the palace of Oz and pulls back the curtain to reveal the "mighty" wizard as nothing but a quivering little man.[74]

Maass goes on to describe this man as a classic bureaucrat, and this passage is strikingly reminiscent of descriptions of Adolf Eichmann, the archetypical bureaucrat of the Holocaust for whom Hannah Arendt coined the now famous phrase "the banality of evil."[75]

To sum up, bureaucrats and bureaucracies often play extremely important roles in facilitating genocide. This reliance upon organizations and organizational processes raises several important questions. First, what are the specific mechanisms that facilitate the participation of nonmilitaristic organizations in genocide? That is, what factors promote the conformity of organizations to genocidal processes? Second, how do individuals working within those organizations come to accept their individual roles in genocide? Are there organizational inducements to their compliance? In order to address these questions, it is useful to examine the literature on organizational crime. For a number of years now, scholars exploring the causes and correlates of organizational crime have identified certain structural characteristics that play a role in encouraging and accommodating participation in criminal enterprises. While the individual organizations may vary greatly in their organizational structures, fields of business, and illegal behavior, they nevertheless share certain motivations for their crimes. This is as true for companies participating in genocidal crimes as it is for those engaged in price fixing, deceptive advertising, or any other corporate criminality.

Profit

One common theme in the literature on organizational crime is profit. Profit appears time and again as an underlying motive for organizational criminality.[76] In the words of Lydia Voigt et al.,

Despite elaborate rationalizations, including alleged altruistic desires to help their organizations, the vast majority of "respectable" criminals are motivated by personal gain.[77]

James William Coleman puts it more simply when he writes, "White-collar criminals break the law . . . because it is the easiest way for them to make a lot of money."[78] This is true for the individuals working within organizations as well as the organization as a whole. Businesses, after all, exist to make money. While genocide may not appear to revolve around profit and money, examination quickly reveals that profit affects genocide in two significant ways.

First, some genocides are perpetrated primarily for profit.[79] For example, we find instances of economically motivated genocide, or socioeconomic genocide, as it has been termed by some,[80] in the rain forests of South America as the region became a frontier of economic exploitation. While some question whether or not the destruction of the Native peoples of South America constitutes genocide on the grounds of definitional issues such as intent, few question the destruction and loss of habitat and life suffered by these people.

In the mid-1970s a mineral survey of the rain forest found large quantities of uranium, gold, diamonds, and tin ore. Soon after, mining companies in several South American countries began operations in the rain forest, while hundreds of independent miners also invaded the region in search of wealth. Inevitably, conflicts between the miners, the military, and the Indigenous peoples developed, with the usual negative consequences for the Native groups. Ironically, in Brazil, many Indians have been killed, not only by soldiers and miners, but also by agents of the government's Indian Protection Agency.[81] While Indian tribes have been exterminated at varying rates throughout the twentieth century, the conflicts and pressures of mining have accelerated their destruction. Irving Horowitz points out that

> Of 19,000 Munducurus believed to have existed in the thirties, only 1,200 were left. The strength of the Guaranis had been reduced from 5,000 to 300. There were 400 Carajas left out of 4,000. Of the Cintas Largas, who had been attacked from the air and driven into the mountains, possibly 500 had survived out of 10,000. The proud and noble nation of the Kadiweus . . . had shrunk to a pitiful scrounging band of about 200. A few hundred only remained of the formidable Chavantes. . . . Many tribes were not represented by a single family, a few by one or two individuals. Some, like the Tapaiunas—in this case from a gift of sugar laced with arsenic—had disappeared altogether. It is estimated that between 50,000 and 100,000 Indians survive today. Without active intervention, the Indian population of Brazil seems doomed to extinction in the name of developmentalism.[82]

This process is being repeated throughout South America. There are reports of entire tribes being bombed into extinction, poisoned food being dropped into villages, and military boats cruising the rivers and machine-gunning any Indians who appear on the banks.[83] Some Indigenous peoples have been forced into settlements, where disease soon kills them off. Roads and towns built in the jungle have destroyed traditional ways of life, disrupted food supplies, and otherwise threatened the Amazon tribes in Brazil. The Yanomamö, for example, have lost fully 15 percent of their population, roughly 2000 people.[84] In 1979, the Fourth International Russell Tribunal found that genocide was being committed against many South American Native peoples as governments in countries such as Columbia and Brazil attempted to "de-indianize" the rain forest.[85]

Another example is the destruction of the Achè people of Paraguay, who, because they stood in the way of the lumber and cattle industries, were systematically killed off. Estimates suggest that over 85 percent of the Achè population were hunted down and murdered by roving death squads.[86] In describing the genocide committed against native peoples in Latin America and elsewhere, Roger Smith writes,

> Indians have been subjected to genocidal attacks in the name of progress and development. . . . the object has been Indian land—for the timber it contains, the minerals that can be extracted, and the cattle it can feed. . . . They are being killed, were killed, because of a combination of ethnocentrism and simple greed.[87]

While Indigenous peoples are not the only group to have had genocide inflicted on them, they have borne the brunt of economic genocides. These types of genocides are often bolstered by dehumanizing and racist stereotypes and ideologies that portray the victims as little more than savages in an effort to justify the atrocities. Many of those responsible for the destruction of the Yanomamö people have portrayed their behavior as beneficial to the Indians and argue that they are helping to raise the Indians out of savagery by bringing them the benefits of modern technological life.[88] This misleading claim dates back to the first European conquests in the Americas, when the invaders argued that they were bringing civilization and Christ to the savages.

Thus, some genocides are perpetrated primarily for profit. In the second form of interaction between profit and genocide, various organizations make use of genocide to generate profits. In November 1938, the German Reich began compulsory "Aryanization" of Jewish property and businesses; the government seized Jewish assets and sold them off to Aryan-owned businesses. This process provided much profit not only to the Reich, but also to private businesses who saw competition eliminated and their own assets increased for a pittance. As Simpson notes, "These institutions saw Aryanization as a legitimate business opportunity that they could not afford to pass up."[89] German industry also exploited the Holocaust for corporate gain. While the concentration camps and death camps are notorious for their brutality, it is less well known that these camps also provided a ready pool of slave labor for various companies. For example, the prisoners of Auschwitz were exploited by a large number of outside businesses, including IG Farbenindustrie and Bismarckhütte, Oberschlesische Hydrierwerke, Siemens-Schuckert, Hermann Göring Werke, Ost Maschinenebau, Grün & Bilfinger, Homzmann, Königshütter Metallwerke, Emmerich Machold, Borsig Koks-Werke, Rheinmettall Borsig, and Schlesische Feinweberei.[90] These firms made use of tremendous numbers of prisoners, approximately thirty-seven thousand in 1944 alone.[91] So ubiquitous were German businesses in the German camp system that at the Nuremburg trials the court found that for all practical purposes "Auschwitz was financed and owned by Farben."[92] While the firms paid the SS only a token amount for the use of the prisoners, the profits reaped by the German state were nonetheless immense. Auschwitz alone earned the government more than sixty million reichsmarks during the years it was in operation. Franciszek Piper writes that "Cheap prisoner labor, combined with low cost of upkeep of prisoners, made the prisoners a source of profits for the state, the SS, and the industrial firms involved."[93]

The businessmen who exploited the camps knew the status of these prisoners, yet did nothing to improve their lot. Managers toured the camps and helped select the workers that their businesses could exploit; moreover, work sites were often located within or next to the camps. Prisoners were routinely beaten, sometimes to death, and if a worker collapsed he would be kicked to determine whether he was alive or dead. The managers and executives could not help but see this horrific treatment meted out, yet at post-war trials, they claimed that they had noticed nothing wrong. They often provided alternative explanations of the camps. Benjamin Ferencz summarizes them:

> They never heard of "selections" at Auschwitz, they said, until after the war. The supplementary "Buna soup," which the inmates described as "nauseating," was praised by one German defense witness as "delicious." To him, the macabre skeletons with their zebra-striped pajamas, their wooden shoes, and shaved heads looked "splendid." Former inmates testified that they were forced to carry unbearable loads until they collapsed, and that they were not permitted to use even a piece of newspaper or a scrap of clothing to protect their bleeding shoulders or hands, yet Farben's witness, Engineer Häfele, characterized Monowitz as a "convalescent camp."[94]

These statements indicate a real unwillingness on the part of the managers to own up to their exploitation of the inmates. To the firms, the prisoners were a never-ending supply of incredibly cheap labor that could be utilized to turn a profit and then be discarded and forgotten. These prisoners were valuable tools only so long as they could work and be productive. Once used up, they could be easily replaced without any sentimentality or emotion. It was a policy of *Vernichtung durch Arbeit*, destruction through work.[95]

The case of Topf and Sons also illustrates the ways in which profit could be generated from genocide. Topf and Sons was an Erfurt-based company that manufactured blast furnaces and crematoria. Actively in competition with the rival firm of Kori, Topf and Sons worked hard to win contracts to supply the crematoria for many concentration and death camps, including Dachau, Buchenwald, Flossenburg, and Auschwitz.[96] Men like Topf and Sons engineer Kurt Prüfer clearly knew what these crematoria would be used for. They supervised the construction at the camps and attended meetings in which the crematoria and their use were discussed in great detail. Nevertheless, the knowledge that their labor would be used to dispose of the victims of mass murder did not dissuade them from supplying the camps with incinerators. Working closely with SS officers at the camps, these engineers moved from passive acceptance of genocide to active participation. The lure of profits and commissions was simply too enticing for these educated professionals to resist. Profit, however, is not the only motivation that executives and the organizations they work for have to participate in genocide.

Organizational Size

Another important factor that sometimes contributes to genocidal participation is organizational size.[97] A general rule of thumb is that the larger the organization, the more often it violates laws. The size of the organization does not itself facilitate criminality; rather, larger structures are typically more complex and specialized, and their complexity and specialization facilitate criminality, since they serve to limit individual responsibility. In fact, some scholars assert that the likelihood of corporate crime is directly related to the structural and procedural complexity of the organization.[98] Katherine Jamieson writes that

> Both organizational differentiation and decentralization require a greater diffusion of responsibility because authority becomes dispersed throughout the corporation. . . . The decentralized nature of large companies facilitates individual participation in corporate crime.[99]

In large organizations individuals typically work in narrowly defined areas of expertise, constrained by departmental or structural boundaries that delimit areas of responsibility. The tasks and functions of bureaucrats tend to be fragmented into discrete steps, with different actors handling different duties. This mode of organization encourages the functionaries to focus on only the immediate task at hand rather than the larger ramifications of their collective accomplishments. In other words, they see only the individual links rather than the entire chain. In the words of Todorov,

> Those who made all this possible—Speer, Eichmann, Höss, and all the countless other intermediaries, the police, the bureaucrats, the railway employees, the manufacturers of the deadly gas, the suppliers of barbed wire, the builders of the high-performance crematoriums—can always shift their responsibility onto the next link in the chain.[100]

While specialization is an efficient way to achieve the goals of the organization, "specialization, decentralization, and delegation are often cited as conducive to corporate crime by allowing for the diffusion of responsibility throughout the organization."[101] No single person is directly responsible for any decision or task since numerous individuals, committees, and divisions within the organization contribute to the final outcome. Zygmunt Bauman points out that in this type of situation, any individual task is

> devoid of meaning, and the meaning which will be eventually bestowed on it is in no way pre-empted by the actions of its perpetrators. It will be "the others" (in most cases anonymous and out of reach) who will some time, somewhere, decide that meaning.[102]

The individuals working on those discrete tasks do not interpret or assign meaning to them. This is as true of those engaged in ordinary bureaucratic tasks as it is of those engaged in genocide. Kren and Rappoport put it this way:

> The routinized genocide program in our judgement influenced the mentality of the killers in much the same way as other repetitive, rationalized forms of industrial work influences the ordinary worker. That is, the activity becomes relatively meaningless and quite detached from the actor's sense of self.[103]

Like embezzlers and other white-collar criminals, the bureaucrats who contribute to genocide typically do not see themselves as deviant, evil, or criminal. Their acts are divorced from their sense of identity: "The route to evil often takes the form of a sequence of seemingly small, innocuous incremental steps, in each of which one tries to solve a problem within one's immediate situation."[104] During Adolf Eichmann's trial in Jerusalem he consistently held that he had no "blood guilt," since he was not personally responsible for killing any Jews. He contended that the Nazi leadership was responsible, since they understood the overall plan of extermination, but he himself was only a petty bureaucrat. All he did was to organize the trains for those who would be deported. In his own words:

> The only matters we dealt with in IV B 4 were purely technical. . . . As for who was going to the gas chamber and who wasn't, or if it was time to begin or not, or if we were supposed to stop or speed up, . . . I had nothing to do with any of that.[105]

In other word, these results were not his responsibility; they were someone else's burden in some other department or organization. This is a clear example of what some scholars have termed compartmentalization.

Compartmentalization is the process by which individuals intellectually separate different arenas of their life from one another. Bureaucrats engage in this as much as those who actually kill. Franz Stangl, the commandant of Treblinka, referred explicitly to this process when he stated that

> The only way I could live was by compartmentalizing my thinking. . . . There were hundreds of ways to take one's mind off it [the liquidations]. I used them all . . . I made myself concentrate on work, work, and again work.[106]

Finding himself in a horrible job, Stangl separated his work into small tasks, which allowed him to continue functioning. He focused on the logistical minutiae of running an extermination camp, not on the reality of extermination. Even so, he was not entirely successful in divorcing himself from the reality of his actions, as indicated by his reliance on alcohol to dull his senses.[107]

Executives perpetrating other types of organizational crime also compartmentalize in this way. Kermit Vandivier reports on an engineer working for a firm that was developing a braking system for aircraft. Even though the brake was shown to be inadequate and prone to failure, the management of the company pushed for favorable reports. One engineer who was initially opposed to sending forward favorable reports justified his eventual acquiescence this way:

"we're just drawing some curves, and what happens to them after they leave here, well, we're not responsible for that."[108]

Even those who try to ameliorate the effects of genocide must sometimes compartmentalize. The journalist David Rieff was told by one U.N. Civil Affairs official in Bosnia that

> You have to learn to compartmentalize in this job. I know what the Serbs have done in Bosnia. I've seen the corpses, heard the women weep. But it doesn't matter where my sympathies lie, or what I might say or want done if I were a journalist like you. My job is neither to fight the Serbs nor to denounce them. I'm here to help Bosnia as much as I can, and to do that I not only have to appear impartial, to treat Serbs and Muslims just the same, but, because the Serbs have all but won this war, and you need their permission to do most things here, I have to stay on good terms with them.[109]

In this way, genocide even forces compartmentalization on those who work to end the killing and violence.

Organizational Conformity and Subcultures

One criminologist notes that "organizations are machines for controlling human behavior."[110] That is, in order to function, bureaucracies must constrain and regulate their employees so that they perform in ways that benefit the agency rather than harm it. Personnel must be trained in specific skills so that the goals of the organization can be reached, and they must be taught what not to do. Just as importantly, they must be socialized into the culture of the workplace, which allows them to function in that setting. Human beings are cultural animals and we make sense of our world through various culturally transmitted symbols. This is as true in the work setting as it is in the larger social world. In the workplace, shared understandings, beliefs, and codes of conduct provide employees with the intellectual tools to interact with other workers, understand the motives and rationales for the tasks, and gain fluency in the normative system of that institution. Coleman summarizes this process when he writes,

> A large organization harbors a unique social world all its own, and the subculture embodied in the organization shapes its members' behavior in countless ways, many times without much conscious awareness on the part of the employees. At the most fundamental level, the way an organizational subculture defines the work situation and the role of various employees creates the context for all organizational behavior. The ethos of a corporation also helps to shape the moral sensibilities and perspectives of its employees. . . . Certainly any decision to engage in illegal activity is profoundly affected by the social world sheltered within the organization.[111]

This socialization process helps to enforce conformity to the goals of the organization by shaping awareness of the nature of the work. While it is not as intense in business as in militaristic organizations, it nonetheless creates a shared reality among members of organizations. In this setting, the ethical climate of the corporation is very important. Many companies, for example, create cultures of amoral calculation in which values and ethics are of less importance than eliminating competition and increasing profits. In a place with such a moral tone, employees and executives see their behavior not as criminal, but as that of aggressive or competitive businessmen. Are they any different from the Nazi bureaucrats who defined their co-workers as "hard" if they could stomach their participation, or as "soft" if they were at all squeamish?[112] The subculture shared by fellow workers helps indoctrinate them so that the illegal behavior of one is justified and reinforced by the others. Morton Mintz captures this beautifully when he writes,

> A human being who would not harm you on an individual face-to-face basis, who is charitable, civic-minded, loving and devout, will wound or kill you from behind the corporate veil. He may do this without qualm because he has been conditioned to drop a curtain between his private moral and religious self and his corporate immoral and irreligious self.[113]

In such a setting, with attitudes buttressed by the prevailing corporate ethos, immoral or harmful behavior simply appears to be a normal part of the operational routines of the office. Given the bureaucratic distance from genocide, this socialization process must be no different in those organizations that are complicit in genocide.

Organizational Coercion and Reward

For individuals, the impetus to participate in illegal behavior for the sake of the organization is often assisted by various structural mechanisms of punishment or reward. The most obvious and powerful punishment in nonmilitary institutions is dismissal. When an engineer at Ford was asked if anyone had told Lee Iacocca, the president of the company, that the now infamous Pinto had an unsafe gas tank, he replied, "Hell no. That person would have been fired. Safety wasn't a popular subject around Ford in those days."[114] Similarly, another auto executive at a different company who objected to dangerous flaws in a car's design was told, "You're not a member of the team. Shut up or go looking for another job."[115] Demotion, loss of a promotion, or transfer are also possible punishments for employees who do not meet performance expectations or fail to conform to the required behavior or ideology. In one case, executives caught in a price-fixing scheme participated because they feared, not job loss, but loss of prestigious assignments and harm to their future advancement. As one said, "If I didn't do it, I felt someone else would. I would be removed, and somebody else would do it."[116] On the opposite side of the coin, we find numerous rewards for participation: promotion or advancement within the organization, pay increases, and choice assignments.

Coercion and reward are certainly evident in bureaucratic participation in genocide. During the Nazification of the German civil service, one scholar notes, dismissal and transfer were used to ensure compliance.[117] One Nazi confided that "I thought that if I asked him to release me from having to take part in the executions it would be over for me as far as he was concerned and my chances of promotion would be spoilt or I would not be promoted at all."[118] Solving the "Jewish question" was a high priority for the Reich, as indicated by the fact that "abundant resources were put at the disposal of those who chose to take the initiative and to show enterprise in the pursuit of the Final Solution."[119] An ambitious functionary or businessman therefore could see ample opportunity for advancement and reward. Adolf Eichmann was nothing if not a careerist who saw his expertise on Jewish issues as a means to professional elevation. Kurt Prüfer, the engineer from the Topf company, received a 2 percent commission from the profits of each order that the SS placed for furnaces and crematoria.[120] Not only was Prüfer helping his company meet its goals and stay profitable in a competitive business environment, he also saw an opportunity for personal gain. Similarly, a foreman for Krupp received a pay raise in 1943 because "in these recent months Herr Hassel has been especially efficient."[121] It turns out that this efficiency meant an ever more brutal regime of beatings, torture, and abuse of slave laborers in order to extract greater amounts of work from them. The head of another company wrote that he was proud of the "initiative displayed by my staff in the procurement of labor,"[122] by which he was referring to his company's acquisition of prisoners at Auschwitz. It is obvious that the executives who had secured those arrangements were acting as good competitive businessmen for their organization and no onus was attached to their actions. On the contrary, they were rewarded for their entrepreneurial skills.

In summary: genocidal killers commit crimes as members of various types of institutions that provide structural inducements and rewards to those who are called upon or volunteer to assist in genocidal processes. Without minimizing the importance of this level of genocide, we must not forget that the entire apparatus of death is contingent upon individual human beings deciding to participate in this crime.

5   Accommodating Genocide

The novelty of totalitarian crimes lies less in the fact that heads of state could conceive of such projects . . . than in the fact that these men were able to realize their projects, an accomplishment that required the collaboration of thousands and thousands of individuals acting on the state's behalf and at its behest. . . . The key factor is the transformations that all these thousands of individuals underwent so that they could suspend their usual responses to fellow human beings.

—Tzvetan Todorov[1]

Most of the harm in the world is done by those who are dogmatically certain that they are right. For being absolutely right means that those who disagree are absolutely wrong. Those who are absolutely wrong are of course dangerous to society and must be restrained or eliminated. That is the beginning of the road to the torture chamber and the gas oven.

—Anthony Storr[2]

The massacre at the Nyarabuye church is a particularly powerful example of the type of killing that marked the Rwandan genocide.[3] When the killing erupted throughout that country, several thousand Tutsis gathered at the church, many on the advice of the local bourgemestre, or mayor, Sylvestre Gacumbitsi. They were seeking shelter and protection from the roving bands of the *Interahamwe* militia as well as from many of their Hutu neighbors. Men, women, and children set up camp, prayed for help, scavenged for food, and tried to stay alive. After having successfully beaten off one half-hearted attack, they were surprised to find Gacumbitsi leading a troop of soldiers, police officers, and militiamen in another attack several days later. After Gacumbitsi handed out machetes to his followers, the Hutus attacked and slaughtered the Tutsis. There were too many to kill in one day, so they ended by slitting the Achilles tendons of many survivors to prevent them from escaping. Then, hungry from their day's labor, they went off to feast on roasted beef and banana beer.[4] They returned the next morning and finished their horrific task.

Since that massacre, the site has been left as it was as a memorial to the genocide. Bodies, now desiccated, still lie as they fell: men and women who were hacked to death with arms raised to ward off the blows that killed them; young children decapitated or cut in half; bodies piled outside the door to the church where they sought shelter as they were cut down; mothers surrounded by the bodies of their children.[5] Various accounts describe the shock and outrage felt by visitors to the site of the slaughter. As he wandered through the killing grounds, a journalist was asked if he could imagine what the victims had endured. He replied that he could not, because his "powers of visualization cannot possibly encompass the magnitude of the terror."[6] Like that reporter, most people recoil in shock from such abominations. Our sensibilities may refuse to accept such a pornography of violence. Even secondhand, these images produce extreme feelings of disbelief, revulsion, and outrage. Perhaps we may even feel shame: shame that fellow human beings could inflict such pain and terror upon others of their kind. Our awareness of these atrocities also poses some very difficult questions. What kind of people are able to hack women and children to death while ignoring their pleas and agony? Don't the perpetrators of genocide feel the same things you and I feel? More disturbingly, might we ourselves be capable of such deeds?

Thus far we have examined genocide at the level of the state and the organization. This chapter continues this multitiered analysis by focusing on the last level of genocide: the individual. As we have seen, it is the state that provides the resources and rationale for genocide. This impetus is filtered through various organizations and institutions that provide the framework, the structure, and the means for its implementation. Ultimately, however, it is the individual who must actually carry out the policies and murder other humans. At its essence, genocide is about people killing other people.

It is important to note that those who perpetrate genocide conduct themselves in conformity to established authority structures and legal codes, not in opposition to them. Genocide is protected and sanctioned by the state. Social scientists have long recognized the power of the state and of the group in fostering conformity, even if the group is composed of strangers and regardless of the individual's personal feelings.[7] Even when placed in situations that require them to participate in genocide, people are predisposed to participate and conform. Individuals tend to defer to the group and not assert their individual will, even if their beliefs differ from those of the group. If the authority of the state is embodied in that group, then the pressure to conform is even greater. This does not mean, however, that personal beliefs and feelings are somehow lost or discarded. Rather, they are deferred, repressed, or neglected, and may in fact create a conflict if they clearly oppose the mandated behavior. The relevant question, then, is, how do participants define their actions in order to resolve such conflict and comply? This is a different question from the one more commonly asked: why didn't more individuals resist or refuse to comply?

While the killers act in conformity to laws, their participation usually conflicts with internalized social norms and morals. For most people this disjunction poses a problem, since participation in genocide, especially for those on the front lines of the killings, is so far removed from routine behavior; some form of internal normative adjustment is necessary. Confronted with the reality and horror of the killing, many participants are forced to grapple with the dichotomy between their actions and their beliefs. One military historian analyzed why so many soldiers are unable to kill during war and concluded that "the average and healthy individual . . . has such an inner and usually unrealized resistance towards killing a fellow man that he will not of his own volition take life if it is possible to turn away from that responsibility."[8] If this is true of soldiers, how much more difficult it must be for civilians, who lack the indoctrination that soldiers receive. How can these internal oppositions to killing be overcome?

While the state does usually legalize and legitimate the mistreatment of its victims, the process it authorizes is often problematic for many people. The architects of genocide recognize this difficulty; if they did not, they would not go to such lengths to legitimize their actions and policies. Internal systems of belief do not change as quickly or as easily as legal statutes. The cultural values of most perpetrators are not often compatible with genocidal action. Those who participated in the Holocaust, for example, had not been socialized into a belief system in which genocidal behavior was normative. They were products of European culture, and more specifically the Enlightenment, with its emphasis on the sanctity of individual rights and the expression of noble sentiments in art, music, literature, and law.[9] They condemned murder and extolled charity, compassion, and the value of human life.

Many accounts of Yugoslavia emphasize that, prior to the ethnic violence of the 1990s, the country had been well along the path toward a tolerant multicultural society with a cosmopolitan and relatively sophisticated population more intent on improving their standard of living than victimizing their neighbors.[10] Let us also not forget that it was Americans who in cold blood massacred four hundred men, women, and children in the Vietnamese hamlet of My Lai.[11] The young American men who brutally murdered these civilians were raised in a society in which idealistic humanitarian values were deeply embedded in the culture and its institutions. We cannot simply assume that those who engage in genocide or extreme acts of violence come from cultures with value systems antithetical to human rights. Supposedly civilized people can murder just as cruelly as anybody else.

Another way to illustrate that genocide violates many normative standards is to point out the protests against the killing that sometimes take place. In Germany, for example, widespread public outrage and condemnation brought an official end to the T4 euthanasia program that targeted the physically and mentally handicapped.[12] There are many other examples of Germans exercising moral agency, such as the German wives in Berlin who secured the release of their imprisoned Jewish husbands after three days of protest,[13] the widespread condemnation of the rampant street violence,[14] and the German military officer who told his superiors that he could not assist in clearing out a local ghetto because "he could not ask his handful of men to undertake such a morally burdensome task."[15] In other words, a normative base existed that often served to protect stigmatized groups, sometimes even Jews. Zygmunt Bauman goes so far as to assert that "the perpetration of the Holocaust required the neutralization of ordinary German attitudes toward the Jews, not their mobilization."[16]

The selective application of compassion and morality has surfaced during other examples of genocide as well. For example, a young Rwandan named Richard, along with other Tutsi refugees, was taken from a truck by a band of Hutus engaged in mass killing. Marched to the edge of a mass grave, Richard had prepared himself for death when an old school friend, a member of the gang of killers, recognized him and spared his life because of their past relationship.[17] After saving Richard, the friend then presumably returned to his task of slaughtering other Tutsis. Such differentiation among Tutsis happened fairly frequently. Phillip Gourevitch writes,

> Many people who participated in the killing—as public officials, as soldiers or militia members, or as ordinary citizen butchers—also protected some Tutsis, whether out of personal sympathy or for financial or sexual profit. It was not uncommon for a man or a woman who regularly went forth to kill to keep a few favorite Tutsis hidden in his or her home.[18]

While some, as Gourevitch notes, had less than honorable motives, many must have been motivated by nothing more than past friendships or a burst of morality brought about by some individual or situational characteristic.

This still leaves unresolved the question of how participants were able to violate deep-seated morals and beliefs in other cases, and how they then coped with the contradiction between their beliefs and their actions. As Bauman puts it, we must explain the

> mechanism of "overcoming the animal pity"; a social production of conduct contrary to innate moral inhibitions, capable of transforming individuals who are not "moral degenerates" in any of the "normal" senses, into murderers or conscious collaborators in the murdering process.[19]

An argument first proposed by Gresham Sykes and David Matza is useful in answering this question.[20] Sykes and Matza found in their research on youth crime that most delinquents relied on very similar definitional processes to justify their criminal behavior. These processes, or techniques of neutralization, allowed delinquents to suppress their normative system of values and engage in deviant behavior. This is the same process engaged in by participants in genocide. In short, these techniques are the ways in which "ordinary" men and women define behavior or a situation in such a way that their moral prohibitions are not violated. Internal constraints are suppressed or neutralized in that specific context, but not necessarily in others. These techniques contribute to our understanding of the mechanisms by which individuals accede to and perpetrate "crimes of obedience," to borrow Kelman and Hamilton's terminology, even if this participation is in opposition to their personal normative system.[21]

Those who perpetrate genocide are not necessarily wholly committed to the killing; they must negotiate their positions vis-a-vis their internalized value systems. As discussed earlier, conformity to the state and to the group is a powerful force for compliance and action, and this compliance often occurs in spite of and in opposition to internal systems of belief. With this knowledge as our starting point, we can explore the techniques of neutralization by which the opposing forces (belief and behavior) are reconciled.

In reference to values and beliefs, Fred Katz writes,

> At any one time, each of us has a number of different values . . . at any one time these values are arranged in a definite order. Some things are more important than others. Some things can be achieved right away, while others must be held in abeyance. Some things can be neglected. Others have priority and must be tackled immediately. In short, at any one time, our values are unequal. They are organized— they are *packaged*—in definite ways.[22]

The techniques of neutralization allow values to be repackaged in various ways, which we can explore. Beliefs in opposition to participation are minimized, suppressed, or deferred, while others conducive to participation are increased in priority. Tzvetan Todorov puts it this way:

> Guards who committed atrocities never stopped distinguishing between good and evil. Their moral faculty had not withered away. They simply believed that the "atrocity" was in fact a good thing and thus not an atrocity at all—because the state, custodian of the standards of good and evil, told them so. The guards were not deprived of a moral sensibility but provided with a new one.[23]

In recognizing and explaining how values are repackaged in order to resolve disjunctions between beliefs and actions, the techniques of neutralization offer us a way to explain "ordinary" civilized people's widespread participation in atrocities and their selective and situational application of compassion and mercy.

In the course of their research, Sykes and Matza uncovered specific techniques consistently used by delinquents to neutralize normative dissonance. Perpetrators of genocide use similar techniques to repackage values and neutralize internal normative barriers. Identification of these consistent and patterned modes of adjustment is important because we can then recognize the culturally mediated discursive themes used by "ordinary" people in order to participate in genocide. People do not rely on purely individualistic arguments to repackage their values; rather, they refer to larger culturally created images and ideas. These "vocabularies of motive," as Mills labeled them,[24] reflect socially constructed symbols and messages that participants can draw upon to accommodate themselves to killing. In other words, the arguments utilized by perpetrators follow common patterns because they are in large part created and reinforced by the larger political and cultural context. Identification of these arguments, therefore, allows us to understand how individuals suppress internal opposition to participation, but also illustrates the relationship between individual accommodation and cultural milieu.

For these reasons, an understanding of the techniques of neutralization illustrates the specific processes by which ordinary citizens come to participate in genocide. At this point, a brief review of neutralization theory may assist in illustrating its relevance and explanatory power.

Techniques of Neutralization

Sykes and Matza originally developed neutralization theory to explain how teenagers engage in delinquent behavior.[25] Specifically, they argued that youthful offenders are not always engaged in delinquent and criminal activity, and consequently even the most chronic teenage offenders tend to hold conventional beliefs and values that support conformity and law-abiding behavior in some social arenas. Delinquents spend much of their time engaged in legitimate and socially acceptable behavior, or, as Sykes and Matza assert,

> the juvenile delinquent would appear to be at least partially committed to the dominant social order in that he frequently exhibits guilt or shame when he violates its proscriptions, accords approval to certain conforming figures, and distinguishes between appropriate and inappropriate targets for his deviance.[26]

How then are these young offenders able to engage in criminal behaviors in violation of their conformist beliefs and attitudes? This is essentially the same question raised in regard to genocide, albeit with different populations. Sykes and Matza argue that delinquent youth develop a set of justifications for their criminal behavior that serve to nullify their conventional values. What allows them to commit deviant acts is not the adoption of deviant values, but rather utilization of certain perceptual tools that serve to suppress their conformist value system under certain conditions. These techniques of neutralization allow youths to define a situation in such a way that conventional values, which would normally prevent them from engaging in behavior contradictory to their beliefs, cease to operate. Sykes and Matza identified five techniques of neutralization commonly used by delinquents:

Denial of Responsibility. In this case the delinquent argues the behavior was not his or her fault, that it was caused by accident or by forces beyond his or her control. As Sykes and Matza assert, "In so far as the delinquent can define himself as lacking responsibility for his deviant actions, the disapproval of self or others is sharply reduced in effectiveness as a restraining influence."[27]

Denial of Injury. In this case, the offender defines the act as a prank or as mischief, which is socially and individually much more acceptable than something defined as criminal or deviant. The delinquent might, for instance, also point out that the victim has insurance, so no harm has been done. The key concept here is that since there is no obvious or significant harm being done to anyone or anything, it is acceptable to engage in the behavior.

Denial of Victim. The argument here is that the victim caused his or her own victimization or somehow deserved it. This definitional about-face changes the perpetrator's role from that of criminal or delinquent to that of justified avenger. Correspondingly, the victim is transformed from a wrongfully aggrieved innocent into someone who is responsible for his or her own victimization because of actions, beliefs, background, or race.

Condemning the Condemners. This technique asserts that everyone is corrupt or unfair, so what right do others have to judge the offender? The delinquent offender shifts the focus away from his or her own actions, directing it toward figures who represent the conformist world (e.g., teachers, police officers, public officials). By portraying them as corrupt, fallible, or hypocritical, the delinquent is able to accept and validate his or her own deviant or criminal activities.

Appeal to Higher Loyalties. This is the assertion that the offender's actions are not motivated by personal or selfish reasons like greed, but are undertaken on behalf of the group to which he or she owes primary loyalty, such as a gang or family. As Sykes and Matza summarize, "deviation from certain norms may occur not because the norms are rejected but because other norms, held to be more pressing or involving a higher loyalty, are accorded precedence."[28]

Over the years, neutralization theory has been tested and utilized in a variety of situations,[29] many of which have provided empirical support for and refinement of it.[30] It should be noted that these techniques are not rationalizations. Rationalizations are attempts to ease the conscience after the fact. Instead, these techniques are utilized *prior* to the behavior, not after, and are what make it possible to engage in otherwise unacceptable activities. Agnew's longitudinal analysis found evidence for the a priori utilization of neutralizations to lower normative boundaries and thus facilitate criminality.[31] An understanding of neutralization techniques helps to illuminate the strategies individuals engage in when called on to participate in genocide.

Genocide and the Techniques of Neutralization

Denial of Responsibility

Denial of responsibility is evident in the argument raised by many perpetrators that they were only following orders. This can be interpreted as an attempt on the part of the participants to shed the burden of responsibility by arguing that they were forced to kill. Orders or authoritarian commands allow individuals to "see themselves as having no choice as long as they accept the legitimacy of the orders and of the authorities who give them."[32] Arad points out that to Franz Stangl, the commandant of Treblinka,

> The motive to murder did not originate with him. He "only" carried out the order he had received in the best possible way. Looking at the situation in this way relieved his conscience and enabled him to oversee the death factory in which hundreds of thousands of people were murdered.[33]

Eichmann's defense, as related by Arendt, follows the same logic:

> The court did not understand him: he had never been a Jew-hater, and he had never willed the murder of human beings. His guilt came from his obedience, and obedience is praised as a virtue. His virtue had been abused by the Nazi Leaders. But he was not one of the ruling clique, he was a victim, and only the leaders deserved punishment.[34]

In much the same vein, one perpetrator of the Rwandan genocide asked pardon from a Tutsi woman by saying that "It was the fault of the authorities who led us in these acts, seeking their own gains."[35] These killers believed themselves innocent of wrongdoing because they were only following orders and were, therefore, not personally responsible for their crimes.

While some might argue that this tactic is merely an after-the-fact defense intended to exculpate the offenders and protect them from war-crimes trials, it is used throughout a genocide. At every step of the annihilation process, officials work to remove personal responsibility and place it elsewhere, usually higher up the hierarchy of command. Kelman and Hamilton specifically assert that

> the basic structure of the authority situation is that actors often do not see themselves as personally responsible for the consequences of their actions. . . . They were not personal agents, but merely extensions of the authority. Thus when their actions cause harm to others, they can feel relatively free of guilt.[36]

The Nazi leadership, for example, made sure that the killers were explicitly ordered to carry out their tasks and to do so in certain prescribed ways, a tactic designed to relieve the individual participant of any sense of guilt or responsibility.[37] Similarly, the Bosnian Serb leadership constantly emphasized that all the actions of their soldiers were justified and authorized.[38] The participants were thus able to allay their qualms about their actions and could proceed with a clear conscience, certain that they remained decent people who were forced to do a dirty job.

Orders were utilized not only to remove guilt, but also to weaken ethical and moral restraints. An order, especially a military one, is an authoritative direction usually accompanied by the threat of punishment for failure to comply. Serbs in Bosnia, for example, might have been punished or murdered if they refused to take part in or at least support the killing. When the journalist Michael Palaich interviewed a convicted Serb war criminal named Borislav Herak, he asked Herak if he felt any remorse for his participation in numerous atrocities. Herak replied,

> I felt sorry, but I could not talk to anyone, because they would think that I was a coward. I could not refuse because the order was that everyone had to do it. And if I refused to carry out the order they would kill me.[39]

The same situation prevailed in Rwanda, where one perpetrator put it this way:

> at that time we were called on by the state to kill. You were told you had the duty to do this or you'd be imprisoned or killed. We were just pawns in this. We were just tools.[40]

Here, too, perpetrators could assert that they really had no choice in the matter and were not fundamentally responsible. However, different offending groups faced different levels of compulsion. While Serbs and Rwandan Hutus who refused to participate were punished, there is no evidence that German soldiers or officials who refused to obey orders to execute Jews were punished in any significant way.[41] As one member of an *Einsatzkommando* killing squad related, "It was made clear to us that we could refuse to obey an order to participate in the Sonderaktionen ['special actions'] without adverse consequences."[42] It is extremely unlikely that other participants in the Holocaust were unaware of this, and yet most continued to participate.

Whether subject to punishment or not, without the reference to authority, many participants would otherwise feel themselves bearing personal responsibility and confronting a disjunction between self-concept and behavior. The surrender of individual choice through submission to authority was and is an important step in the process of removing normative barriers.

Depending on the social context, deferring to authority is much easier for some perpetrators than others. Members of tightly knit organizations, such as the SS, the Rwandan *Interahamwe* militia, and the Serbian White Eagles, as well as Arkan's Tigers, are more easily able to neutralize their values and evade responsibility. The socialization processes of these groups stress conformity, obedience to authority, ideological homogeneity, duty, and loyalty, all of which tend to relieve the individual of moral responsibility. In such a setting, the morality of the group takes precedence over individual morality. As long as the primacy and legitimacy of the group remain unchallenged, individual choice is abrogated. Groups themselves, by their very nature, tend to diffuse responsibility away from the individual. In any organization that emphasizes ideological indoctrination and unquestioning obedience, the member surrenders individual identity and choice to the group and its leaders. In such a context, it is indeed a rare individual who can break the powerful compulsion to conform to the group and assert individual (and in this context, ironically, "deviant") identity. Rudolf Höss, the commandant of Auschwitz, relates that "The goal of the many years of rigid SS training was to make each SS soldier a tool without its own will who would carry out blindly all of Himmler's plans. That is the reason why I also became a blind, obedient robot who carried out every order."[43] Höss was able to convince himself that he had no choice, he was not responsible for his actions, he was simply a tool.

By denying individual responsibility for their actions and emphasizing the authorized or "coerced" nature of their participation, perpetrators allow themselves to believe that their actions have been both legitimated and forced on them by persons in authority.

Denial of Injury

The technique of denying injury is most visible in the terminology employed by the perpetrators when referring to their actions. The participants in the Holocaust developed a special language of camouflage and deception.[44] Words like "genocide," "murder," and "killing" were not often used by the participants, because of their negative connotations. Instead, they referred to their actions only indirectly, and in euphemistic disguise. Thus, genocide became a final solution *(Endlösung)*, and killing became special treatment *(Sonderbehandlung)*, appropriate treatment *(entsprechende Behandlung)*, or cleansing *(Sauberung)*, to name just a few of many such euphemisms.[45] In fact, special language rules *(Sprachregelungen)* were instituted to regulate the terms that could and could not be used in reference to the policies and actions of the Holocaust. These euphemisms were utilized not only to conceal actions, but also to define actions as acceptable. As Hilberg asserts, bureaucracies used these euphemisms "to conceal the destructive process not only from all outsiders, but also from the censuring gaze of its own conscience."[46] By applying positive terms to the Holocaust, the participants portrayed their actions in the most favorable light. To find the "solution" to a "problem" is acceptable and even praiseworthy, while to exterminate innocent men, women, and children is reprehensible. To cleanse Germany of a cancer or plague was admirable, to perpetrate genocide was not.

The Serbian use of the term "ethnic cleansing" served many of the same functions as the German euphemisms of the Holocaust. It is rather ironic that the term "cleansing" *(čišćenje)* was actually originated by Croatians who were ridding their territories of Serbs earlier in the century.[47] Norman Cigar is clearly cognizant of the power of euphemisms during the Bosnian genocide when he writes,

> Perhaps nowhere was the power of language to categorize and destroy as evident as the choice of the term "cleansing," used freely in unofficial discourse to describe the violent removal of Muslims. Logically, a procedure with such a name . . . could only be viewed as positive and desirable, the implicit antithesis and correction of an assumed impure, unnatural, and demeaning state. When the commander of a Serbian militia unit was able to report that "this region is ethnically clean," for example, he was clearly proud of what he viewed as an achievement.[48]

In Rwanda, the killing was referred to as *umuganda* or "work," while cutting down men was "bush clearing," and killing women and children was "pulling out the roots of the bad weeds."[49] These were familiar analogies in the largely agricultural and peasant-based Hutu society.

The Argentine death squads during the "dirty war" of the 1970s came up with *chupado* (sucked up) to refer to kidnap victims, and *traslado* (transferred) to describe people who were thrown out of airplanes into the sea.[50] Similarly, the language of the American military is replete with terms such as "collateral damage" for the killing of civilians, "neutralizing the enemy" for killing other people, "surgical strike" for a precise attack designed to kill specific targets, "pacification" for making an area safe by killing all opponents within it, "delivery vehicle" for a bomber or missile, and "countervalue" for destroying a city. Enemy soldiers are not killed; instead they are wasted, greased, taken out, hosed, or zapped.[51] All these terms are designed to conceal the unpleasant realities of modern warfare.

Euphemisms also shape perceptions of the very nature of the act. Through the use of ambiguous, sterile, and technical language, the participants in genocide are able to deny to themselves and others that people are being injured and killed. Carol Cohn asserts that

> Learning the language is a transformative, rather than an additive, process. When you choose to learn it you are not simply choosing to add new information, new vocabulary, but to enter into a mode of thinking.[52]

Someone physically removed from the killing centers can employ this linguistic distancing much more easily than can those involved in the actual killing. As David Rieff puts it, "the opaque, banal language of the Serb bureaucracy allowed people to pretend to themselves that the ethnic cleansing was not really going on."[53] But even on the front lines of genocide, the same linguistic manipulations are employed by those holding the guns and running the camps. The participants consciously and consistently work to distance themselves psychologically from the horrible reality of their actions.

Additionally, the progression of killing techniques from mass shootings to gassing during the Holocaust not only meant an increase in efficiency, but also served to further distance the participants from their victims, thus making it easier to participate in mass murder. Rudolf Höss was relieved at this change in technique because he and his men were spared the trauma and blood of mass shooting.

In addition to techniques that increase physical distance, such as gassing, euphemisms are constantly utilized not only to deceive the victims and make them more compliant, but also to neutralize the participants' personal morality. The language of the camps was usually technical, filled with the imagery of processing and exploiting cargo and material (that is, human beings) as quickly and as efficiently as possible. In fact, the victims were not even referred to as human beings; Lang points out that they were often referred to as *Figuren* (figures or pieces),[54] or, as Motke Zaïdl and Itzhak Dugin, two survivors of Sobibor, related:

> The Germans even forbade us to use the words "corpse" or "victim." The dead were blocks of wood, shit, with absolutely no importance. Anyone who said "corpse" or "victim" was beaten. The Germans made us refer to the bodies as Figuren, that is, as puppets, as dolls, or as Schmattes, which means "rags."[55]

Franz Stangl, the former commandant of Treblinka, was once asked if he did not believe that his victims were human. Stangl replied that they were cargo, merely cargo.[56] And what does one do with cargo except process it? Similarly, a Soviet gulag survivor describes one victimizer this way:

> He derived no satisfaction from our sufferings. He was simply oblivious to them because in the most sincere way imaginable, he did not regard us as human. Wastage among the convict work force was to him no more than a routine malfunction.[57]

During the Second World War, the Japanese conducted various biological and chemical experiments on unwilling human guinea pigs, including civilians and prisoners of war. These victims were referred to by the Japanese as *maruta,* or logs.[58] Thus language allows killers to define themselves as technicians, soldiers, and laborers, rather then as murderers and genocidal killers.

Significantly, euphemisms are often dominated by scientific and technical terms. This is no accident. The language of science is seen as nonjudgmental, nonemotional, and nonbiased, and carries with it no obvious moral imperatives, values, or connotations. It is perceived to be objective, rational, and nonthreatening. Technical terminology and euphemistic jargon camouflage the suffering, pain, and inhumanity they describe, and thereby condone and perpetuate indifference and inhumanity in their users. They offer a linguistic refuge from the horror found in "everyday" language. Kren and Rappoport summarize the importance of euphemistic language when they write,

> In connection with the planning and implementation of the genocide program, for example, the capacity to think and act according to euphemistic language became a widespread and apparently effective form of individual psychological adjustment. Euphemisms such as "final solution," "relocation," and "shower bath" seemed to work nicely for the SS as a means of imposing a rationalized, business-as-usual emotional framework upon activities too atrocious to be contemplated in the raw.[59]

This same idea is discussed by Herbert Hirsch, who writes that, "Blinded by the myths of objectivity and the mask of scientific methodology, professionals are able to distance themselves, in the name of scientific rigor, from emotional confrontation with mass death."[60] With the use of these kinds of linguistic tools, the perpetrators become more concerned with purely technical problems than with issues of life and death. In short, they detach themselves from the underlying reality that they are murdering other human beings, and instead focus on efficiently dealing with a logistical problem.

In summary, language is a mechanism through which the participants are able to define events in such a way that participating in genocide becomes an acceptable thing to do. The language defines the intended victims as "things" to be disposed of and distances the participants from the frightful reality of their actions.

Denial of Victim

Denying the victim is of central importance to the facilitation of mass murder since, as Vulliamy suggests, "our century tells us that the fabrication of giant conspiracies against a besieged race is a necessary prerequisite to unleashing the kind of violence that was to follow."[61] The assertion that the victims cause their own victimization and deserve whatever happens to them makes it easier to kill them. The killing is defined, not as murder, but as self-defense, which has very different legal and social connotations. Most cultures traditionally accept violence when it occurs within the specific context of self-defense.[62] This technique allows the perpetrators to apply long-accepted traditions of self-defense to the realm of mass killing. As one prominent Rwandan mayor put it, "If the reasons are just, the massacres are justified."[63]

The Serbs attempted to portray the Bosnian Muslims as representing a clear threat to their Serbian neighbors. From this viewpoint, the Serbs were facing an enemy intent on destroying them as a people. General Ratko Mladić, the commander of the Bosnian Serb army, said that the goal of the Muslims was the "complete annihilation of the Serbian people."[64] In fact, much propaganda asserted, without apparent irony, that the Serbs were victims of genocidal policies.[65] One Orthodox bishop warned that Bosnian Serbs were living "under the threat that genocide will again be visited upon them,"[66] while Slobodan Milošević derided trade sanctions against Serbia by saying,

I do not know how you will explain to your children, on the day when they discover the truth, why you killed our children, why you led a war against three million of our children, and with what right you turned twelve million inhabitants of Europe into a test site for the application of what is, I hope, the last genocide of this century.[67]

In this way, the perpetrators of genocide convinced themselves that they themselves were the victims of genocide. The violence they employed was not aggressive, but merely defensive. As one Serb Army officer claimed, "We have not done ethnic cleansing. The other side began with ethnic cleansing of Serbs and imposed the war on us."[68] When combined with a steady diet of propaganda reciting a litany of atrocities inflicted by Muslims upon innocent and unarmed Serbs, the genocidal policies came to seem a necessary response to the Islamic onslaught. Not even children were immune to this propaganda campaign. One twelve-year-old Serb boy related that "I do not miss my Muslim classmates one bit. It has been explained to me that while we were playing together, they were actually plotting behind my back."[69]

Serbs were also warned that they needed to protect themselves from more insidious forms of Muslim aggression. One argument relied on the notion of excessive Muslim fertility. Serb propaganda repeatedly emphasized that the Muslims were deliberately outbreeding the Serbs. One Serb put it this way:

The only good Muslim is a dead Muslim. Their women are bitches and whores. They breed children like animals, more than ten per woman . . . Down there, they are fighting for a single land that will stretch from here to Tehran, where our women will wear shawls, where there is bigamy.[70]

Croatia's Franjo Tudjman made the same argument against Bosnian Muslims when he asserted that

The Muslims want to establish an Islamic fundamentalist state. They plan to do this by flooding Bosnia with 500,000 Turks. Izetbegović has also launched a demographic threat. He has a secret policy to reward large families so that in a few years the Muslims will be a majority in Bosnia.[71]

These arguments asserted that the Muslims were attempting to make Bosnia into an Islamic state, subject to Islamic laws, under which Serbs would be killed or at the very least become second-class citizens. Procreation was portrayed as a potent weapon against the Serbs, which may in part explain the systematic use of rape as a weapon of ethnic cleansing. The rapes were a way to turn the Muslims' reproductive weapon against them. Rather than producing excessive numbers of Muslim babies, their women would bear Serb children.

From its inception, the Nazi party consistently used the Jews as a scapegoat for the defeat Germany had suffered in the First World War, for the subsequent economic collapse, and for a host of other real and imagined social woes. Updating medieval anti-Semitic themes and incorporating pseudo-scientific racial theories, the Nazis were able to portray the Jews as the source of Germany's troubles. Goldhagen asserts that anti-Semitism was the most powerful factor in the inception and perpetration of the Holocaust.[72] Nazi propaganda, as Sarah Gordon writes, had as its primary focus "the overriding theme . . . that the Jews were the Enemy."[73] The propaganda concerning the Jews expounded three primary messages: that they were subhuman vermin; that they threatened the racial purity of Aryans; and that they threatened the German state.[74]

This image of the Jew as representing a mortal threat became a potent rallying symbol for the Nazi power structure and ultimately the German people. The demonization of the Jews allowed the Nazis to construct themselves as the idealized symbols of Aryan purity and as Germany's only hope for survival. Accepting this constructed image, the participants in genocide were then able to define themselves as victims of the Jews and their actions as therefore justifiable. Letters from participants in the Holocaust to colleagues, friends, and families often reflected this message. Gendarmie Chief Fritz Jacob, in a letter to a superior, once wrote,

> We men of the new Germany have to be very tough with ourselves even when we are forced by circumstances to be separated from our families for quite a long time. This is the case right now. We have to settle up with the war criminals once and for all so that we can build a more beautiful and eternal Germany for our children and our children's children.[75]

Similarly, SS soldier Karl Kretschmer wrote,

> The sight of the dead (including women and children) is not very cheering. But we are fighting this war for the survival or non-survival of our people. . . . My comrades are literally fighting for the existence of our people.[76]

To reassure his troubled troops, Höss had to "tell them that it was necessary to destroy all the Jews in order to forever free Germany and the future generations from our toughest enemy."[77] Portrayal of the Jews as the enemy allowed the participants in the Holocaust to believe that they were in a position of moral superiority and to define their actions as absolutely just, moral, and necessary. In other words, they were able to assert that they had no choice but to defend themselves. Definitionally, the killing of the Jews was transformed from genocide to justifiable homicide, from a wrong to a right. Himmler summarized this transformation when he wrote, "We had the moral right vis-a-vis our people to annihilate this people which wanted to annihilate us."[78] Many must have comforted themselves with the belief that they had no choice but to defend themselves and their way of life.

The portrayal of the victimized population as the enemy is common in other examples of genocide as well. For example, the Rwandan genocide was ignited by the announcement on the state-owned radio station, Radio Rwanda, that a secret Tutsi plan to slaughter the Hutu population had been discovered. This is why one participant could believe that "I defended the members of my tribe against the Tutsi,"[79] while another pointed out, "The government told us that the RPF is Tutsi and if it wins the war all the Hutus will be killed. As of now I don't believe this is true. At the time I believed the government was telling the truth."[80] This latter Hutu was an eighteen-year-old *Interahamwe* member who admitted to killing fifteen of his neighbors. This self-defense argument became the immediate pretext for the killing. Denial of the victim allows the perpetrators to reconcile their actions with their morals and values. They do not have to redefine themselves as murderers; rather, they are defenders, protectors, and guardians of a way of life.

Condemning the Condemners

In Sykes and Matza's description, the technique of condemning the condemners consists of pointing out the shortcomings, deviance, and criminality of others in order to deflect criticism and justify one's own deviant or criminal actions. The perpetrators of genocide can refer to many historic instances of inhumane policies and practices similar in intent, if not in scale. The treatment of Blacks and Native Americans in the United States, the abuse of Native peoples by the British, French, and Spanish in their colonies, the pogroms in Tsarist Russia, the extermination of the Kulaks in the Soviet Union, and the persecution of the Armenians by the Turks can all be used to illustrate that the actions of the genocidal regimes are, historically speaking, not aberrant. The Bosnian Serb commander Ratko Mladić provided an example of this when he was asked by an American general by what right the Serbs were conducting their violent attacks against the Muslims. Mladić replied, "by the same right by which you Americans admit to having carried out chemical cleansing of the Indian tribes."[81] By referring to America's past, Mladić was denying the United States any moral authority over the Serbs on this issue.

In the case of the Holocaust, the Western countries' reluctance to raise their immigration quotas and accept more Jews expelled by the Nazis, and their failure to either decry the Holocaust or try to impede it (e.g., by bombing the railway terminus at Auschwitz), could be interpreted by the participants as tacit approval of their actions and could be used to neutralize prohibitions against such actions. Hitler certainly believed that what he was doing was for the sake of all races, not for Aryans alone.[82] Dismissing the risk of world criticism with the question "Who, after all, speaks today of the annihilation of the Armenians?"[83] he reasoned that since no one had spoken up then, no one would speak up now. The Allies had credible evidence of the nature and extent of the geno-cidal policies of the Nazi regime, yet refused to speak out or take direct action against those policies.[84] Even the Vatican never specifically denounced the treat-ment of the Jews. While it can be argued that the Pope feared the Nazi seizure of the Vatican and reprisals against Catholic laity and clergy, it can be equally well argued that an unequivocal condemnation of the treatment of the Jews would have had a powerful impact on many of the perpetrators of the Holo-caust.[85] Sadly, this censure never came. In fact, it was not until March of 1998 that the Vatican specifically denounced the Holocaust.

Ward Churchill goes so far as to suggest that the Holocaust was largely mod-eled on earlier examples of genocide. As he states,

> Not only was the Armenian holocaust a "true" genocide, the marked lack of re-sponse to it by the Western democracies was used by Adolf Hitler to reassure his cabinet that there would be no undue consequences if Germany were to perpetrate its own genocide(s). Not only were Stalin's policies in the Ukraine a genuine holo-caust, the methods by which it was carried out were surely incorporated into Ger-many's *Generalplan Ost* just a few years later. Not only was the Spanish policy of conscripting entire native populations into forced labor throughout the Caribbean, as well as much of South and Central America holocaustal, it served as a prototype for nazi policies in eastern Europe. Not only were U.S. "clearing" operations di-rected against the indigenous peoples of North America genocidal in every sense, they unquestionably served as a conceptual/practical mooring to which the whole Hitlerian rendering of *Lebensraumpolitik* was tied.[86]

Condemnation of the condemners is triggered by condemnation of them. In the absence of external condemnation, the need to utilize this particular neu-tralization is minimal. When they need to, however, participants can easily rec-ognize connections between current genocides and historical precedents. The more that perpetrators are able to contextualize their genocidal actions within a historical framework replete with numerous other genocidal episodes, the easier it is to reconcile those actions with internal norms.

Appeal to Higher Loyalties

As shown above, the Nazis consistently portrayed the Jews as a serious threat to the German people. Thus, when the perpetrators were put in the po-sition of having to contribute in some way to the "Final Solution," they could assert that they were doing so for their people and their country. The appeal to patriotism and protection of the "Fatherland" was a powerful means of lower-ing normative boundaries and overcoming any possible resistance. In general, the perpetrators of genocide portray their actions as a hard but necessary duty that is carried out not for personal motives, but for patriotic ones. For Ger-mans, "Ideological indoctrination made killing Jews the fulfillment of a 'higher' ideal,"[87] which allowed the participants to portray the situation as one in which the needs of Germany and the German people outweighed their individual internal prohibitions against killing and genocide. In his memoirs, Höss echoed this sentiment when he wrote,

> My tremendous love for my country and my feeling for everything German brought me into the NSDAP [the Nazi Party] and into the SS. I believed that the National Socialist world philosophy was the only one that suited the German people. The SS was, in my opinion, the most energetic defender of this philosophy, and the only one capable of leading the German people back to a life more in keeping with its character.[88]

SS member Karl Frenzel evoked the same type of rationale:

> To my regret, I was then convinced of its necessity. I was shocked that just during the war, when I wanted to serve my homeland, I had to be in such a terrible extermination camp. But then I thought very often about the enemy bomber pilots, who surely were not asked whether they wanted to carry out their murderous flights against German people in their homes in such a manner.[89]

Almost identical sentiments were expressed by the killers and torturers in Argentina during that country's "dirty war." Interviewed in 1995, one participant stated that "What I did I did for my Fatherland, my faith, and my religion," while another asserted that throwing drugged but living victims of the military regime into the ocean from aircraft was "a supreme act we did for the country."[90] To these men, both Argentinean and German, their acts were simply a service to their homelands and their duty as loyal and patriotic citizens.

For the Serbs in Bosnia, participating in the genocide was a duty not only to the Serb peoples, but to all of Western civilization. One Serb asserted, "We Serbs are saving Europe, even if Europe does not appreciate our efforts, even if it condemns them,"[91] while Radovan Karadžić, the leader of the Bosnian Serbs, said, "we defended Europe from Islam six hundred years ago. . . . We are defending Europe again . . . from Islamic fundamentalism."[92] Another soldier believed that "For five hundred years we Serbs have been defending Western civilization against the Turks."[93] Murder is therefore elevated from a criminal act into an almost sacred obligation. Patriotism, duty, and loyalty are generally idealized as virtues. This is why SS member Karl Jäger could proudly say after his arrest, "I was always a person with a heightened sense of duty."[94] When killing is linked to these higher principles, it is much easier to accept.

Denial of Humanity

Much of the research on genocide emphasizes the process of dehumanization that invariably precedes and accompanies the killing. It is one of the key elements needed to understand participants' accommodation to the act. Kelman and Hamilton perceive it as one of three critical elements in facilitating mass murder.[95] Considering dehumanization extends the established categories or techniques outlined by Sykes and Matza and suggests the denial of humanity as a new and separate technique by which internal prohibitions against killing are neutralized. Psychologists generally refer to this differentiation as *pseudo-speciation,* the process by which one's own group is considered human in contrast to subhuman others.[96]

The Rwandan Hutu extremists constantly portrayed the Tutsis as lesser forms of life, sometimes as *inyenzi,* literally cockroaches, or as devils, complete with horns, tails, hooves, pointed ears, and eyes that glowed in the dark.[97] As one radio broadcaster said, "You cockroaches must know you are made of flesh. We won't let you kill. We will kill you."[98]

Along the same lines, the Nazis worked diligently to define their victims as less than human. Much of the German propaganda machine was focused specifically on dehumanizing Jews and other groups. A pamphlet put out by the SS command to describe the Jews is illustrative of this theme:

> From a biological point of view he seems completely normal. He has hands and feet and a sort of brain. He has eyes and a mouth. But, in fact, he is a completely different creature, a horror. He only looks human, with a human face, but his spirit is lower than that of an animal. A terrible chaos runs rampant in this creature, an awful urge for destruction, primitive desires, unparalleled evil, a monster, subhuman.[99]

This same imagery is evident throughout most of the anti-Semitic propaganda promulgated by the Nazis. Julius Streicher's newspaper, *Der Stürmer,* relied heavily on political cartoons that often depicted the Jews as a race as snakes or demons, with a star of David to identify them. Individually, Jews were caricatured in stereotyped exaggerations: fat and stooped, with brutish features and expressions, scruffy beards and large hooked noses, clawlike hands and taloned nails heavy with skull-shaped rings. Films like *Jud Süss* and *Der Ewige Jude* reinforced and perpetuated these grotesque images of the Jew as a creature fundamentally different from and beneath humanity.

The Serbs also defined and treated their Muslim neighbors as less than human. In one instance a group of Serbs who were calling for the death of Bosnian Muslims yelled, *"Zaklaćemo vas! Zaklaćemo vas!"* or "Butcher them! Butcher them!" The term refers to the slaughter of animals, not human beings.[100] The Islamic faith was also equated with disease, as indicated by Karadžić's statement that the Serbs were trying to make sure "Islamic fundamentalism doesn't infect Europe from the south."[101] Another prominent politician argued that "genetically deformed material . . . embraced Islam. And now, of course, with each successive generation this gene simply becomes concentrated."[102] The equation of specific groups with disease or illness is a metaphor commonly used by perpetrators of genocide. The Jews were similarly identified. A German judge once said, "the Jew is not a human being. He is a symptom of putrefaction."[103] In another case, Fritz Klein, an SS doctor, in explaining his respect for human life, stated, "Out of respect for a human life I would remove a purulent appendix from a diseased body. The Jews are the purulent appendix in the body of Europe."[104]

This process is hardly unique to genocide. Even in the United States, the dehumanization of certain groups has been a prominent feature of intergroup relationships. For example, African Americans,[105] Native Americans,[106] Chinese,[107] and Japanese[108] have all been the targets of dehumanizing stereotypes and images.

This process of dehumanization serves many important functions in facilitating genocide. It acts as a mechanism for distancing participants from intended victims. When a group's identity as human beings has been stolen, the act of killing does not then violate religious and philosophical traditions that define human life as sacred and special. To overcome a lifetime of socialization that breeds a deep-seated revulsion toward killing fellow humans, perpetrators must be able to define the victims as separate from humanity; doing so removes the victims from the "universe of obligations," to borrow Fein's term.[109] The "universe of obligations" is the recognition of shared humanity that conveys a sense of commonality and moral obligation. To acknowledge a person's humanity is to recognize that he or she is subject to feelings, emotions, aspirations, dreams, and fears. To destroy another human being is to destroy someone like yourself. In contrast, it is far easier to destroy that which shares no commonality with you, that which is beneath you. As John Dower writes,

> What we are concerned with here is something different: the attachment of stupid, bestial, even pestilential subhuman caricatures on the enemy, and the manner in which this blocked seeing the foe as rational or even human, and facilitated mass killing. It is, at least for most people, easier to kill animals than fellow humans.[110]

Conversely, what distinguished those who aided or rescued victims of genocide, often at great personal and familial risk, was an inability to dehumanize them, to move them out of the universe of shared humanity and the corresponding moral obligations.[111] As has been shown, the ability to harm others depends in part on psychological distance. Those who are unable to distance themselves from and thereby devalue their fellow human beings are consequently unable to turn away those in need of protection.

Another aspect of the dehumanization process can be seen in the specific treatment meted out to the persecuted. During the Holocaust, those who were rounded up, transported, worked, and died in the camps were deliberately kept in appalling circumstances. They were, as Des Pres maintains, "systematically subjected to filth . . . the deliberate target of excremental assault."[112] Heads shaved, covered in their own waste, emaciated beyond recognition, the inmates of the camps were hardly recognizable as human beings. Aside from stifling any possible will to resist, this policy of degradation and humiliation helped the participants carry out their duties. The physical appearance of the victims helped define them as beings who were less than human. Gitta Sereny writes that when asked why their victims were subjected to these seemingly unnecessary cruelties, Franz Stangl answered, "To condition those who actually had to carry out the policies—to make it possible for them to do what they did."[113] Similarly, Tom Segev relates that Ruth Kalder, the widow of the commandant of Plascow, told an interviewer that "They were not human like us. They were so foul."[114] Names, the hallmark of individuality, were removed in favor of impersonal numbers tattooed on the arms of the inmates.

The treatment of Bosnian Muslims illustrates the same design. Michael Sells writes that

> Captives would be held for months in extremely cramped quarters without toilets or sanitary facilities. Women spoke of the shame of being forced to wear clothes stained with menstrual blood. Weeks of a starvation diet, lack of water, and lack of hygiene would turn captives into filthy, emaciated shadows of the persons they had once been.[115]

In short, perpetrators create situations in which their victims lose the outward appearance of humanity, and this serves to reinforce their definition as nonhuman. In effect, a self-fulfilling prophecy is created. Without these ceremonies of degradation it would be much harder for participants to psychologically distance themselves from their intended victims. As Goldhagen summarizes,

> the Germans succeeded in making many of the camp system's inhabitants take on the appearance—including festering, open wounds, and the marks of disease and illness—and behavioral attributes of the "subhumans" that the Germans imagined them to be. The sight . . . could only confirm in the Germans' mind how devoid of dignity these creatures were, how far removed they were from being humans worthy of respect and full moral consideration.[116]

To symbolically and physically diminish the worth of other human beings seems to be a prerequisite to the subsequent destruction of those so defined, a fact genocidal regimes have exploited to the utmost in their policies of extermination. It is questionable whether any genocide could be carried out without this method of neutralizing internal values.

Defining the Situation

It should be pointed out that the use of these techniques does not merely involve a single internal readjustment, but depends on an ongoing process. These are not only a priori techniques used to overcome initial normative hurdles. Once engaged in genocidal activities, participants constantly utilize these techniques in order to allow themselves to continue. As people become more inured to, brutalized by, or comfortable in their actions and as the process in some cases becomes more routinized and "sanitized" (e.g., a change from shooting to gassing), these techniques became easier for the participants to utilize and maintain.

It should also be noted that utilization of these techniques is not always a completely conscious process. Neutralization of norms often involves a subtle shift in the definition of a situation. Human beings need to frame their actions and experiences within an acceptable and understandable construct of referents. Genocide falls outside most people's normative boundaries, and when individuals are placed in such a context they must somehow define their actions in a way that is consistent with their self-concept. In other words, they must reconcile the disjunction between belief and behavior, or, as Fred Katz suggests, repackage their values.[117] They are not always successful. Rubenstein and Roth illustrate this when they write,

> The heavy drinking and the emotional disturbances experienced by many of the men indicate that no amount of legalistic reconstruction of human reality could wholly eradicate the normal human response to grievous human suffering.[118]

Given the social, political, and psychological pressures to conform, it is understandable that participants are able to neutralize or repackage internal values and beliefs antithetical to genocide, and thus to participate in it. The historic materials very clearly suggest that perpetrators manifest a priori justifications for their genocidal actions. Many must feel in moral conflict with themselves over their supposed duty and struggle to frame their actions in such a way that their doubts and hesitancies are quelled. As Primo Levi asserts,

> The best way to defend oneself against the invasion of burdensome memories is to impede their entry, to extend a cordon sanitaire. It is easier to deny entry to a memory than to free oneself from it after it has been recorded. This, in substance, was the purpose of many of the artifices thought up by the Nazi commanders in order to protect the consciences of those assigned to do the dirty work and to ensure their services, disagreeable even for the most hardened.[119]

Finding themselves in situations in which they are asked or ordered to engage in activities initially repugnant to or difficult for them, many participate because they feel that they have no choice. Others, who perceive a choice, take part because it is easier to neutralize internal opposition than to deviate from expectations and risk censure or condemnation or, in some cases, physical harm. Regardless of whether or not the participants perceive themselves to have a choice, all need to define the situation in such a way that their actions become acceptable. They rely upon neutralizations or vocabularies of motive that are largely derived from and reinforced by the propaganda, culture, and political and social climate of the times. It is crucial to understand this dialectic, since it provides a sobering warning of the potential for harm inherent in all human communities. Genocide is a type of criminality that is carried out by law-abiding citizens and is not possible without the consent, compliance, and cooperation of large numbers of ordinary men and women. In this chapter, it has become clear that it is eminently possible for "ordinary" men and women to become active and willing agents of genocide. "Normal" people can in clear conscience commit the most horrific crimes. This leaves us, therefore, with the last and most important question concerning genocide: how can we predict and prevent further occurrences?

6   Confronting Genocide

Few countries can be considered immune to a future tide of violence generated by intolerance, lust for power, economic difficulties, religious or political
fanaticism, and racialist attritions. It is therefore necessary to sharpen our
senses, distrust the prophets, the enchanters, those who speak and write
"beautiful words" unsupported by intelligent reasons.

—Primo Levi[1]

... human society has thus far failed, one can say almost completely, to take
strong and effective stands against ongoing events of genocide or genocide
which threatens to occur in the foreseeable future.

—Israel Charny[2]

Genocide often evokes images of inexplicable and powerful natural and supernatural forces. One survivor said the Holocaust "was storm, lightning, thunder,
wind, rain,"[3] while Rezak Hukanović, a survivor of the camps at Omarska and
Manjača, described the genocide in Bosnia this way: "Bosnia trembled as if it
had been hit by a powerful earthquake. But an earthquake comes and goes. This
upheaval just kept on coming."[4] During the Second World War, a Bosnian Muslim named Alija Mehmedović wrote, "We can control the flood, but what can
we do against the cyclone? We can only pray to Allah for mercy."[5] Similarly, the
Serb Draža Mihailović, during his trial in 1946, stated that "Destiny was mer-
ciless towards me when it threw me into the most difficult whirlwinds. I wanted
much, I began much, but the whirlwind, the world whirlwind, carried me and
my work away."[6] While these words are over fifty years old, they could just as
easily have been uttered or written during the 1990s. A missionary in Rwanda
trying to make sense of that country's genocide put it this way: "We were overwhelmed, you see. We were overwhelmed by this great evil, by these acts of
wickedness."[7]

These allusions to natural disasters capture a sense of being caught up in
forces beyond one's control. After all, who can control nature, much less predict
it? When people are "swept up" by natural disasters or "engulfed" by evil, they
are helpless victims of unavoidable and spontaneous misfortunes. Trapped in
the middle of titanic events, individuals feel themselves to be at the mercy of
inescapable forces that profoundly alter or threaten their lives. But these images, while emotive and moving, are misleading because they implicitly suggest
that genocide is both unpredictable and inexplicable.[8] The wars, massacres, and
genocide that have marked the global landscape are not natural and unpre-

dictable. While resonating among those who struggle to make sense of the chaos and violence that have descended upon their communities, these analogies obscure the human agency behind genocide.

The victims of hurricanes in the Caribbean, floods in China, or earthquakes in Turkey are different from victims of genocide. The former are struck down by impersonal and essentially random forces of nature; by acts of God, if you will. The victims of genocide, on the other hand, are struck down by other human beings who rationally and cold-bloodedly go about the job of targeting and eliminating specific groups within society. It is the difference between the power of nature and the power of politics. By these comments I do not imply criticism of those who endure victimization. To the victims of genocide, these metaphors make sense and explain what might otherwise appear unexplainable. For those who live through terrible times, a storm has indeed swept away rationality and reason and uprooted their lives from the normal and the safe. Perhaps these explanations make victimization more endurable, if such a thing is possible. It may be easier to attribute genocide to some mysterious natural or supernatural force than to accept that human beings have selected their fellows for extermination. These metaphors, however, overshadow the political and human impulses to destruction that underlie most examples of genocide. In other words, genocide is conceived and carried out by human beings, and therefore it is certainly not inevitable. It can be subverted and even stopped. While the forces that compel participation, or at least inaction, are powerful, there are many examples of individuals, organizations, and even entire communities resisting and subverting the process of genocide.

Witness, for example, the case of the village of Le Chambon in the Haute-Loire region of France. During the Second World War, the inhabitants of this village repeatedly risked everything to save the lives of thousands of Jewish strangers. The rescue efforts were led by the pastor of the village, Andre Trocmé, and his wife, Magda, although the village as a whole was instrumental in saving the lives of many persecuted Jews.[9] The villagers conducted these rescue efforts at great risk, since the Germans and their French Vichy accomplices often arrested, tortured, and killed those who aided Jewish refugees. The entire village of Oradour-sur-glane was destroyed and all its inhabitants massacred in German reprisals for French resistance to the Nazis. In spite of these dangers, the villagers of Le Chambon worked diligently to save as many Jews as possible from deportation and death. While their resistance did not hasten the end of the war, it certainly affected the lives of those they saved and serves as an object lesson in moral behavior even in the face of tremendous pressure and danger.

Resistance to genocide is not limited to individuals or isolated villages; it can be quite widespread. Approximately 85 percent of the Jews in Italy survived, a much higher proportion than in many other European countries.[10] Only 25 percent of Dutch Jews survived, while Lithuania and Poland, for example, had Jewish survival rates of less than 10 percent.[11] These different mortality rates were the result of different situational and political factors that included the nature of the German presence in that country, the presence or absence of a history of anti-Semitism, and the willingness of individuals and groups to shelter and protect Jews. In Italy, for example, there was a great deal of resistance to the anti-Semitic policies of the Italian fascists and German Nazis. As one Italian put it, "I was always a fascist. I will not deny being a fascist, but I will never accept anti-Semitism and the persecution of Jews."[12] This protection was extended not merely to Italian Jews, but to non-Italian Jewish refugees and to Jews inhabiting countries occupied by Italian troops. In fact, Jews in occupied nations received more protection from the Italian government than did Jews in Italy itself. Susan Zuccotti points out that

> Nothing demonstrates the paradox more clearly than the exceptional measures of the Italian army, Foreign Ministry, and entire diplomatic corps to protect all Jews in Italian-occupied territories. Italy occupied much of Greece in 1941, part of Croatia at about the same time, and eight departments in southern France in November 1942. In all three areas, military and diplomatic personnel, often without instructions or coordination, acted similarly. They resorted to every imaginable scheme and subterfuge to resist repeated German demands for the deportation of Jews. They ignored Mussolini's directives, occasionally with his tacit consent. They neglected to pass on instructions, made orders deliberately vague and imprecise, invented absurd bureaucratic excuses, lied, and totally misled the Germans.[13]

The Italians pursued this strategy of succor even though it weakened their relationship with Germany and consequently the security and independence of their country. They did it nonetheless and saved the lives of many thousands of Jews throughout southern Europe. In countries where the government and its bureaucracies cooperated more with the mechanics of genocide, a far greater percentage of the Jewish population perished in the camps and crematoria of the Holocaust. In short, not all European Jews were equally at risk during the Holocaust. Even though the pressure to assist the Nazis was tremendous, involving military, political, and social coercion, many individuals and organizations chose not to comply. These examples illustrate that genocide can be resisted and subverted. It is important to recognize that it can also be prevented.

The prevention of genocide is dependent upon two linked elements: detection and intervention. Detection refers to the identification of precursors to this crime, while intervention concerns the various mechanisms that members of the international community can implement to either deter or curtail it. Early intervention depends upon the accurate identification of genocidal intentions and planning, and so detection is the first step toward prevention.

Detection

As discussed earlier in this book, genocides don't just happen. They are not spontaneous eruptions of ethnic, religious, or racial hatreds. Rather, they are planned strategies calculated to destroy a targeted population. Because specific tactics must be initiated before the killing can take place, it becomes possible to identify precursors to the killing. The patterns of genocide are laid down months or even years before the actual killings begin. Raul Hilberg, for example, argued that the Holocaust went through several prefatory stages, definition, expropriation, and concentration, before the final stage of annihilation began.[14] Hitler began targeting Jews years before the Holocaust was finally implemented. In Yugoslavia, nationalistic rhetoric from politicians like Tudjman of Croatia and Milošević of Serbia began the process of fragmentation and antagonism years before violence actually broke out. Because of this consistency in preparation for genocide, many experts have advocated the early identification of genocidal trends.

David Callahan, for example, suggests three predictive factors for ethnic warfare: a history of state repression of an ethnic minority or encouragement of violence toward a minority; a history of violence among ethnic groups; and the existence of ethnic pockets within newly independent states.[15] His work mirrors that of Helen Fein, whose research indicates that ethnic discrimination and the polarization of populations are a powerful warning of future genocides.[16] However, as Callahan himself readily admits, none of these indicators is sufficient to determine whether genocide will occur. They merely represent situational and historical realities that may or may not escalate into systematic lethal persecution of specific groups. Callahan also limits himself to a discussion of precursors specifically of ethnic conflict. Genocide, however, can target a variety of groups independent of ethnicity, which makes the applicability of the precursors he identifies problematic. Nonetheless, his work does point to certain hostile and polarized situations that make genocidal violence more likely.

Barbara Harff similarly recognizes the importance of ethnic polarization. In her work describing the etiology of genocide, Harff asserts that a "factor leading to the development of genocide is the existence of sharp internal cleavages combined with a history of struggle between groups prior to the upheaval."[17] The greater the divisions between groups, the easier it is to escalate conflict or tension into violence. In addition, Harff also notes the necessity for structural change. By this she intends to highlight the idea that genocides are typically preceded by some sort of national upheaval, which she defines as "an abrupt change in the political community."[18] In other words, a coup, war, or revolution is necessary for genocide. A last factor is the absence of outside deterrents, or even international support for the genocidal state. As discussed earlier, assistance from the international community, or at least its inaction, is necessary for genocide to occur.

One of the most comprehensive attempts to grapple with the problem of preventing genocide is the work of Israel Charny, who has written about the need for a "world genocide early warning system" that would identify and observe human rights violations in order to identify societies on the path toward genocide.[19] Specifically, Charny argues for a system that would collect information on human rights violations, genocides, and massacres. This information would be used to conduct research on the ways in which genocidal forces build up in a society and are unleashed. Importantly, it would also be used to call attention to genocidal societies as a first step toward intervention. Charny's system is notable in that it differentiates between ongoing processes and critical incidents:

> the first refers to, for instance, the degree of protection of free speech, or the degree of discrimination of minorities, while the second refers to dramatic events such as a major turn in policy as a result of the emergence of a new leader, the impact of going to war, or economic breakdown.[20]

Essentially, this distinction allows the identification of both precursors and specific triggers and thus offers a more precise estimate of genocidal inclinations. A brief review of the ten variables identified by Charny illustrates the range of genocidal precursors.

1. *The Valuing of Human Life:* Where life is cheap, genocide is much more likely. Genocide is, after all, the destruction of human beings, and societies that do not value or respect life find it much easier to contemplate and enact genocidal policies.
2. *Concern with the Quality of Human Experience:* A state that tries to ensure that its citizens have adequate food, shelter, medical care, work, etc., is less likely to pursue genocidal policies.
3. *The Valuing of Power:* Charny recognizes that power can be used in constructive and positive ways, but when power is used to dominate and exploit people, this is a powerful warning sign of potential massacres and genocides. It indicates a fundamental disregard for the well-being of others and a willingness to use force against people.
4. *Machinery for Managing Escalations of Threat:* All states and societies have to deal with threats to their integrity or survival. In places where established mechanisms exist to deal with these threats rationally, where decision makers are constrained by checks and balances, there is little danger of succumbing to genocidal paranoia.
5. *Orientation toward Force for Self-Defense and in Solution of Conflicts:* States that prefer violent or brutal strategies of conflict resolution are more likely to foster genocidal solutions to problems perceived to be posed by specific groups.
6. *Overt Violence and Destructiveness:* As Charny suggests, "A society that limits exposure to violence in its media, and develops more mature attitudes in its journalistic reports of actual events of violence, can also be expected to be less susceptible to being drawn into genocidal violence toward others."[21] In short, societies that glamorize and glorify violence are more likely to ultimately perpetrate violence.
7. *Dehumanization of a Potential Victim Target Group:* Such dehumanization is, as we have seen, an absolutely essential component of genocide. The first step in targeting a population for destruction is to remove their identity as human beings and replace it with a lesser, subhuman identity. Hannah Arendt once said that "it is easier to kill a

dog than a man, easier yet to kill a rat or frog, and no problem at all to kill insects."[22] The more removed a victim's identity is from human, the easier it is to kill. Leo Kuper echoes this when he asserts that the dehumanization of a population is a common forerunner of genocide.[23]

8. *Perception of the Victim Group as Dangerous:* Populations targeted for destruction are invariably portrayed as presenting a threat to their subsequent attackers. In this way, justifications for self-defense are invoked, which help legitimize the violence.

9. *Availability of the Victim Group:* Genocide can only take place where a power differential exists. The more marginalized a group is politically, socially, and economically, the more defenseless it is against genocidal regimes. When targeted groups are well entrenched within a society, active measures are taken to reduce their power and push them to the periphery of that society.

10. *Legitimation of Victimization by Leadership Individuals and Institutions:* Human beings are social beings first and foremost, and look to authority figures and social institutions for guidance and inspiration. As Supreme Court Justice Louis Brandeis once wrote,

> Our government is the potent, the omnipresent teacher. For good or ill, it teaches the whole people by its example. Crime is contagious. If the government becomes a lawbreaker, it breeds contempt for the law.[24]

When influential people encourage violence against a population group, many others will be persuaded or prompted to participate.

The variables identified by Israel Charny are remarkably comprehensive and capture most of the precursors to genocide. They are, however, somewhat abstract and difficult to translate into measurable indicators. How does one measure the relative value of human life in a given society, or an orientation toward force? Nevertheless, Charny's conceptualization offers a theoretical framework with which to begin identifying the various processes that signal genocidal intentions.

Kurt Jonassohn and Karin Solveig Björnson have developed a somewhat more specific list of warning signs that is intended to reveal a genocide in its initial stages. These are official statements of genocidal intentions, the appearance of refugees, legal changes intended to deprive a group of human rights, and misleading and damaging news reports that target a specific group.[25] These are all steps taken in preparation for genocide, and they are readily identifiable. While individually these indicators may not be definitive proof of an impetus toward mass killing, in the aggregate they demonstrate genocidal planning and intent. As all of these examples suggest, enough indicators exist to raise warning signals that a society is engaged in potentially genocidal activities. But at some point the identification and monitoring of warning signs becomes meaningless unless it is linked with strategies for intervention in genocidal societies. What good is studying and identifying warning signs if the international community then sits idly by and watches genocides come to fruition? Intervention is consequently a natural and necessary outgrowth of detection.

Intervention

Intervention, by definition, involves the violation of another state's sovereignty. Its legitimacy derives from various principles of international law, especially in regard to human rights issues. While many of these precepts date back to the Middle Ages, most owe their articulation to the ideals established by the Nuremberg trials that followed the Second World War. The Holocaust largely ended the belief that a state has free rein in how it treats its own citizens and that the international community should not interfere in purely domestic issues.

Foremost among recent innovations is the development of international human rights law, which is largely based on the concept that every state must protect the human rights of its people. If it violates those rights, then the international community has the right to intervene.[26] This means that no nation can now consider itself immune from responsibility for genocidal crimes, since international human rights law is considered binding upon all states even if those states have not ratified specific human rights treaties and conventions.[27] While the principles of territorial integrity and political independence known collectively as sovereignty are protected by international law, they are increasingly defined as being of lesser importance than protecting the rights and lives of human beings in those sovereign states. As the International Criminal Tribunal for the Former Yugoslavia recently articulated, "State sovereignty must give way in cases where the nature of the offenses alleged does not affect the interests of one state alone but shocks the very conscience of mankind."[28] The tribunal also asserts that national borders "should not be considered as a shield against the reach of the law and as a protection for those who trample underfoot the most elementary rights of humanity."[29] Intervention, then, in its many forms, is increasingly accepted as a legitimate response to human rights violations around the world. One of the most widely practiced strategies of intervention is diplomacy.

Diplomacy

Diplomacy is a process of communication that involves negotiation, coercion, and clarification of intentions and reactions. In one sense it is the umbrella under which various forms of intervention are sheltered and may "rely on simple persuasion and moral authority, coercive threats and intimidation, or some mix of these elements."[30] Diplomats cajole and try to convince state leaders that their genocidal policies are ill advised or immoral. They may also suggest that certain policies, if implemented, would lead to other more serious interventions, such as sanctions or military action. If nothing else, diplomats can assure the leaders of a genocidal regime that their actions have not gone unnoticed and, more importantly, that those responsible may be held accountable for those actions. The fact that many perpetrators of genocide seek to conceal their crimes illustrates the power that international recognition and condemnation have on the actions of state leaders. Perpetrators may believe that by cloaking their actions they can avoid decisive intervention and act with impunity. Diplomats can inform them that they are wrong. Worldwide censure, spurred on by diplomacy, can also serve to remove the illusion of legitimacy from genocidal actions and may also inhibit genocidal politicians.

The difficulty with diplomacy and diplomats is that they are often held hostage to *Realpolitik* strategies that place a higher value on protecting national security than on protecting an oppressed group. Just before Indonesia invaded East Timor in 1975 and began its brutal repression of the East Timorese population, the Australian ambassador to Indonesia wrote that Australia should assume "a pragmatic rather than a principled stand," because "that is what national interest and foreign policy is all about."[31] American diplomats were similarly directed to avoid the issue of East Timor and, just days before the invasion, Henry Kissinger and Gerald Ford met with Indonesian president Suharto and essentially gave him the go-ahead for the invasion. Approximately two hundred thousand East Timorese have been killed under the Indonesian occupation.[32] In this particular case, diplomacy worked against the interests of the population at risk. Another example of the failure of diplomacy is the Rwandan genocide of the 1990s. James Woods, a U.S. deputy assistant secretary of defense, placed Rwanda-Burundi on a list of potential trouble spots just before the killing began but was told by a superior,

> if something happens in Rwanda-Burundi, we don't care. Take it off the list . . .
> U.S. national interest is not involved . . . we can't put all these silly humanitarian
> issues on lists like important problems like the Middle East and North Korea and
> so on.[33]

After the genocide began, the U.S. government tried to put diplomatic pressure on the Hutu government, but to no avail. Clearly, diplomacy does not always serve as an effective means of intervention.

Additionally, diplomacy relies upon the good faith of those involved. A genocidal regime may engage in diplomacy simply to appear reasonable and open. In this sense, diplomacy may allow the leadership to project an image of legitimacy and a willingness to negotiate simply as a stalling tactic while they continue the killing and repression. In one interview, Bosnian Serb general and indicted war criminal Ratko Mladić asserted, "In order to succeed, you have to be devious; tell them one thing one time, another thing at another time."[34] To Mladić, deception in diplomacy was an acceptable strategy. Evidencing the same attitude, Radovan Karadžić, the political leader of the Bosnian Serbs, told fellow Serbs, "Pay no attention to what we do at the conferences, as all the maps are transient, and only what you hold is eternal. Hold every village of ours, and do not worry."[35]

Mediation

Another possible form of intervention is mediation, in which a third party resolves the dispute. In recent years, mediation has become popular in the United States as individuals and organizations increasingly perceive it as a viable alternative to more traditional forms of conflict resolution. However, as David Callahan points out,

> The United States has sought to mediate nearly every major ethnic conflict in the past thirty years. Only on rare occasions have such efforts succeeded. More often, U.S. mediation attempts have failed or have produced mixed results.[36]

This poor track record invites the question: why has mediation been so unsuccessful? One obvious answer is that this form of intervention is dependent upon all the involved parties presenting their case before a mediator, and then abiding by the mediator's decision. State leaders involved in genocidal policy may feel that it is strictly an internal matter or that too much is at stake for them to rely on mediation. It also presupposes a legitimate dispute to be resolved, yet, as we know, many conflicts are manufactured and have no basis in reality. The threat that the Jews posed to Germany was nonexistent, as was the threat from the Rwandan Tutsis. How can a mediator reconcile opposing positions on an issue when one side has no objective legitimacy and the other no power? Mediation, therefore, is somewhat limited as an effective tool of intervention.

Sanctions

Another type of intervention is the imposition of sanctions. The United Nations charter defines sanctions as the "complete or partial interruption of economic relations and of rail, sea, air, postal, telegraphic, radio, and other means of communication, and the severance of diplomatic relations."[37] Sanctions, therefore, generally involve isolating a country and severing some or all of its linkages with other nations. Since most states are heavily involved in world trade and depend upon imports and exports to maintain their economic health, this form of intervention can be a very potent weapon for inducing change in a state's policies. Economic sanctions are also important because they do not need to be implemented by state or intergovernmental organizations. Governments are often unwilling to institute sanctions because they feel sanctions may undermine their own economic health or destroy any leverage they may exert over the targeted nation. Private organizations and groups of concerned citizens, on the other hand, can launch campaigns to boycott a nation's goods and services, or alternatively boycott businesses in their own country that do business in the genocidal society. These boycotts can be fairly effective at producing change, as evidenced by the boycott of South African products that helped bring about the end of apartheid. Like other forms of intervention, however, sanctions do have drawbacks.

Perhaps the greatest drawback of sanctions is that civilian populations are the ones most affected. When food supplies, medical equipment, drugs, heating fuel, and other necessities become scarce or unavailable because of sanctions, typically it is the civilians who suffer the most. The leaders of a state and the military are often insulated from the worst effects of sanctions and consequently may not be inclined to halt their actions. In fact, their domestic support may be strengthened as the population turns its anger against those imposing the sanctions and rallies around its leadership.

It is also possible that, because of their impact on civilians, many sanctions may actually violate international law. Various protocols to the Geneva Conventions ban measures that reduce the ability of civilians to survive, such as Article 54 of Protocol 1 of the Geneva Conventions, which asserts that "starvation of civilians as a method of warfare is prohibited."[38] However, many economic and trade sanctions have just such an effect and may therefore violate some types of international law. The best example of this is the sanctions imposed on Iraq in the wake of the 1991 Gulf War.[39] These sanctions have resulted in a tremendous increase in mortality rates for children under five years of age, the elderly, and the chronically ill. Malnutrition is rampant, with corresponding increases in disease. Shortages of food and medical supplies have been exacerbated by the widespread destruction of Iraq's infrastructure that occurred during the war. In short, the group most affected by the sanctions in Iraq is the civilian population, which has the fewest resources with which to resist. How can one impose sanctions on a country for human rights violations when those sanctions themselves violate human rights?

Military Action

Another type of intervention is direct military intervention. Of all strategies, this one carries the most risk. This form of intervention is the most aggressive, since it involves the direct use of force to violate another nation's sovereignty. In some situations it has proven quite effective. The Dayton Peace Accords were signed only after the U.N. and NATO began a sustained bombing campaign in 1995. Prompted into action by years of Serb intransigence, the massacres at Zepa and Srebrenica, and the shelling of a Sarajevan marketplace, the U.N. and NATO forces quickly brought the siege of Sarajevo to an end and forced the Serbs to the negotiating table. In this they were assisted by Croatian troops who, trained and armed in large part by the United States, were given the green light to attack Serb-held territory.[40] In this case, military intervention brought to an end the killing and massacres that had wracked this Balkan country, although the Croatians carried out massacres of their own in the course of expelling Serbs from the territory they captured.

However, when done incorrectly or for the wrong reasons, military intervention can be disastrous. When NATO launched its air campaign against Serbia because of the violence and repression in Kosovo, the two most immediate results were devastating. First, the attacks incited the Serb leadership to speed up its policies of ethnic cleansing of Kosovar Albanians, resulting in wide-spread massacres and the uprooting and dislocation of the majority of the population. Second, they also strengthened Milošević's support among the Serbs. Conflict with an outside group always serves to strengthen the ties of members within a group. The NATO bombing campaign reinforced a sense of persecution among Serbs, strengthened their collective identity, and elevated Milošević in their eyes as a man who was willing to stand up to the NATO allies.

Additionally, military intervention runs the risk of both increasing the geographic area of a conflict and intensifying the violence. Many states engaged in genocidal repression have the military capability to actively resist armed intervention. Both sides may increase their commitment in troops and materiel, or the fighting may spill over into neighboring states. War also tends to brutalize and dehumanize, and a military intervention, unless it is swift and decisive, runs the risk of exacerbating the violence as populations are further exposed to the debasing aspects of military conflict.

Electronic Jamming

One last, nontraditional form of intervention is suggested by Norman Cigar, who proposes that the electronic media be jammed in the genocidal state.[41] Genocide is preceded and accompanied by a concerted media campaign that targets a population by portraying it as the enemy and as a threat and assists in creating a climate of hatred and distrust. The electronic media are a significant facilitator for genocidal violence, since states most likely to pursue destructive policies almost always monopolize sources of information. Not only does Cigar suggest blocking hate propaganda, he also proposes that alternative perspectives and information be broadcast so that the population can see how the actions of their society are perceived by others and what the possible implications of those actions are. In her work on totalitarianism, Hannah Arendt argues that fact-based information can minimize the ability of propaganda to organize a population around myths and lies; this helps explain why many dictatorial regimes routinely prohibit access to outside sources of information.[42] In Cambodia, the citizens were deprived of all sources of information except the political education lessons controlled by the state.[43] In Rwanda and Serbia the state controlled all the media, so that the official government position was the only one many citizens of those states knew of. It may be that, as one commentator suggests, "the broadcasting of truth . . . upends the torturer's boastful claim that no one will ever know."[44]

The difficulty with this strategy is that "the population may already be so indoctrinated that an outside information campaign may have only a marginal, or slow, impact on public opinion."[45] Moreover, the population for whom it is intended may, ironically, see the outside information as propaganda while the domestic media are seen as broadcasting only the truth.

As this discussion indicates, all forms of intervention carry with them significant problems and risks. But even with the limitations inherent in each form of intervention, the risks of not doing anything are far greater. For all their shortcomings, interventions offer at least the possibility of preventing or curtailing the crime of genocide. This is especially important given that inaction often acts as tacit approval and encourages repetition. Helen Fein has found that "genocide unchecked also leads to more genocide: I found that most users of genocide . . . were repeat offenders."[46] The authors of a recent biography of Slobodan Milošević suggest that he interpreted the U.S. lack of interest in his machinations as unspoken approval.[47] The U.S. position was summed up by George Bush's secretary of state, James Baker, who repeatedly stated, "We don't have a dog in this fight."[48] Roger Smith makes essentially the same argument in regard to the Armenian genocide and the lack of effective intervention.[49] The lessons learned by genocidally inclined states from these kinds of examples are easy to imagine. Intervention is a necessity.

It is clear, however, that intervention strategies must be carefully thought out before being applied. Bazyler suggests that five criteria need to be met for intervention to take place:

1. Large-scale atrocities must be occurring or contemplated;
2. The overriding concern in intervention must be humanitarian;
3. The intervention must be conducted by a variety of states, not one acting unilaterally;
4. The intervention must be limited to stopping the killing and, if necessary, removing the leader responsible;
5. Other, more peaceful remedies must be first exhausted.[50]

Not all genocides occur for the same reasons, and the approaches utilized by those working to prevent human rights abuses must be tailored to the specifics of each case. For economic genocide, economic sanctions may be entirely sufficient, since they may change the cost/benefit equation for the leadership of the genocidal state. Ideological genocides, on the other hand, motivated as they are by aberrant belief systems, may require other methods or even multiple intervention strategies, such as diplomacy backed up by the threat or actual use of sanctions or military intervention.

Implementation

One important issue raised by this discussion of detection and intervention is implementation. Although it is possible to identify potential genocide, it is unclear how an effective monitoring system can be instituted. Logistical issues must be resolved that concern which agencies or organizations should or could conduct the monitoring, who would be warned if danger signals appeared, and what types of intervention strategies would then be implemented.[51] The most significant of these issues is the first. Three different types of structures could undertake such a mission: governments or states, nongovernmental organizations (NGOs), and intergovernmental organizations (IGOs).

Governments are the leading contender for this responsibility. After all, international relations are based upon national governments empowered to negotiate, ally with, threaten, and compromise with each other. International law is based upon the primacy of the sovereign rights of states. There are, however, significant problems with relying upon states to intervene in the actions of other states.

States have a terrible track record in regard to human rights interventions. Israel Charny writes that the history of governmental intervention against genocidal states is "a sorry one of indifference, cynicism, impotence, and most outrageous manipulations by member nations."[52] One important reason for this is that states have not wanted to violate the sovereignty of other nations lest their own sovereignty be violated in turn. Nationalistic sentiments often depend upon the perceived inviolability of sovereign states. Most nations do not feel secure enough to open their internal policies and practices to international scrutiny by relaxing their stance on sovereign immunity. However, it should be pointed out that this hesitancy is not always unwarranted. The history of colonial exploitation is filled with states exploiting ethnic and racial tensions in other countries for their own political and economic advantage. State intervention in the affairs of other nations, even for the most humanitarian of reasons, carries with it a significant amount of historical baggage. Since most states practice variants of *Realpolitik*, a policy that values pragmatic self-interest through the pursuit of power, individual states may be inappropriate agents for genocide identification and intervention.

Another possibility is nongovernmental organizations (NGOs). Since the Second World War, NGOs have proliferated across the globe, with many devoting themselves to human rights and related issues. The United Nations database of NGOs lists 21 organizations dedicated to conflict resolution, 8 devoted to refugees and displaced persons, 22 focused on economic, humanitarian, and disaster-relief assistance, and 167 committed to human rights. These numbers represent only a small fraction of all NGOs. While many of these are limited in scope to a particular geographic area or a specific demographic or interest group, others are not. Groups such as Amnesty International and Human Rights Watch are dedicated to monitoring violations of human rights around the world and could easily serve as genocide watchdogs. Alternatively, some have argued for the establishment of an International Genocide Bureau or a World Genocide Tribunal that would focus exclusively on genocidal crimes.[53] Such an organization not only would gather information on and monitor states pursuing destructive policies, but would also be authorized to function as both a civil and a criminal court in order to try and punish those responsible for genocide.

NGOs are often among the first to alert the international community to potentially lethal regimes and have played key roles in international efforts to ameliorate crises around the world. During the crisis in Burundi that followed in the wake of the Rwandan genocide just over its borders, dozens of NGOs worked on different aspects of the crisis, monitoring massacres in the countryside, seeking to prevent the delivery of new arms, promoting peaceful dialogue between Hutu and Tutsi, addressing discrimination in work and education, trying to counter hate radio, dealing with nutritional and medical needs, attempting to strengthen government organs like the judiciary, aiding efforts to bring war criminals from the 1993 massacres to justice, and so on.[54]

One significant advantage of NGOs is that they are not typically constrained by the political considerations that states are subject to, since they usually operate without formal ties to specific states. Governments are notoriously loath to call attention to human rights outrages in nations with which they are cultivating relations, or to which they have strong economic and political ties. In contrast, NGOs do not operate under such impediments. Members of NGOs are mostly volunteers and often racially, ethnically, and socially diverse, and are directly motivated by humanitarian ideals rather than political issues. However, NGOs have some important weaknesses that ultimately relegate them to a secondary status in strategies of intervention.

The most relevant problem for NGOs is that they have no official power to mandate intervention or force compliance with humanitarian initiatives. Many interventions require the violation of a nation's sovereignty, and NGOs simply do not have the international legitimacy or the resources to forcefully intervene when necessary. NGOs have nonetheless been remarkably effective in calling attention to human rights outrages and in pressuring states to intervene. In the modern era, images and information concerning human rights violations and genocide can be disseminated around the world within a matter of hours. NGOs can often call upon thousands of associates and supporters to lobby for action and educate the public. They have also proven adept at mobilizing resources in order to deliver assistance to people uprooted and devastated by genocide. This power, however, is dependent upon the cooperation of the host nation, or the assistance and protection of larger, more powerful groups, such as the United Nations. NGOs, therefore, can never shoulder the burden alone.

The last category of organization to be considered is intergovernmental organizations, of which the most relevant example is the United Nations. The United Nations was created in the wake of the Second World War as a means of ensuring international security.[55] Consequently, the major goal of the U.N. has been to prevent conflict between nations, to regulate and limit those conflicts that do break out, and to restore peace in their wake.[56] Because of this orientation, the United Nations has become the primary focus of global human rights initiatives and operations.[57] Its charter specifically affirms human rights, and it has been instrumental in developing international law in order to protect those rights. In 1948, the General Assembly of the United Nations adopted the Universal Declaration of Human Rights, and that same year the U.N. also adopted the Convention on the Prevention and Punishment of Genocide. These documents have provided the legal framework for intervention in the internal affairs of sovereign states. Many of the strides taken in ameliorating genocide and punishing perpetrators can be traced to United Nations initiatives. The U.N.'s successes, however, have often been matched by its failures.

In Rwanda, the United Nations was repeatedly warned that plans were being developed to begin a genocide. One informant advised the U.N. that death lists were being drawn up and weapons were being distributed to Hutus, but U.N. officials chose to ignore his news. Other clear warning signs included the creation, training, and arming of militias and the nonstop radio propaganda calling for the destruction of the Tutsi population. The United Nations chose to ignore these signals and became a bystander to the subsequent killings. Even though there were over 2500 United Nations troops in Rwanda at the outbreak of the killing, they did nothing.[58] In one instance, the prime minister, Agathe Uwilingiyimana, was taken away from U.N. troops who were ostensibly protecting her and was murdered, along with her U.N. protectors.[59] Another time, Tutsis were taken off trucks headed for the airport and murdered while French and Belgian U.N. troops watched.[60]

In Bosnia, the U.N. proved similarly ineffective, and in fact sometimes even served to assist the Bosnian Serbs in their genocidal activities. During the siege of Sarajevo, the United Nations patrolled the airport and would spotlight Sarajevans who were trying to escape the siege by traversing the airport at night. They did this in order to appear neutral to the Serbs in the surrounding hills, who otherwise might force the closure of the airport. Caught in the light of United Nations searchlights, some escapees were killed by Serb snipers.[61] One of the most infamous genocidal bloodbaths occurred in and around the town of Srebrenica and was similarly facilitated by poorly thought out United Nations policies. This example is poignantly illustrated by the experiences of one survivor.

Hurem Suljić is, depending on your point of view, either very lucky or very unlucky. A Bosnian Muslim in his mid-fifties, Suljić lived in the small village of Potočari, located outside Srebrenica. Disabled by a bad fall years before, Suljić was employed as a night watchman in a local factory. He was unlucky enough to be living in the Srebrenica enclave when it fell, yet lucky enough to escape the worst European massacre since the Holocaust.[62]

In 1993, the United Nations made Srebrenica and the area surrounding the town into what was to be the first of several U.N.-protected safe zones. The Bosnian Serbs had overrun the eastern part of Bosnia, and communities such as Goražde, Žepa, Sarajevo, and Srebrenica found themselves cut off and surrounded by hostile Serb forces. These communities were swollen with Muslim refugees fleeing the fighting and its accompanying "ethnic cleansing." It was at this point that the United Nations stepped in to protect the encircled enclaves. One U.N. policy, with ultimately tragic consequences, was to disarm the inhabitants of those safe areas.[63] Inevitably, when the Serbs attacked Srebrenica, the United Nations lacked the ability or the will to resist, while the inhabitants lacked the weapons. Not surprisingly, the safe area soon fell to the Serbs, who quickly forced the Muslim inhabitants to evacuate their homes and gather in central areas where the men, Hurem Suljić among them, were separated from their families. For several days these men were penned up in various warehouses and transported to different locations, all the while subjected to beatings and torture, and sometimes killed. Suljić, for example, witnessed Serbs executing Muslims with axes and knives. Others were killed by grenades thrown into crowded rooms. With their ranks thinned out, the survivors were eventually loaded onto trucks and transported to a field littered with the bodies of dead Muslim men, and in which had been dug a mass grave. It was a scene horribly familiar to anyone with knowledge of the infamous Nazi *Einsatzgruppen* and places such as Babi Yar. The prisoners, no doubt fully aware of what was about to happen, were forced to stand at the end of the line of dead bodies. They were then executed. Miraculously, Hurem Suljić was not hit by bullets and survived by playing dead, shielded by corpses. Crawling away after dark, he survived to be reunited with his family. His luck did not extend to the other men from his village; he is the only known survivor. The United Nations not only failed to protect the Muslims of Srebrenica, it actually contributed to their destruction. Creating the illusion of safety, they attracted refugees to this "safe haven" who were then disarmed and ultimately left to the not-so-tender mercies of the Serbs when the U.N. troops pulled out. With failures like these to its credit, is it any wonder that the reputation of this organization has been seriously compromised over the years? Tadeusz Mazowiecki, a special rapporteur for the U.N., resigned after the fall of Srebrenica and wrote,

> One cannot speak about the protection of human rights with credibility when one is confronted with the lack of consistency and courage displayed by the international community and its leaders. . . . Crimes have been committed with swiftness and brutality, and by contrast, the response of the international community has been slow and ineffectual.[64]

In fairness to the soldiers and others working for the U.N., they are often hampered by the rules under which they are forced to serve. U.N. peacekeeping troops are usually lightly armed and their rules of engagement allow them to use their weapons only as a last resort. Officially, the U.N. is supposed to maintain a posture of neutrality and keep the belligerents apart, thus making sure the peace is maintained. Too often these constraints serve only to make the U.N. "a symbol of weakness and a candidate for blackmail."[65]

Despite the clear failure of the United Nations to effectively intervene during genocides, it remains the best possibility for effective intervention in the future. It has the experience, the trained personnel, and the legal framework within which any prevention of genocide must of necessity operate. Flawed as it has been, it still has the potential to make a lasting and significant impact on the global stage in regard to human rights and genocide. One area in which the United Nations has already begun to have an effect is in the punishment of perpetrators. The establishment of war crimes tribunals in the 1990s is a significant step against genocide, because if genocide is to truly be eradicated, its perpetration must be clearly linked to legal consequences. A fundamental principle of Western law is that without punishment there is no crime.[66] After all, what use are laws if they are not accompanied by some form of penalty? The post-Holocaust years have seen the implementation of various legal mechanisms that increasingly hold violators of human rights and perpetrators of genocide responsible for their crimes and have the potential to deter future genocides. The abduction and trial of Adolf Eichmann, the prosecution of five hundred members of Argentina's military dictatorship implicated in the "disappearances," Germany's prosecution of East German border troops involved in killing would-be escapees, and, most recently, the indictment of the former dictator of Chile, Augusto Pinochet, on October 16, 1998, all indicate the growing power of international law to punish the guilty.

War Crimes Tribunals

Dusko Tadic is, by all accounts, a coarse and brutal man. He also has the distinction of being the first person convicted of crimes against humanity and war crimes by the first international war crimes tribunal since the Second World War.[67] Described by a neighbor as a "trouble-maker, not very bright, but he was not evil,"[68] Tadic was the owner of a pub called "Nippon," as well as a karate teacher in the Bosnian town of Kozarac. Prone to violence, and with a history of failed business attempts, he was tailor-made for the Nationalist Serbs intent on creating a Greater Serbia and recapturing a glorious past. When the violence began, Tadic targeted Muslim homes for artillery attacks, and after Kozarac fell, he identified leading members of the town's Muslim community for murder, and even participated in some of the murders himself. After so-called detention camps were established nearby, Dusko Tadic was a frequent visitor, seeming to enjoy torturing and killing the Muslim inmates. In one of the most horrendous and widely publicized atrocities of that entire period, Tadic forced a prisoner to castrate a fellow inmate by making him bite off the other's testicles.

In 1993 Tadic and his family moved to Munich, Germany, either because he fell out of favor with local Serb officials or because he wanted to avoid being drafted into the Bosnian Serb army. Quickly recognized by the large community of Bosnian exiles in Munich, he went into hiding at his brother's apartment. Several months later, on the morning of February 12, 1994, as Tadic left the apartment, he was arrested by German police who, under international law, charged him with aggravated assault, murder, crimes against humanity, and genocide. In November of that year, the International Criminal Tribunal for the Former Yugoslavia asked Germany to forgo prosecuting Tadic and instead remand him into the custody of the tribunal, which Germany did in April of 1995. At his trial, Tadic was found guilty of crimes against humanity and violations of the customs of war and was sentenced to twenty years' imprisonment on July 14, 1997. His trial and subsequent conviction are important, not because of who Dusko Tadic is, but because of what it represents. Dusko Tadic is essentially a low-level thug who never possessed official rank or status among the Bosnian Serb forces. His trial, however, represents not only a commitment to the principles of international law established at Nuremberg, but also a renewed willingness to apply them. In its first annual report, the Tribunal articulated that resolution when it wrote,

> The United Nations, which over the years has accumulated an impressive corpus of international standards enjoining States and individuals to conduct themselves humanely, has now set up an institution to put those standards to the test, to transform them into living reality. A whole body of lofty, if remote, United Nations ideals will be brought to bear upon human beings. Through the Tribunal, those imperatives will be turned from abstract tenets into inescapable commands.[69]

The trial of Dusko Tadic therefore represents a milestone in the application of international law to crimes against humanity. But does it represent "a new age of human rights enforcement," as one commentator suggested?[70] The jury is still out.

Located at The Hague in the Netherlands, the International Criminal Tribunal for the Former Yugoslavia (ICTY) was established on May 25, 1993, by the United Nations Security Council and is mandated to prosecute people "responsible for serious violations of international humanitarian law committed on the territory of the former Yugoslavia since 1991." Specifically, the tribunal is empowered to prosecute grave breaches of the 1949 Geneva Conventions, violations of the laws or customs of warfare, genocide, and crimes against humanity.[71] On November 8, 1994, the U.N. Security Council's Resolution 955 also established the International Criminal Tribunal for Rwanda (ICTR), empowered to prosecute those responsible for genocide and other serious violations of international humanitarian law in Rwanda (and Rwandan citizens who committed such acts in neighboring countries) during 1994.[72] Additionally, on July 17, 1998, the United Nations Diplomatic Conference of Plenipotentiaries on the Establishment of an International Criminal Court adopted a resolution permanently establishing such a court, with jurisdiction over genocide, crimes against humanity, war crimes, and crimes of aggression. Replacing tribunals created ad hoc, with all of the start-up difficulties experienced by the ICTY and ICTR, this court will have the authority to investigate and prosecute these types of crimes on a permanent and ongoing basis and represents a significant step forward for the application of international humanitarian law.

When first established, these tribunals were criticized by some for being ineffective and largely symbolic. Shortly after the foundation of the ICTY, one of the appointed judges found that

> There was zero! Nothing! We had four secretaries, a few computers, and the UN had rented a meeting room and three small offices in the Peace Palace. The rent was paid for two weeks.[73]

With these few resources they were expected to investigate and prosecute war crimes in the former Yugoslavia. In spite of these difficulties, the tribunal underwent significant transformations, and by 1999 its annual budget had been increased by $94 million and almost eight hundred people were employed.[74] The tribunal now sends numerous teams into the field every year gathering depositions, reports, photographs, and other evidence of war crimes and genocide and collects information from government and media sources. The tribunal also relies on forensic scientists to exhume individual and mass graves. In order to prove genocide, it must be shown that a population was targeted for deliberate mass destruction. The investigators can not only show that civilians were cold-bloodedly executed, but also assist in identifying the dead in order to bring some closure to the families of the missing. As Elizabeth Neuffer writes,

> A forensic team will begin probing the grave, often with a metal rod, seeking to test its consistency and detect the smell of dead bodies. Once investigators have dug down to the level of bodies, they will sift the earth for shreds of evidence and dust off each body. Bodies are carefully examined before being removed. Valuable evidence can include blindfolds, bullets and bonds that will indicate how a victim was killed. Jewelry or papers will help with identification.[75]

The exhumations of the mass graves in Srebrenica, for example, showed that many of the victims had their hands tied behind their backs and were blindfolded, while the presence of religious artifacts indicated that they were Bosnian Muslims.[76] When combined with other evidence, the data collected is used to build a case against those indicted of perpetrating or masterminding the killing.

One significant hurdle for the ICTY has been getting custody of indicted suspects. Early on, hampered by lack of cooperation from the states of the former Yugoslavia, the tribunal had limited success. More recently, however, the tribunal has been more forceful in seeking the arrest and extradition of those indicted. In July of 1997, NATO troops captured three Bosnian Serbs indicted for war crimes and killed a fourth who resisted arrest and wounded a British soldier,[77] and in December of 1998, American troops in Bosnia arrested Radislav Krstic, a Bosnian Serb general. His indictment was based on evidence that he, along with Ratko Mladić, had organized and carried out the massacres of Bosnian Muslims after the fall of Srebrenica. On December 20, 1999, NATO troops arrested Stanislav Galic, a general who commanded the Bosnian Serb troops who laid siege to the city of Sarajevo,[78] while on April 3, 2000, NATO troops arrested the Bosnian Serb Momcilo Krajisnik, the highest-ranking official yet apprehended by the ICTY. These arrests, while mandated by the Dayton Peace Accords, departed from the NATO policy of trying to avoid conflict by turning a blind eye to indicted war criminals.

The Tribunal for Yugoslavia has begun to aggressively seek custody of those it has indicted, and it has leveled indictments against not only low-level perpetrators such as Tadic, but also those responsible at the highest level. As of August 1999, the tribunal has indicted ninety-one individuals, although six of them have died, and charges have been dropped against eighteen others. The indicted include Radovan Karadžić, Ratko Mladić, and Slobodan Milošević.

The Tribunal for Rwanda, similarly located at the Hague, has also overcome initial difficulties and charges of inefficiency and corruption to begin prosecuting the perpetrators of the genocide. As of August 1999, the ICTR operates with a budget of over $68 million and employs 688 people, and it has issued twenty-eight indictments against forty-eight people, of whom thirty-eight are in custody. Importantly, this tribunal has successfully prosecuted high-ranking Rwandans for the crime of genocide. Jean-Paul Akayesu was found guilty of genocide and crimes against humanity on September 2, 1998, and Jean Kambanda, the former prime minister of Rwanda, was also found guilty of six counts of genocide on May 1, 1998. Both were sentenced to life imprisonment. In 1999, four more individuals were found guilty of genocide and received various sentences. The last was handed down on December 6 to Georges Rutaganda, a former businessman who was the vice president of the *Interahamwe* militia.[79] He was convicted on three counts of genocide and crimes against humanity.[80] These convictions are the first ever for the crime of genocide. This stands in marked contrast to the Tribunal for Yugoslavia, which has not convicted anyone of genocide. Its only convictions have been for war crimes and crimes against humanity. Additionally, the ICTR has successfully prosecuted the man who was the prime minister of Rwanda during the genocide and is considered one of the ringleaders of the killing, while the ICTY has yet to even apprehend any of the leaders of the killing in Bosnia. As the ICTY brings to trial higher-ranking Serbs who bear greater responsibility, however, this may well change. The first prosecutor for the ICTY, Justice Richard Goldstone, explained,

> Our strategy includes the investigation of lower-level persons directly involved in carrying out the crimes in order to build effective cases against the military and civilian leaders who were party to the overall planning and organization of these crimes.[81]

The new government of Rwanda has also implemented a domestic system of genocide trials, which began in 1996. The government trials rank participants by their culpability. The planners and leaders of genocide, as well as notorious killers and torturers, are subject to the full penalty of the law; other killers can reduce their punishment by providing a full confession and information on accomplices; and those who perpetrated other crimes against individuals, or crimes against property, are not subject to criminal penalties.[82] In April of 1998, twenty-one men and one woman were executed after having been found guilty of genocide. They were tied to posts and killed by firing squads in public executions throughout the country.[83]

Prosecutions of war crimes and genocide serve several purposes. Neil J. Kritz writes that

> They can provide victims with a sense of justice and catharsis—a sense that their grievances have been addressed and can more easily be put to rest, rather than smoldering in anticipation of the next round of conflict. In addition they can establish a new dynamic in society, an understanding that aggressors and those who attempt to abuse the rights of others will henceforth be held accountable. Perhaps most important for purposes of long-term reconciliation, this approach makes the statement that specific individuals—not entire ethnic or religious or political groups—committed atrocities for which they need to be held accountable. In so

doing, it rejects the dangerous culture of collective guilt and retribution that often produces further cycles of resentment and violence.[84]

In short, the tribunals not only serve the traditional roles of retribution and deterrence, but play an educational role as well. They remain the best weapon for ensuring a more peaceful future, or, as Peter Maass beautifully sums up, "Peace is not guaranteed by a thick treaty or enforcement troops; it is guaranteed by justice."[85] Whether or not the tribunals and the international criminal courts will fully live up to the expectations of the humanitarian ideals they embody is yet to be seen.

Individual Resistance

Thus far, we have examined the role that various institutions can play in first identifying and then preventing or halting genocidal processes. While this is a necessary and important part of any discussion of genocide, it is not the only problem that this discourse should address. It is important to recognize that the responsibility for making this world safer rests not only with institutions, but with individuals as well. Jonassohn and Björnson make this point eloquently when they write,

> In order to prevent genocides in the future, it is futile to rely exclusively on the United Nations or on its member governments. Instead, it is imperative to educate a generation of citizens who will not be prepared to be passive bystanders to the violation of human rights, but who will actively criticize and/or oppose their governments when they want to engage in such violations.[86]

For genocide to truly become a historical artifact, individuals must take responsibility for their own actions, the actions of their neighbors, and the actions of their government. The history of the twenty-first century has yet to be written. Whether it is inscribed in the blood of innocent victims, or whether we break free of this escalating cycle of killing, depends upon the choices that the citizens of this world make to either resist or cooperate. Israel Charny argues that "To fight genocide, one has to have a conviction that, at no point in history and despite any self-interest, one must never cooperate with any form of mass killing, genocidal massacre, or genocide."[87] Importantly, it is not enough to refrain from participating; one must actively fight against intolerance, hatred, and genocide. Citizens of all societies must refuse to comply with or tolerate political leaders intent on pursuing destructive policies. This is by no means an easy objective, since such a position involves taking a stand against one's nation, community, friends, and family. Nonetheless, it must be done. The reason why this stand must be taken is articulated by one former KGB member who resigned, became an activist, and was ultimately imprisoned. He realized "that human values have supremacy over state ones. From the perspective of the state, I had betrayed it. But I didn't betray myself."[88] Genocide depends upon the participation of many and the acquiescence of others, or, as the Marquis de Custine once wrote, "Tyranny is the handiwork of nations, not the masterpiece of a single man."[89] Without the active and passive complicity of the masses, genocide cannot be perpetrated.

It is important to emphasize that resistance to genocide can be difficult and exceedingly dangerous, but it occurs nonetheless. Some individuals do not turn aside from their fellow humans, even in the face of death. During the genocide in Rwanda a Hutu Catholic lay worker named Félicité Niyitegeka spirited Tutsi refugees across the border. Even though she was warned that the *Interahamwe* militia were aware of her activities, she continued to aid those in need. Eventually, the inevitable happened and she was caught by the militia, along with thirty Tutsis she was hiding and protecting. Perhaps because she was Hutu like them, or because her brother was an officer in the army, the *Interahamwe* told her that she was free to go. Incredibly, she refused and answered that they would stay together in life or in death. In an attempt to force her to renounce her stand, they began to kill the thirty Tutsis one by one. When they were done, she asked them to kill her also, and just before shooting her, the militia member asked her to pray for his soul.[90] The courage of this woman, even in the face of such cruelty, is remarkable and reminds us that ordinary human beings are capable, not only of terrible crimes, but of acts of incredible humanity and heroism.

The example of Dr. Janus Korczak also inspires and teaches. Dr. Korczak was a prominent Polish neurologist, writer, and educator. During the Holocaust, he ran an orphanage for Jewish children in the Warsaw ghetto, where he devoted himself to the care of his little charges. On August 12, 1942, the Nazis ordered all the children to the trains. As a physician, Dr. Korczak could have stayed in the ghetto and stayed alive, at least for a while. Instead, he decided to accompany his children to the gas chambers so that they would not go to their deaths alone and afraid.[91] He sacrificed his own life in order to give comfort to his young charges in the hour of their death. His example also teaches us that virtuous behavior exists even in the most dire of circumstances. With examples such as these, how can anybody choose to acquiesce to the manipulations of cynical, self-serving, and hate-filled politicians?

Lest one be intimidated or cowed by these examples, however, it is also important to recognize that this resistance is accomplished by "ordinary" people. Research on the rescuers of Jews during the Holocaust reveals that they came from all walks of life, and included educated and uneducated people, rich and poor, and young and old. They were not classically heroic individuals, but rather were as flawed and imperfect as the rest of us. Oliner and Oliner assert that

> Living in any society demands submission to its organized patterns and behavioral requirements. Within such dominating structures, the individual often appears to be powerless. The existence of rescuers informs us, however, that individuals are not entirely powerless.[92]

We must remember this power and recognize that we as individuals have the ability to exercise it even in the most difficult of circumstances. At its most fundamental level, genocide is about the choices people make. Adam Hochschild believes that "We all carry in us the embryos both of an executioner and of a teacher or healer; it is the communities we build for ourselves that call forth a little less of the one and a little more of the other."[93] Individuals must choose to embrace humanity and tolerance instead of hatred and intolerance. The future depends upon it. We have seen what the choices of the past have produced, and it is now time to make sure that we learn from those mistakes and do not repeat them.

Notes

Introduction

1. Michael Freeman, "The Theory and Prevention of Genocide," *Holocaust and Genocide Studies* 6 (1991), 185.

2. Sarah Berkowitz, *Where Are My Brothers?* (New York: Helios, 1965), 43.

3. Helen Fein, "Is Sociology Aware of Genocide? Recognition of Genocide in Introductory Sociology Texts in the US, 1947–1977," *Humanity and Society* (1979): 177–193.

4. Zygmunt Bauman, *Modernity and the Holocaust* (Ithaca: Cornell University Press, 1989), 3.

5. Eric Markusen and David Kopf, *The Holocaust and Strategic Bombing: Genocide and Total War in the Twentieth Century* (Boulder: Westview Press, 1995), 3.

6. Herbert Hirsch, *Genocide and the Politics of Memory: Studying Death to Preserve Life* (Chapel Hill: University of North Carolina Press, 1995), 75.

7. Of the social scientists, psychologists have been among the most active in pursuing research on genocide. Since by definition psychologists tend to explain individual processes and motivations, research in this area has focused on examining authoritarian personality types prone to support fascism, individual obedience to authority figures, and internal adaptations such as psychological doubling. More recently, sociologists have entered the debate: Everett Hughes and his notion of "good people" doing "dirty work," Helen Fein's work on definitional development and clarification, and Zygmunt Bauman's ideas on modern rationality and morality and how they have contributed to genocide, to name some of the more prominent examples. For examples of this work see Theodore W. Adorno, Else Frenkel-Brunswik, Daniel J. Levinson, and Nevitt Sanford, *The Authoritarian Personality* (New York: Harper and Row, 1950); Bauman, *Modernity and the Holocaust;* Helen Fein, *Genocide: A Sociological Perspective* (London: Sage Publications, 1993); Everett C. Hughes, "Good People and Dirty Work," *Social Problems* 10 (1962): 3–11; Robert J. Lifton, *The Nazi Doctors: Medical Killing and the Psychology of Genocide* (New York: Basic Books, 1986); Robert J. Lifton and Eric Markusen, *The Genocidal Mentality: Nazi Holocaust and Nuclear Threat* (New York: Basic Books, 1990); Stanley Milgram, *Obedience to Authority* (New York: Harper Torchbooks, 1969).

8. There are a few exceptions to this statement. In recent years David Friedrichs has published theoretical research on state crime that explicitly examines genocide. Similarly, Augustine Brannigan has published a criminological article on the Holocaust, while Margaret Vandiver and L. Edward Day have been effective advocates for criminological attention to this crime. They have, for example, developed a Web site on genocide for scholars, and have been ac-

tive in developing an agenda for genocide research at professional conferences. In a recent book on political crime Hagan addresses genocide, as does Galliher in his criminology text. These examples, while important in their own right, remain the exception to the rule. See Augustine Brannigan, "Criminology and the Holocaust: Xenophobia, Evolution, and Genocide," *Crime and Delinquency* 44 (1998): 257–276; David O. Friedrichs, "Criminological, Sociolegal, and Jurisprudential Dimensions of the Holocaust: A Pedagogical Approach," in *Proceedings of the Fourth Biennial Conference on Christianity and the Holocaust: The Fiftieth Anniversary of the Nuremberg War Crimes Trials: Their Effectiveness and Legacy* (Rider University, 1996); David O. Friedrichs, "Governmental Crime, Hitler and White Collar Crime: A Problematic Relationship," *Caribbean Journal of Criminology and Social Psychology* 1 (1996): 44–63; David O. Friedrichs, ed., *State Crime: Defining, Delineating, and Explaining State Crime* (Dartmouth: Ashgate, 1998); John F. Galliher, *Criminology: Human Rights, Criminal Law, and Crime* (Englewood Cliffs, N.J.: Prentice Hall, 1989); Frank E. Hagan, *Political Crime: Ideology & Criminality* (Boston: Allyn and Bacon, 1997).

9. Max Weber, *The Theory of Social and Economic Organization* (New York: Oxford University Press, 1947), 88.

10. Gregg Barak, "Crime, Criminology, and Human Rights: Toward an Understanding of State Criminality," in *Varieties of Criminology: Readings from a Dynamic Discipline,* ed. Gregg Barak (Westport, Conn.: Praeger, 1994), 253.

11. Gregg Barak, "Newsmaking Criminology: Reflections on the Media, Intellectuals, and Crime," *Justice Quarterly* 5 (1988): 565–587.

12. Ray Surette, *Media, Crime, and Criminal Justice: Images and Realities,* 2nd ed. (Belmont, Calif.: West/Wadsworth, 1998), 63.

13. Roger W. Smith, Eric Markusen, and Robert Jay Lifton, "Professional Ethics and the Denial of Armenian Genocide," *Holocaust and Genocide Studies* 9 (1995), 14.

14. Smith, Markusen, and Lifton, "Professional Ethics," 16.

15. Bruno Bettelheim, *Surviving* (New York: Alfred A. Knopf, 1979), 97.

16. Hirsch, *Genocide and the Politics of Memory,* 158.

17. Samuel Totten and William S. Parsons, "Introduction," in *Century of Genocide: Eyewitness Accounts and Critical Views,* ed. Samuel Totten, William S. Parsons, and Israel W. Charny (New York: Garland Publishing, 1997), xxxi.

18. Peter Hayes, "Introduction," in *Lessons and Legacies: The Meaning of the Holocaust in a Changing World,* ed. Peter Hayes (Evanston: Northwestern University Press, 1991), 16.

19. Frank P. Williams III, "The Demise of the Criminological Imagination: A Critique of Recent Criminology," *Justice Quarterly* 1 (1984): 91–106.

20. Williams, "Demise," 97.

21. Williams, "Demise," 98.

22. For a review of the difficulties in conducting cross-national research on crime, see Dane Archer and Rosemary Gartner, *Violence and Crime in Cross-National Perspective* (New Haven: Yale University Press, 1984).

23.   Frank Chalk and Kurt Jonassohn, *The History and Sociology of Genocide: Analyses and Case Studies* (New Haven: Yale University Press, 1990); Laurence M. Hauptman, *Tribes and Tribulations* (Albuquerque: University of New Mexico Press, 1995); Lyman H. Legters, "The American Genocide," *Policy Studies Journal* 16 (1988): 768–777; David E. Stannard, *American Holocaust: The Conquest of the New World* (New York: Oxford University Press, 1992).

24.   See for example Ward Churchill, *A Little Matter of Genocide: Holocaust and Denial in the Americas: 1492 to the Present* (San Francisco: City Lights Books, 1997).

25.   Ward Churchill, *Indians Are Us? Culture and Genocide in Native North America* (Monroe, Maine: Common Courage Press, 1994).

26.   Alain Destexhe, *Rwanda and Genocide in the Twentieth Century* (New York: New York University Press, 1995), 33.

27.   Marguerite Feitlowitz, *A Lexicon of Terror: Argentina and the Legacies of Torture* (New York: Oxford University Press, 1998).

28.   See for example Susanne Jones, *The Battle for Guatemala: Rebels, Death Squads, and U.S. Power* (Boulder: Westview Press, 1991); Mark Danner, *The Massacre at El Mozote* (New York: Vintage Books, 1993).

29.   David P. Chandler, *Brother Number One: A Political Biography of Pol Pot* (Boulder: Westview Press, 1992); Stan Sesser, *The Lands of Charm and Cruelty: Travels in Southeast Asia* (New York: Vintage Books, 1989).

30.   See for example Churchill, *A Little Matter of Genocide;* Joe Kane, *Savages* (New York: Vintage Books, 1995).

31.   Kenneth D. Tunnell, "Prologue," in *Political Crime in Contemporary America: A Critical Approach,* ed. Kenneth D. Tunnell (New York, Garland Publishing, 1993), 101.

32.   Kenneth D. Tunnell, "Political Crime and Pedagogy: A Content Analysis of Criminology and Criminal Justice Texts," *Journal of Criminal Justice Education* 4 (1993), 101–114.

33.   R. A. Wright and David Friedrichs, "White-Collar Crime in the Criminal Justice Curriculum," *Journal of Criminal Justice Curriculum* 2 (1991): 96–121; Friedrichs, "Governmental Crime."

34.   Markusen and Kopf, *The Holocaust and Strategic Bombing,* 243.

35.   See for example William C. Bailey, "Poverty, Inequality, and City Homicide Rates," *Criminology* 22 (1984): 531–550; Carolyn R. Block, "Race/Ethnicity and Patterns of Chicago Homicide, 1965 to 1981," *Crime and Delinquency* 31 (1985): 104–116; Roland Chilton, "Twenty Years of Homicide and Robbery in Chicago: The Impact of the City's Changing Racial and Age Composition," *Journal of Quantitative Criminology* 3 (1987): 195–214; Leslie W. Kennedy and Robert A. Silverman, "The Elderly Victim of Homicide: An Application of the Routine Activities Approach," *The Sociological Quarterly* 31 (1990): 307–319; Kenneth C. Land, Patricia L. McCall, and Lawrence E. Cohen, "Structural Covariates of Homicide Rates: Are There Any Invariances across Time and Social Space?" *American Journal of Sociology* 95 (1990): 922–963; Steven F. Messner, "Regional Differences in the Economic Correlates of the Urban Homicide

Rate: Some Evidence on the Importance of Cultural Context," *Criminology* 21 (1983): 477–488; Robert N. Parker, "Poverty, Subculture of Violence, and Type of Homicide," *Social Forces* 67 (1989): 983–1007.

36.   See for example Alexander Alvarez, "Trends and Patterns of Justifiable Homicide: A Comparative Analysis," *Violence and Victims* 7 (1992): 347–357; Arnold Binder and Peter Scharf, "Deadly Force in Law Enforcement," *Crime and Delinquency* (1982): 1–23; James J. Fyfe, "Blind Justice: Police Shootings in Memphis," *The Journal of Criminal Law and Criminology* 73 (1982): 421–470; David Jacobs and David Britt, "Inequality and Police Use of Deadly Force: An Empirical Assessment of a Conflict Hypothesis," *Social Problems* 26 (1979): 403–411; Jack Kuykendall, "Trends in the Use of Deadly Force by Police," *Journal of Criminal Justice* 9 (1981): 359–366; William B. Waegel, "How Police Justify the Use of Deadly Force," *Social Problems* 32 (1984): 144–155.

37.   See for example Steven A. Egger, *The Killers among Us: An Examination of Serial Murder and Its Investigation* (Upper Saddle River, N.J.: Prentice Hall, 1998); Eric W. Hickey, *Serial Murderers and Their Victims,* 2nd ed. (Belmont, Calif.: Wadsworth Publishing, 1997); Ronald M. Holmes and James De Burger, *Serial Murder* (Newbury Park, Calif.: Sage Publications, 1988).

38.   See for example Dane Archer, Rosemary Gartner, and M. Beittel, "Homicide and the Death Penalty: A Cross-National Test of a Deterrence Hypothesis," *The Journal of Criminal Law and Criminology* 3 (1983): 991–1013; S. D. Arkin, "Discrimination and Arbitrariness in Capital Punishment: An Analysis of Post-Furman Murder Cases in Dade County, Florida, 1973–1976," *Stanford Law Review* 33 (1980): 75–101; William C. Bailey, "Capital Punishment and Lethal Assaults against Police," *Criminology* 19 (1982): 608–625; William C. Bailey and R. D. Peterson, "Police Killings and Capital Punishment: The Post-Furman Period," *Criminology* 25 (1987): 1–25; William C. Bailey and R. D. Peterson, "Murder, Capital Punishment, and Deterrence: A Review of the Evidence and an Examination of Police Killings," *Journal of Social Issues* 50 (1994): 53–74; William J. Bowers, *Legal Homicide* (Boston: Northeastern University Press, 1984); William J. Bowers and Glenn L. Pierce, "Arbitrariness and Discrimination under Post-Furman Capital Statutes," *Crime and Delinquency* 26 (1980): 563–635; Derral Cheatwood, "Capital Punishment and the Deterrence of Violent Crime in Comparable Counties," *Criminal Justice Review* 18 (1993): 165–181; T. J. Keil and Gennaro F. Vito, "Race, Homicide Severity, and Application of the Death Penalty: A Consideration of the Barnett Scale," *Criminology* 27 (1989): 511–535; Gary Kleck, "Racial Discrimination in Criminal Sentencing: A Critical Evaluation of the Evidence with Additional Evidence on the Death Penalty," *American Sociological Review* 46 (1981): 783–805; R. Lempert, "The Effect of Executions on Homicides: A New Look in an Old Light," *Crime and Delinquency* 29 (1983): 88–115; R. D. Peterson and William C. Bailey, "Murder and Capital Punishment in the Evolving Context of the Post-*Furman* Era," *Social Forces* 66 (1988): 774–807; R. D. Peterson and William C. Bailey, "Felony Murder and Capital Punishment: An Examination of the Deterrence Question," *Criminology* 29 (1991): 367–395; C. D. Phillips, "Exploring Relations among Forms of Social Control: The Lynching and Execution of Blacks in North Carolina, 1889–1918," *Law & Society Review* 21

(1987): 361–374; Michael L. Radelet, "Racial Characteristics and the Imposition of the Death Penalty," *American Sociological Review* 46 (1981): 918–927; Marvin E. Wolfgang and Mark Riedel, "Race, Judicial Discretion, and the Death Penalty," *The Annals of the American Academy of Political and Social Science* 407 (1973): 119–133; H. Zeisel, "Race Bias in the Administration of the Death Penalty: The Florida Experience," *Harvard Law Review* 95 (1981): 456–468.

39.   Piers Beirne and James Messerschmidt, *Criminology,* 2nd ed. (Fort Worth: Harcourt Brace College Publishers, 1995); Alan A. Block, "Violence, Corruption, and Clientelism: The Assassination of Jesús de Galíndez, 1956," *Social Justice* 16 (1989): 64–88; William J. Chambliss, "State-Organized Crime," in *Making Law: The State, the Law, and Structural Contradictions,* ed. William J. Chambliss and Marjorie S. Zatz (Bloomington: Indiana University Press, 1993), 290–314; Mark S. Hamm, "State-Organized Homicide: A Study of Seven CIA Plans to Assassinate Fidel Castro," in *Making Law: The State, the Law, and Structural Contradictions,* ed. William J. Chambliss and Marjorie S. Zatz (Bloomington: Indiana University Press, 1993), 315–343.

40.   James Q. Wilson, *Thinking About Crime* (New York: Basic Books, 1975), 209.

41.   Markusen and Kopf, *The Holocaust and Strategic Bombing,* 1.

1. The Age of Genocide

1.   Richard L. Rubenstein, *The Cunning of History: The Holocaust and the American Future* (New York: Harper Colophon, 1975), 6.

2.   Roger W. Smith, "Human Destructiveness and Politics: The Twentieth Century As an Age of Genocide," in *Genocide and the Modern Age: Etiology and Case Studies of Mass Death,* ed. Isidor Wallimann and Michael N. Dobkowski (New York: Greenwood Press, 1987), 21.

3.   Helen Fein, *Genocide: A Sociological Perspective* (London: Sage Publications, 1993).

4.   In his exhaustive work, Rummel has documented and extrapolated the most likely death tolls of twentieth-century genocides. See R. J. Rummel, *Death by Government* (New Brunswick: Transaction Publishers, 1994); R. J. Rummel, "Democracy, Power, Genocide, and Mass Murder," *Journal of Conflict Resolution* 39 (1995): 3–26.

5.   Omer Bartov, *Murder in Our Midst: The Holocaust, Industrial Killing, and Representation* (New York: Oxford University Press, 1996), 3–4.

6.   Frank Chalk and Kurt Jonassohn, *The History and Sociology of Genocide: Analyses and Case Studies* (New Haven: Yale University Press, 1990); Vahakn N. Dadrian, "The Role of Turkish Physicians in the World War I Genocide of Ottoman Armenians," *Holocaust and Genocide Studies* 1 (1986): 169–192; Vahakn N. Dadrian, "Genocide As a Problem of National and International Law: The World War I Armenian Case and Its Contemporary Legal Ramifications," *The Yale Journal of International Law* 14 (1989): 221–334; Vahakn N. Dadrian, "The Documentation of the World War I Armenian Massacres in

the Proceedings of the Turkish Military Tribunal," *International Journal of Middle East Studies* 23 (1991): 549–576; Vahakn N. Dadrian, *The History of the Armenian Genocide: Ethnic Conflict from the Balkans to Anatolia to the Caucasus* (Providence, R.I.: Berghahn Books, 1995); Robert Melson, "Revolution and Genocide: On the Causes of the Armenian Genocide and the Holocaust," in *The Armenian Genocide: History, Politics, Ethics,* ed. Richard G. Hovannisian (New York: St. Martin's Press, 1992), 80–102.

7.   As if these figures are not extreme enough, recently uncovered information indicates that the numbers may well need to be revised upward. See "Decoded German Reports Shed New Light on the Holocaust," *The Arizona Republic,* November 11, 1996. For historical examinations of the Holocaust see Martin Gilbert, *The Holocaust: A History of the Jews of Europe during the Second World War* (New York: Henry Holt, 1985); Raul Hilberg, *The Destruction of the European Jews* (New York: Holmes and Meier, 1985); Leni Yahil, *The Holocaust: The Fate of European Jewry* (New York: Oxford University Press, 1987).

8.   The T4 program was named for the address of the administrative headquarters of the project: Tiergartenstrasse No. 4, Berlin. Martin Gilbert, *Holocaust Journey: Travelling in Search of the Past* (New York: Columbia University Press, 1997).

9.   In recent years, much has been made of the earlier euthanasia program, with scholars specifically arguing that the groundwork for the Holocaust was laid in the T4 program. See Michael Burleigh, *Death and Deliverance: "Euthanasia" in Germany 1900–1945* (Cambridge: Cambridge University Press, 1994); Michael Burleigh and Wolfgang Wipperman, *The Racial State: Germany 1933–1945* (Cambridge: Cambridge University Press, 1991); Willi Dressen, "Euthanasia," in Eugen Kogon, Hermann Langbein, and Adalbert Rückerl, eds., *Nazi Mass Murder: A Documentary History of the Use of Poison Gas* (New Haven: Yale University Press, 1993): 13–51; Henry Friedlander, *The Origins of Nazi Genocide: From Euthanasia to the Final Solution* (Chapel Hill: University of North Carolina Press, 1995); Daniel Goldhagen, *Hitler's Willing Executioners: Ordinary Germans and the Holocaust* (New York: Alfred A. Knopf, 1996).

10.   Gerald Astor, *The "Last" Nazi: The Life and Times of Dr. Joseph Mengele* (New York: Donald I. Fine, 1985), 106–107.

11.   Both Hilberg and Rubenstein argue that the efficiency of a rational bureaucratic organization, when linked to the depersonalization and dehumanization produced in bureaucracies, was a necessary element in creating an efficient genocidal machine. See Hilberg, *The Destruction of the European Jews;* Rubenstein, *The Cunning of History.*

12.   Robert E. Conot, *Justice at Nuremberg* (New York: Carroll and Graf, 1983); Bradley F. Smith, *Reaching Judgement at Nuremberg* (New York: Basic Books, 1977).

13.   Human Rights Watch, *Slaughter Among Neighbors: The Political Origins of Communal Violence* (New Haven: Yale University Press, 1995); Neil J. Kressel, *Mass Hate: The Global Rise of Genocide and Terror* (New York: Plenum Press, 1996); Gérard Prunier, *The Rwanda Crisis: History of a Genocide* (New York: Columbia University Press, 1995).

14. Human Rights Watch, "Zaire: Forced to Flee: Violence against the Tutsis in Zaire," report for Human Rights Watch/Africa, vol. 8, no. 2 (A) (July 1996).

15. Chalk and Jonassohn, *The History and Sociology of Genocide;* Robert Conquest, *The Harvest of Sorrow: Soviet Collectivization and the Terror-Famine* (New York: Oxford University Press, 1986); Robert W. Thurston, *Life and Terror in Stalin's Russia, 1934–1941* (New Haven: Yale University Press, 1996); James E. Mace, "Genocide by Famine: Ukraine in 1932–1933," in *State Violence and Ethnicity,* ed. Pierre L. van den Berghe (Niwot, Colo.: University Press of Colorado, 1990): 53–71.

16. Human Rights Watch/Middle East, *Iraq's Crime of Genocide: The Anfal Campaign against the Kurds* (New Haven: Yale University Press, 1995).

17. Chalk and Jonassohn, *The History and Sociology of Genocide.*

18. Robert K. Hitchcock and Tara M. Twedt, "Physical and Cultural Genocide of Various Indigenous Peoples," in *Century of Genocide: Eyewitness Accounts and Critical Views,* ed. Samuel Totten, William S. Parsons, and Israel W. Charny (New York: Garland Publishing, 1997): 372–407.

19. Thomas Hobbes, *Leviathan* (New York: Macmillan, 1947 [originally published 1651]), pt. I, ch. 13.

20. Rubenstein, *The Cunning of History,* 7.

21. See for example Herbert Hirsch, *Genocide and the Politics of Memory: Studying Death to Preserve Life* (Chapel Hill: University of North Carolina Press, 1995).

22. Robert Melson, *Revolution and Genocide: On the Origins of the Armenian Genocide and the Holocaust* (Chicago: University of Chicago Press, 1992), 2.

23. See for example Deborah Lipstadt, *Denying the Holocaust: The Growing Assault on Truth and Memory* (New York: Plume, 1993); Steven Katz, *The Holocaust in Historical Context,* vol. 1, *The Holocaust and Mass Death before the Modern Age* (New York: Oxford University Press, 1992); Steven T. Katz, "Ideology, State Power, and Mass Murder/Genocide," in *Lessons and Legacies: The Meaning of the Holocaust in a Changing World,* ed. Peter Hayes (Evanston: Northwestern University Press, 1991), 47–89; Steven T. Katz, "The Uniqueness of the Holocaust: The Historical Dimension," in *Is The Holocaust Unique: Perspectives on Comparative Genocide,* ed. Alan S. Rosenbaum (Boulder: Westview Press, 1996), 19–38.

24. The most eloquent spokesman for this point of view is arguably Elie Wiesel, the noted writer, Holocaust survivor, and Nobel prize winner, who contends that the Holocaust stands outside of history. See Gerd Korman, "The Holocaust in Historical Writing," *Societas* 2 (1972), 15–16.

25. Scholars such as Fred Katz, Ervin Staub, and Robert Melson, to name a few, make essentially the same argument. Fred E. Katz, *Ordinary People and Extraordinary Evil: A Report on the Beguilings of Evil* (Albany: State University of New York Press, 1993); Melson, "Revolution and Genocide"; Ervin Staub, *The Roots of Evil: The Origins of Genocide and Other Group Violence* (Cambridge: Cambridge University Press, 1989).

26. The writings of Primo Levi, Tadeusz Borowski, Haing Ngor, and Rezak

Hukanović come to mind as prime examples of autobiographical writing on genocide.

27. See for example Roy Gutman, *A Witness To Genocide* (New York: Macmillan Books, 1993); David Rieff, *Slaughterhouse: Bosnia and the Failure of the West* (New York: Touchstone Books, 1995).

28. See for example Gilbert, *The Holocaust;* Hilberg, *The Destruction of the European Jews;* Nora Levin, *The Holocaust: The Destruction of European Jewry, 1933–1945* (New York: Shocken Books, 1973).

29. To these can be added the recent Goldhagen thesis, which asserts that the single most powerful cause of the Holocaust was a particular form of racially based hatred of the Jews that he terms "eliminationist antisemitism." His thesis is worth reviewing, since it has generated such a storm of attention and controversy. He argues that the Nazi leadership was able to tap into and mold the pervasive anti-Semitic ideology present in Germany and utilize it for the destruction of European Jewry. For Goldhagen, the Germans' demonized conception of Jews not only provided the stimulus for genocidal policies, but also made ordinary Germans willing to contribute to the genocide. Their stigmatized image of Jews provided a distinguishing, tainted identity that served to set the Jews apart and thus made it easier to victimize them. While Goldhagen's work illustrates well the role of anti-Semitic ideology in providing a powerful impetus to the Holocaust, his argument has some limitations. First, he himself recognizes that the anti-Semitism prevalent throughout Germany was highly abstract. The ideology of hatred was focused against an anonymous "other," not against individual Jews.

I would argue that when confronted with the reality of killing or assisting in the killing of real breathing individuals, victims who were not demonized abstractions but recognizable human beings, many participants had to neutralize internal moral opposition to that act. While the symbolic image of the Jew certainly facilitated murder, it alone cannot account for the social-psychological adjustment that allowed participation. Goldhagen's work is also unable to address the victimization of non-Jewish targets of genocide. While Jews were the primary targets of the Holocaust, they were not its only victims. Homosexuals, Communists, Jehovah's Witnesses, and especially the Sinti and Roma (more commonly known as Gypsies) were all targeted as undesirables and subjected to many of the same horrors visited upon the Jews. As virulent and lethal as "eliminationist antisemitism" was, it alone cannot explain how participants were able to justify the killing of members of these other marginalized groups, who, even though stigmatized and discriminated against, were not subjected to the same intensity and volume of hate ideology.

One final limitation of Goldhagen's argument centers on his assertion that eliminationist antisemitism was unique to German society. The evidence, however, shows that many citizens of other countries collaborated significantly in the process of destruction. While Goldhagen minimizes the role of non-German participants, their frequent assistance suggests that we must look beyond eliminationist antisemitism in our attempts to explain the Holocaust. For a thorough review and critique of Goldhagen's work see Norman G. Finkelstein and Ruth Bettina Birn, *A Nation on Trial: The Goldhagen Thesis and Historical Truth* (New York: Owl Books, 1998).

30. Rummel, *Death by Government*, 17.

31. Rummel, *Death by Government*, 86.

32. Dave Grossman, *On Killing: The Psychological Cost of Learning to Kill in War and Society* (Boston: Little, Brown, 1995), 160.

33. Hilberg, *The Destruction of the European Jews;* Rubenstein, *The Cunning of History.*

34. Max Weber, *The Theory of Social and Economic Organization* (New York: Oxford University Press, 1947).

35. Herbert C. Kelman and V. Lee Hamilton, *Crimes of Obedience: Toward a Social Psychology of Authority and Responsibility* (New Haven: Yale University Press, 1989).

36. Fred Katz, *Ordinary People and Extraordinary Evil,* 25.

37. John J. Macionis, *Sociology,* 5th ed. (Englewood Cliffs, N.J.: Prentice Hall, 1995), 102.

38. Fein, *Genocide,* 36.

39. Herbert C. Kelman, "Violence without Moral Restraint: Reflections on the Dehumanization of Victims and Victimizers," *Journal of Social Issues* 29 (1973): 25–61.

40. Kelman and Hamilton, *Crimes of Obedience,* 16.

41. Stanley Milgram, *Obedience to Authority* (New York: Harper Torchbooks, 1969).

42. Milgram, *Obedience to Authority,* xi.

43. Zygmunt Bauman, *Modernity and the Holocaust* (Ithaca: Cornell University Press, 1989); Christopher R. Browning, *Ordinary Men: Reserve Police Battalion 101 and the Final Solution in Poland* (New York: Aaron Asher Books, 1992); Raul Hilberg, *The Destruction of the European Jews.*

44. Robert J. Lifton, *The Nazi Doctors: Medical Killing and the Psychology of Genocide* (New York: Basic Books, 1986); Robert J. Lifton and Eric Markusen, *The Genocidal Mentality: Nazi Holocaust and Nuclear Threat* (New York: Basic Books, 1990).

45. Lifton, *The Nazi Doctors,* 193.

46. Lifton and Markuson, *The Genocidal Mentality,* 106.

47. Rummel, *Death by Government;* Leo Kuper, *Genocide* (New Haven: Yale University Press, 1981).

48. Michael Freeman, "The Theory and Prevention of Genocide," *Holocaust and Genocide Studies* 6 (1991), 188.

49. Samuel Hynes, *The Soldiers' Tale: Bearing Witness to Modern War* (New York: Penguin Books, 1997), 76.

50. Adolf Eichmann, the architect of the Holocaust, made a very similar statement when he asserted that "One hundred dead are a catastrophe, one million dead are nothing but a statistic" (Alan S. Rosenbaum, *Prosecuting Nazi War Criminals* [Boulder: Westview Press, 1993], 16).

51. Tzvetan Todorov, *Facing the Extreme: Moral Life in the Concentration Camps,* trans. Arthur Denner and Abigail Pollak (New York: Henry Holt, 1996), 161.

52. Stéphane Courtois, "Introduction: The Crimes of Communism," in *The Black Book of Communism: Crimes, Terror, Repression,* ed. Stéphane Courtois et al., trans. Jonathan Murphy, and Mark Kramer (Cambridge: Harvard University Press, 1999), 8.

53. Robert G. L. Waite, "The Holocaust and Historical Explanation," in *Genocide and the Modern Age: Etiology and Case Studies of Mass Death,* ed. Isidor Wallimann and Michael N. Dobkowski (New York: Greenwood Press, 1987), 165.

54. In fact, Nora Levin argues that German Jews were among the most assimilated in the world (Levin, *The Holocaust,* 20).

55. Kressel, *Mass Hate,* 94.

56. Roy Gutman, *A Witness to Genocide;* David Rohde, *Endgame: The Betrayal and Fall of Srebrenica: Europe's Worst Massacre Since World War II* (New York: Farrar, Straus, and Giroux, 1997).

57. Peter Maass, *Love Thy Neighbor: A Story of War* (New York: Vintage Books, 1996), 70.

58. Ed Vulliamy, *Seasons in Hell: Understanding Bosnia's War* (New York: St. Martin's Press, 1994), 65.

59. Todorov, *Facing the Extreme,* 159.

60. Rezak Hukanović, *The Tenth Circle of Hell: A Memoir of Life in the Death Camps of Bosnia* (New York: New Republic Books, 1993), 7.

61. Vulliamy, *Seasons in Hell,* 148.

62. Prunier, *The Rwanda Crisis,* 254.

63. Maass, *Love Thy Neighbor,* 6.

64. David Hackworth, *Hazardous Duty* (New York: Avon Books, 1996), 116.

65. Rieff, *Slaughterhouse,* 105.

66. Bruno Bettelheim, *The Informed Heart* (New York: Free Press, 1966).

67. Todorov, *Facing the Extreme,* 137.

68. Primo Levi, *The Periodic Table,* trans. Raymond Rosenthal (New York: Schocken Books, 1984), 151.

69. Primo Levi, *The Reawakening* (New York: Collier, 1965), 228.

70. For example, in films about the Holocaust, such as *The Bunker, Stalag 17, The Boys from Brazil, Marathon Man,* and *Night of the Generals,* the Nazis are usually portrayed as psychopathic fanatics. An excellent recent example of this is the portrayal of the Nazi camp commander Amon Goeth as a cold-blooded, inhuman psychopath in the film *Schindler's List.*

71. Goldhagen, *Hitler's Willing Executioners.*

72. Hilberg, *The Destruction of the European Jews;* Rubenstein, *The Cunning of History.*

73. Götz Aly, Peter Chroust, and Christian Pross, *Cleansing the Fatherland: Nazi Medicine and Racial Hygiene,* trans. Belinda Cooper (Baltimore: The Johns

Hopkins University Press, 1994); Gert H. Brieger, "The Medical Profession," in *The Holocaust: Ideology, Bureaucracy, and Genocide,* ed. Henry Friedlander and Sybil Milton (Millwood, N.Y.: Kraus International, 1980), 141–150; Burleigh and Wipperman, *The Racial State;* Joachim C. Fest, *The Face of the Third Reich* (New York: Pantheon Books, 1970); Raul Hilberg, *Perpetrators, Victims, Bystanders* (New York: Harper Collins, 1992); Lifton, *The Nazi Doctors;* Richard L. Miller, *Nazi Justiz: Law of the Holocaust* (Westport, Conn.: Praeger, 1995); William E. Seidelman, "Medical Selection: Auschwitz Antecedents and Effluent," *Holocaust and Genocide Studies* 4 (1989): 435–448.

74. James E. Mace, "Soviet Man-Made Famine in the Ukraine," in *Century of Genocide,* ed. Samuel Totten, William S. Parsons, and Israel W. Charny (New York: Garland Publishing, 1997), 83.

75. Adam Hochschild, *The Unquiet Ghost: Russians Remember Stalin* (New York: Penguin Books, 1994), 18.

76. S. L. Jacobs, *Raphael Lemkin's Thoughts on Nazi Genocide* (Lewiston, Maine: Edwin Mellen, 1992), 229.

77. George M. Kren and Leon Rappoport, *The Holocaust and the Crisis of Human Behavior* (New York: Holmes and Meier, 1994), 76.

78. See for example Maass, *Love Thy Neighbor.*

79. Goldhagen, *Hitler's Willing Executioners.*

80. Helen Fein, *Accounting for Genocide: National Responses and Jewish Victimization during the Holocaust* (New York: Free Press, 1979); Hilberg, *Perpetrators, Victims, Bystanders;* Kren and Rappoport, *The Holocaust and the Crisis of Human Behavior;* B. F. Sabrin, ed., *Alliance For Murder: The Nazi-Ukrainian Nationalist Partnership in Genocide* (New York: Sarpedon, 1991).

81. Bauman, *Modernity and the Holocaust,* 20.

82. Kren and Rappoport, *The Holocaust and the Crisis of Human Behavior,* 75.

83. Alfred M. de Zayas, *The Wehrmacht War Crimes Bureau, 1939–1945* (Lincoln: University of Nebraska Press, 1989), 21; Richard L. Rubenstein and J. K. Roth, *Approaches to Auschwitz* (Atlanta: John Knox, 1987), 136.

84. Browning, *Ordinary Men;* Rudolph Höss, *Death Dealer,* ed. Steven Paskuly, trans. Andrew Pollinger (Buffalo, N.Y.: Prometheus, 1992).

85. Rubenstein and Roth, *Approaches to Auschwitz,* 134.

86. Hilberg, *The Destruction of the European Jews,* 1008.

87. Kren and Rappoport, *The Holocaust and the Crisis of Human Behavior,* 71; Rubenstein and Roth, *Approaches to Auschwitz,* 135.

88. Michael A. Sells, *The Bridge Betrayed: Religion and Genocide in Bosnia* (Berkeley: University of California Press, 1996), 74.

89. The speaker is Nedžad Jacupović, who is quoted in Vulliamy, *Seasons in Hell,* 109.

90. Fergal Keane, *Season of Blood: A Rwandan Journey* (New York: Penguin Books, 1995); Philip Gourevitch, *We Wish to Inform You That Tomorrow We Will Be Killed with Our Families* (New York: Farrar, Straus, and Giroux, 1998).

91. Michael Ignatieff, *Blood and Belonging: Journeys into the New Nationalism* (New York: Noonday Press, 1993), 246.

92. Warren K. Thompson, "Ethics, Evil, and the Final Solution," in *Echoes From the Holocaust,* ed. Alan Rosenberg and Gerald E. Myers (Philadelphia: Temple University Press, 1988), 184.

93. Gourevitch, *We Wish to Inform You,* 279.

94. Richard Breitman, *The Architect of Genocide: Himmler and the Final Solution* (New York: Alfred A. Knopf, 1991); Burleigh, *Death and Deliverance;* Burleigh and Wipperman, *The Racial State.*

95. Hilberg, *Perpetrators, Victims, Bystanders,* 132.

96. United States Holocaust Memorial Museum, *Historical Atlas of the Holocaust* (New York: Macmillan Publishing, 1996), 195.

97. United States Holocaust Memorial Museum, *Historical Atlas,* 195.

98. United States Holocaust Memorial Museum, *Historical Atlas,* 195.

99. Maass, *Love Thy Neighbor,* 21.

100. Marguerite Feitlowitz, *A Lexicon of Terror: Argentina and the Legacies of Torture* (New York: Oxford University Press), 149–150.

101. Harvey Wallace, *Victimology: Legal, Psychological, and Social Perspectives* (Boston: Allyn and Bacon, 1998), 264.

102. James M. Glass, *"Life Unworthy of Life": Racial Phobia and Mass Murder in Hitler's Germany* (New York: Basic Books, 1997).

103. Eva Fogelman, *Conscience and Courage: Rescuers of Jews during the Holocaust* (New York: Anchor Books, 1994), 47.

104. Keane, *Season of Blood,* 173.

105. Miklos Nyiszli, *Auschwitz: A Doctor's Eyewitness Account* (New York: Arcade Publishing, 1960).

106. Rohde, *Endgame,* 200.

107. Maass, *Love Thy Neighbor,* 242.

2. A Crime by Any Other Name

1. Herbert Hirsch, *Genocide and the Politics of Memory: Studying Death to Preserve Life* (Chapel Hill: University of North Carolina Press, 1995), 75.

2. Leo Kuper, *Genocide* (New Haven: Yale University Press, 1981), 11.

3. Roger W. Smith, "Human Destructiveness and Politics: The Twentieth Century As an Age of Genocide," in *Genocide and the Modern Age: Etiology and Case Studies of Mass Death,* ed. Isidor Wallimann and Michael N. Dobkowski (New York: Greenwood Press, 1987), 28.

4. B. H. Warmington, *Carthage: A History* (New York: Barnes and Noble Books, 1960), 230.

5. Brian Caven, *The Punic Wars* (New York: Barnes and Noble Books, 1980); Michael Grant, *History of Rome* (New York: Charles Scribner's Sons, 1978);

Polybius, *The Rise of the Roman Empire,* trans. I. Scott-Kilvert (New York: Penguin Books, 1979); Warmington, *Carthage.*

6. Erik Hildinger, *Warriors of the Steppe: A Military History of Central Asia, 500 B.C. to 1700 A.D.* (New York: Sarpedon Press, 1997), 128.

7. Donald R. Morris, *The Washing of the Spears* (New York: Simon and Schuster, 1965); E. A. Ritter, *Shaka Zulu* (New York: Penguin Books, 1955).

8. Morris, *The Washing of the Spears,* 20.

9. Noel Mostert, *Frontiers: The Epic of South Africa's Creation and the Tragedy of the Xhosa People* (New York: Alfred A. Knopf, 1992).

10. Robert Payne, *The Dream and the Tomb: A History of the Crusades* (New York: Dorset Press, 1984), 102–103.

11. John J. Robinson, *Dungeon, Fire, and Sword: The Knights Templar in the Crusades* (New York: M. Evans, 1991); Jonathan Riley-Smith, *The Crusades: A Short History* (New Haven: Yale University Press, 1987).

12. Zoé Oldenbourg, *Massacre at Montségur* (London: Phoenix Giant, 1959).

13. D. M. R. Esson, *The Curse of Cromwell: A History of the Ironside Conquest of Ireland* (Totowa, N.J.: Rowman and Littlefield, 1971).

14. Benson Bobrick, *East of the Sun: The Epic Conquest and Tragic History of Siberia* (New York: Henry Holt, 1992); W. Bruce Lincoln, *The Conquest of a Continent: Siberia and the Russians* (New York: Random House, 1994).

15. Bartolomé De Las Casas, *The Devastation of the Indies: A Brief Account* (Baltimore: The Johns Hopkins University Press, 1974); Laurence M. Hauptman, *Tribes and Tribulations* (Albuquerque: University of New Mexico Press, 1995); David E. Stannard, *American Holocaust: The Conquest of the New World* (New York: Oxford University Press, 1992); Ian K. Steele, *Warpaths: Invasions of North America* (New York: Oxford University Press, 1994).

16. Steele, *Warpaths,* 7.

17. Zygmunt Bauman, *Modernity and the Holocaust* (Ithaca: Cornell University Press, 1989); George M. Kren and Leon Rappaport, *The Holocaust and the Crisis of Human Behavior* (New York: Holmes and Meier, 1994); Richard L. Rubenstein, *The Cunning of History: The Holocaust and the American Future* (New York: Harper and Row Publishers, 1975).

18. Rubenstein, *The Cunning of History,* 6.

19. Bauman, *Modernity and the Holocaust,* 206.

20. Bauman, *Modernity and the Holocaust,* 17.

21. Omer Bartov, *Murder In Our Midst: The Holocaust, Industrial Killing, and Representation* (New York: Oxford University Press, 1996), 34.

22. Paul Fussell, *The Great War and Modern Memory* (New York: Oxford University Press, 1989), 74.

23. Yehuda Bauer, *A History of the Holocaust* (New York: Franklin Watts, 1982), 59.

24. Martin Gilbert, *The First World War: A Complete History* (New York: Henry

Holt, 1994); Alistair Horne, *The Price of Glory: Verdun 1916* (London: Penguin Books, 1962).

25. Horne, *The Price of Glory,* 327.

26. Norbert Elias, *The Civilizing Process: The History of Manners* (New York: Urizen, 1978).

27. See for example many of the chapters in Eric A. Johnson and Eric H. Monkkonen, eds., *The Civilization of Crime: Violence in Town and Country since the Middle Ages* (Urbana: University of Illinois Press, 1996). Many of the authors in this work utilize Norbert Elias's thesis in explaining their findings.

28. See R. J. Rummel, *Death By Government* (New Brunswick: Transaction Publishers, 1994); R. J. Rummel, *China's Bloody Century: Genocide and Mass Murder since 1900* (New Brunswick: Transaction Publishers, 1991).

29. Michael Freeman, "The Theory and Prevention of Genocide," *Holocaust and Genocide Studies* 6 (1991): 185–199; Michael Freeman, "Genocide, Civilization, and Modernity," *British Journal of Sociology* 46 (1995): 207–223.

30. Jack Nusan Porter writes that the word "has been applied to all of the following: 'race mixing' (integration of blacks and non-blacks); drug distribution; methadone programs; the practice of birth control and abortions among Third World people; sterilization and 'Mississippi appendectomies' (tubal ligations and hysterectomies); medical treatment of Catholics; and the closing of synagogues in the Soviet Union. In other words when one needs a catch-all term to describe 'oppression' of one form or another, one often resorts to labeling it 'genocide.' The net result is a debasement of the concept" (Jack Nusan Porter, "Introduction: What is Genocide? Notes toward a Definition," in *Genocide and Human Rights: A Global Anthology,* ed. Jack Nusan Porter [Lanham: University Press of America, 1982], 9–10). Similarly, Helen Fein writes, "The wave of misuse and rhetorical abuse parallels the alphabet: abortion, bisexuality, cocaine addiction, and dieting have also been labeled as examples of genocide—as well as suburbanization" (Helen Fein, "Genocide, Terror, Life Integrity, and War Crimes: The Case for Discrimination," in *Genocide: Conceptual and Historical Dimensions,* ed. George J. Andreopoulos [Philadelphia: University of Pennsylvania Press, 1994], 95). Walter Ezell reports that the term has been used to describe United States involvement in Vietnam, family planning efforts that target African Americans, and even the urban sprawl in Great Britain that threatens to overwhelm traditional English village life (Walter K. Ezell, "Investigating Genocide: A Catalog of Known and Suspected Causes and Some Categories for Comparing Them," in *Remembering the Future: The Impact of the Holocaust on Jews and Christians,* ed. Yehuda Bauer et al., vol. 3 [Oxford: Pergamon Press, 1989], 2881).

31. Michael Ignatieff, *Blood and Belonging: Journeys into the New Nationalism* (New York: Farrar, Straus, and Giroux, 1993), 194.

32. Raphael Lemkin, *Axis Rule in Occupied Europe* (Washington, D.C.: Carnegie Endowment for International Peace, 1944); Rummel, *Death By Government.*

33. Frank Chalk, "Redefining Genocide," in *Genocide: Conceptual and Historical Dimensions,* ed. George J. Andreopoulos (Philadelphia: University of Pennsylvania Press, 1994), 47.

34.   Israel W. Charny, "Toward a Generic Definition of Genocide," in Andreopoulos, *Genocide,* 66.

35.   Roger W. Smith, Eric Markusen, and Robert Jay Lifton, "Professional Ethics and the Denial of Armenian Genocide," *Holocaust and Genocide Studies* 9 (1995): 1–22.

36.   David Stannard, preface to *A Little Matter of Genocide: Holocaust and Denial in the Americas, 1492 to the Present,* by Ward Churchill (San Francisco: City Lights Books, 1997), xvii.

37.   The most outspoken proponent of this position is Steven Katz. See Steven Katz, *The Holocaust in Historical Context,* vol. 1, *The Holocaust and Mass Death before the Modern Age* (New York: Oxford University Press, 1992); Steven T. Katz, "Ideology, State Power, and Mass Murder/Genocide," in *Lessons and Legacies: The Meaning of the Holocaust in a Changing World,* ed. Peter Hayes (Evanston: Northwestern University Press, 1991): 47–89; Steven T. Katz, "The Uniqueness of the Holocaust: The Historical Dimension," in *Is The Holocaust Unique: Perspectives on Comparative Genocide,* ed. Alan S. Rosenbaum (Boulder: Westview Press, 1996): 19–38.

38.   Phillip Lopate, "Resistance to the Holocaust," *Tikkun* 4 (1989), 65.

39.   For a thorough and hard-hitting review of the Particularists' positions and motivations, see Churchill, *A Little Matter of Genocide.*

40.   Helen Fein, "Genocide, Terror, Life Integrity, and War Crimes," 98.

41.   Kuper, *Genocide;* Frank Chalk and Kurt Jonassohn, *The History and Sociology of Genocide: Analyses and Case Studies* (New Haven: Yale University Press, 1990), 24–25.

42.   Kuper, *Genocide,* 22.

43.   Lemkin, *Axis Rule in Occupied Europe,* 79.

44.   Raphael Lemkin, "Genocide As a Crime Under International Law," *American Journal of International Law* 41 (1947), 147.

45.   W. Michael Reisman and Chris T. Antoniou, eds., *The Laws of War: A Comprehensive Collection of Primary Documents on International Laws Governing Armed Conflict* (New York: Vintage Books, 1994), 320.

46.   Michael P. Scharf, *Balkan Justice: The Story behind the First International War Crimes Trial since Nuremberg* (Durham, N.C.: Carolina Academic Press, 1997), 10.

47.   Arnold C. Brackman, *The Other Nuremberg: The Untold Story of the Tokyo War Crimes Trials* (New York: Quill, 1987).

48.   Reisman and Antoniou, *The Laws of War,* 84–86.

49.   Reisman and Antoniou, *The Laws of War,* 84.

50.   Kuper, *Genocide,* 24.

51.   For a review of these arguments see Ervin Staub, *The Roots of Evil: The Origins of Genocide and Other Group Violence* (New York: Cambridge University Press, 1989).

52.   The Kulaks were a political group only in the sense that the term arbitrarily referred to any peasant who might offer real or imagined resistance to forced

collectivization. As the historian Moshe Lewin explained, a Kulak was "he who is declared to be such by the authorities" (Moshe Lewin, *Russian Peasants and Soviet Power* [London: George Allen and Unwin, 1968], 508).

53. Marguerite Feitlowitz, *A Lexicon of Terror: Argentina and the Legacies of Torture* (New York: Oxford University Press, 1998); Tina Rosenberg, *Children of Cain: Violence and the Violent in Latin America* (New York: Penguin Books, 1991).

54. Feitlowitz, *A Lexicon of Terror*, 32.

55. Feitlowitz, *A Lexicon of Terror*, 248.

56. United Nations International Criminal Tribunal for the Former Yugoslavia, *Fact Sheet*, posted on the Web at <http://www.un.org/icty/glance/fact.htm>, accessed March 13, 2000.

57. United Nations International Criminal Tribunal for the Former Yugoslavia, *Fact Sheet.*

58. Kuper, *Genocide*, 39.

59. Kuper, *Genocide*, 14.

60. Chalk and Jonassohn, *The History and Sociology of Genocide*, 10.

61. Vahakn Dadrian, "A Typology of Genocide," *International Review of Modern Sociology* 5 (1975), 204.

62. This phrase was originally used by Michel Foucault, in *Discipline and Punish: The Birth of the Prison* (New York: Vintage Books, 1977), 55.

63. Dadrian, "A Typology of Genocide," 205–211.

64. See for example Helen Fein, *Genocide: A Sociological Perspective* (London: Sage Publications, 1993), 12–13.

65. Robert Melson, *Revolution and Genocide: On the Origins of the Armenian Genocide and the Holocaust* (Chicago: University of Chicago Press, 1992), 26.

66. Melson, *Revolution and Genocide*, 29.

67. Chalk and Jonassohn, *The History and Sociology of Genocide*, 23.

68. See for example Eric Markusen and David Kopf, *The Holocaust and Strategic Bombing: Genocide and Total War in the Twentieth Century* (Boulder: Westview Press, 1995).

69. Fein, *Genocide: A Sociological Perspective.*

70. Fein, *Genocide: A Sociological Perspective*, 24.

71. Fein, *Genocide: A Sociological Perspective*, 25–26.

72. Charny, "Toward a Generic Definition of Genocide," 75. I am constantly struck by the humanity and compassion that is so evident in Charny's writing, and only hope that my work is also informed with such a humane orientation.

73. Charny, "Toward a Generic Definition of Genocide," 74.

74. See for example Fein; Irving Louis Horowitz, *Taking Lives: Genocide and State Power*, 4th ed. (New Brunswick: Transaction Publishers, 1997).

75. Horowitz, *Taking Lives*, 80.

76. Charny, "Toward a Generic Definition of Genocide," 64.

77. Charny, "Toward a Generic Definition of Genocide," 77.

78. Horowitz, *Taking Lives*, 21.

79. Irving Louis Horowitz, *Genocide: State Power and Mass Murder* (New Brunswick: Transaction Publishers, 1976), 42–43. This is an earlier version of his book *Taking Lives: Genocide and State Power*.

80. Rummel, *Death By Government*, 36–37.

81. Rummel, *Death By Government*, 42.

82. Rummel, *Death By Government*, 1–27.

83. Feitlowitz, *A Lexicon of Terror*.

84. Barbara Harff and Ted Robert Gurr, "Toward Empirical Theory of Genocides and Politicides: Identification and Measurement of Cases since 1945," *International Studies Quarterly* 32 (1988): 359–371.

85. Harff and Gurr, "Toward Empirical Theory," 363.

86. For a thorough review of these issues see Andreopoulos, *Genocide*; Chalk and Jonassohn, *The History and Sociology of Genocide*; Fein, *Genocide: A Sociological Perspective*.

87. Rosenberg, *Children of Cain*.

88. Martin Gilbert, *The Holocaust: A History of the Jews of Europe during the Second World War* (New York: Henry Holt, 1985), 202–205.

89. See for example Paul Carell, *Hitler Moves East, 1941–1943* (Winnepeg, Manitoba: J. J. Fedorowicz Publishing, 1991); Ronald Headland, *Messages of Murder: A Study of the Reports of the Einsatzgruppen of the Security Police and the Security Service, 1941–1943* (Rutherford, N.J.: Fairleigh Dickinson University Press, 1992).

90. Eric Markusen, "Genocide and Total War," in Wallimann and Dobkowski, *Genocide and the Modern Age*, 101.

91. Lemkin, *Axis Rule in Occupied Europe*, 79.

92. Daniel Goldhagen, *Hitler's Willing Executioners: Ordinary Germans and the Holocaust* (New York: Alfred A. Knopf, 1996).

93. Neil J. Kressel, *Mass Hate: The Global Rise of Genocide and Terror* (New York: Plenum Press, 1996), 200.

94. Thomas Sowell, "Middleman Minorities," *The American Enterprise*, May/June 1993, 30–41.

95. Robert S. Wistrich, *Antisemitism: The Longest Hatred* (New York: Schocken Books, 1991).

96. Aaron T. Beck, *Prisoners of Hate: The Cognitive Basis of Anger, Hostility, and Violence* (New York: Harper Collins, 1999).

97. Rouben P. Adalian, "The Armenian Genocide," in *Century of Genocide: Eyewitness Accounts and Critical Views*, ed. Samuel Totten, William S. Parsons, and Israel Charny (New York: Garland Publishing, 1997).

98. Aryeh Neier, *War Crimes: Brutality, Genocide, Terror, and the Struggle for Justice* (New York: Times Books, 1998).

99. Rubenstein, *The Cunning of History,* 4.

100. See Katherine Bischoping and Natalie Fingerhut, "Border Lines: Indigenous Peoples in Genocide Studies," *Canadian Review of Sociology and Anthropology* 33 (1996): 481–506; Geoffrey O'Connor, *Amazon Journal: Dispatches from a Vanishing Frontier* (New York: Dutton Books, 1997); Napoleon A. Chagnon, *Yanomamö: The Last Days of Eden* (San Diego: Harcourt Brace Jovanovich, 1992).

101. Yehuda Bauer, "Is The Holocaust Explicable," *Holocaust and Genocide Studies* 5 (1990): 145–155.

102. See for example Michael A. Sells, *The Bridge Betrayed: Religion and Genocide in Bosnia* (Berkeley: University of California Press, 1996); Neier, *War Crimes.*

103. Joel Samaha, *Criminal Law,* 3rd ed. (St. Paul, Minn.: West Publishing, 1990), 93–94.

104. For a review of this issue see Fein, *Genocide: A Sociological Perspective.*

105. Hirsch, *Genocide and the Politics of Memory,* 202.

106. Wallimann and Dobkowski, *Genocide and the Modern Age,* xvi.

107. Samaha, *Criminal Law,* 94.

108. Samaha, *Criminal Law,* 95.

109. Samaha, *Criminal Law,* 95.

110. Kuper, *Genocide,* 34.

111. Gitta Sereny, *Into That Darkness* (London: Andre Deutsch, 1974), 164.

112. Sereny, *Into That Darkness,* 164.

113. See Gregg Barak, "Newsmaking Criminology: Reflections on the Media, Intellectuals, and Crime," *Justice Quarterly* 5 (1988): 565–587.

114. Susan L. Woodward, *Balkan Tragedy: Chaos and Dissolution after the Cold War* (Washington, D.C.: The Brookings Institute, 1995).

115. Laura Silber and Allan Little, *Yugoslavia: Death of a Nation* (New York: Penguin Books, 1997).

116. Steven L. Burg and Paul S. Shoup, *The War in Bosnia-Herzegovina: Ethnic Conflict and International Intervention* (Armonk, N.Y.: M. E. Sharpe, 1999).

117. "CIA Says 'Most Ethnic Cleansing' Done by Serbs," *New York Times,* March 9, 1995.

118. For a thorough discussion of the nature of ethnic cleansing see Andrew Bell-Fialkoff, *Ethnic Cleansing* (New York: St. Martin's Press/Griffin, 1999).

119. Burg and Shoup, *The War in Bosnia-Herzegovina;* Norman Cigar, *Genocide in Bosnia: The Policy of "Ethnic Cleansing"* (College Station: Texas A&M University Press, 1995).

120. Cigar, *Genocide in Bosnia;* Roger Cohen, *Hearts Grown Brutal: Sagas of Sarajevo* (New York: Random House, 1998); Warren Zimmermann, *Origins of a Catastrophe* (New York: Times Books, 1999).

3. Deadly Regimes

1. Roger Smith, "Human Destructiveness and Politics: The Twentieth Century As an Age of Genocide," in *Genocide and the Modern Age: Etiology and Case Studies of Mass Death*, ed. Isidor Wallimann and Michael N. Dobkowski (New York: Greenwood Press, 1987), 21.

2. R. J. Rummel, *Death By Government* (New Brunswick: Transaction Publishers, 1994), 1–2.

3. Robin McDowell, "Pol Pot Shows No Remorse for Cambodian Genocide," *Associated Press*, October, 1997, posted on the Web at <http://www.jrnl.net/news/97/oct/jrn179231097.html>, accessed February 12, 1998.

4. Henry Kamm, *Cambodia: Report from a Stricken Land* (New York: Arcade Publishing, 1998).

5. Nate Thayer, "Second Thoughts for Pol Pot: Fallen Tyrant Defends His Brutal Regime but Now Wants Cambodia Tied to West," *Washington Post*, October 28, 1997.

6. David P. Chandler, *Brother Number One: A Political Biography of Pol Pot* (Boulder: Westview Press, 1992).

7. Irving Louis Horowitz, *Taking Lives: Genocide and State Power*, 4th ed. (New Brunswick: Transaction Publishers, 1997), 36.

8. Bruce D. Porter, *War and the Rise of the State: The Military Foundations of Modern Politics* (New York: Free Press, 1994), 5.

9. Horowitz, *Taking Lives*, 149.

10. While I prefer to rely on the term "state crime," a wide range of alternative terminology has developed among scholars of crime. Governmental crime, governmental lawlessness, official deviance and misconduct, crimes of obedience, legal crimes, human rights crimes, political crime, and ideological crime are all often used synonymously with each other and with state crime. See for example Jeffrey Ian Ross, "Controlling State Crime: Toward an Integrated Structural Model," in *Controlling State Crime: An Introduction*, ed. Jeffrey Ian Ross (New York: Garland Publishing, 1995).

11. R. Brian Ferguson and Neil L. Whitehead, eds., *War in the Tribal Zone: Expanding States and Indigenous Warfare* (Santa Fe: School of American Research Press, 1992), 6.

12. David Brown, *The State and Ethnic Politics in South-East Asia* (London: Routledge, 1994).

13. Porter, *War and the Rise of the State*.

14. Daniel Papp, *Contemporary International Relations: Frameworks for Understanding*, 4th ed. (New York: Macmillan College Publishing, 1994), 29–30; James Lee Ray, *Global Politics*, 4th ed. (Boston: Houghton Mifflin, 1990), 185–186.

15. Porter, *War and the Rise of the State*, 1.

16. Anthony Giddens, *The Nation-State and Violence: A Contemporary Critique*

of Historical Materialism, vol. 2 (Berkeley: University of California Press, 1985), 20.

17. Pierre van den Berghe, ed., *State Violence and Ethnicity* (Niwot, Colo.: University Press of Colorado, 1990), 1.

18. Porter, *War and the Rise of the State,* 28.

19. Kamm, *Cambodia,* 152.

20. Ward Churchill, *A Little Matter of Genocide: Holocaust and Denial in the Americas, 1492 to the Present* (San Francisco: City Lights Books, 1997), 363–392; Francis A. Boyle, "The Hypocrisy and Racism behind the Formulation of U.S. Human Rights Foreign Policy: In Honor of Clyde Ferguson," *Social Justice* 16 (1989), 71–93.

21. Churchill, *A Little Matter of Genocide,* 385.

22. Churchill, *A Little Matter of Genocide,* 387.

23. Roger Cohen, *Hearts Grown Brutal: Sagas of Sarajevo* (New York: Random House, 1998), 187.

24. Warren Zimmermann, *Origins of a Catastrophe* (New York: Times Books, 1999), 74.

25. Cohen, *Hearts Grown Brutal,* 192–193.

26. Cohen, *Hearts Grown Brutal,* 193.

27. Dusko Doder and Louise Branson, *Milosevic: Portrait of a Tyrant* (New York: Free Press, 1999), 118.

28. Porter, *War and the Rise of the State,* 123.

29. Joseph R. Strayer, *On the Medieval Origins of the Modern State* (Princeton: Princeton University Press, 1970).

30. Hugh Seton-Watson, *Nations and States: An Enquiry into the Origins of Nations and the Politics of Nationalism* (Boulder: Westview Press, 1977), 465.

31. Michael Ignatieff, *Blood and Belonging: Journeys into the New Nationalism* (New York: The Noonday Press, 1993), 5.

32. John T. Rourke, *International Politics on the World Stage,* 2nd ed. (Guilford, Conn.: Dushkin Publishing Group, 1989), 109.

33. Benedict Anderson, *Imagined Communities: Reflections on the Origin and Spread of Nationalism* (London: Verso, 1983).

34. Ernest Gellner, *Thought and Change* (London: Weidenfeld and Nicholson, 1964), 169.

35. H. F. Stein, "The International and Group Milieu of Ethnicity: Identifying Generic Group Dynamic Issues," *Canadian Review of Studies in Nationalism* 17 (1990), 109.

36. This Freudian concept is discussed in Ignatieff, *Blood and Belonging,* 21–28.

37. Ignatieff, *Blood and Belonging,* 22.

38. Bogdan Denitch, *Ethnic Nationalism: The Tragic Death of Yugoslavia* (Minneapolis: University of Minnesota Press, 1994), 29.

39. See Philip Gourevitch, *We Wish to Inform You That Tomorrow We Will Be Killed with Our Families: Stories from Rwanda* (New York: Farrar, Straus, and Giroux, 1998).

40. Gerard Prunier, *The Rwanda Crisis: History of a Genocide* (New York: Columbia University Press, 1995), 249.

41. Solomon Perel, *Europa, Europa,* trans. Margot Bettauer Denbo (New York: John Wiley and Sons, 1997), 93–97.

42. See for example Michael Burleigh and Wolfgang Wippermann, *The Racial State: Germany 1933–1945* (Cambridge: Cambridge University Press, 1991); James M. Glass, *"Life Unworthy of Life": Racial Phobia and Mass Murder in Hitler's Germany* (New York: Basic Books, 1997); Daniel Goldhagen, *Hitler's Willing Executioners: Ordinary Germans and the Holocaust* (New York: Alfred A. Knopf, 1996).

43. Kamm, *Cambodia.*

44. Branimir Anzulovic, *Heavenly Serbia: From Myth to Genocide* (New York: New York University Press, 1999).

45. Catherine Samary, *Yugoslavia Dismembered,* trans. Peter Drucker (New York: Monthly Review Press, 1995), 39.

46. Herbert Hirsch, *Genocide and the Politics of Memory: Studying Death to Preserve Life* (Chapel Hill: University of North Carolina Press, 1995), 9.

47. Vamik Volkan, *Blood Lines: From Ethnic Pride to Ethnic Terrorism* (New York: Farrar, Straus, and Giroux, 1997), 48–49.

48. Cohen, *Hearts Grown Brutal,* 127.

49. Tim Judah, *The Serbs: History, Myth and the Destruction of Yugoslavia* (New Haven: Yale University Press, 1997).

50. Norman Cigar, *Genocide in Bosnia: The Policy of "Ethnic Cleansing"* (College Station: Texas A&M University Press, 1995).

51. E. J. Hobsbawm, *Nations and Nationalism since 1780: Programme, Myth, Reality,* 2nd ed. (Cambridge: Cambridge University Press, 1990), 12.

52. Hirsch, *Genocide and the Politics of Memory,* 164.

53. Cohen, *Hearts Grown Brutal,* 183.

54. See for example Judah, *The Serbs,* 212, and Cohen, *Hearts Grown Brutal.*

55. Chandler, *Brother Number One;* Kamm, *Cambodia;* Ben Kiernan, *The Pol Pot Regime: Race, Power, and Genocide in Cambodia under the Khmer Rouge, 1975–79* (New Haven: Yale University Press, 1996).

56. Jean-Louis Margolin, "Cambodia: The Country of Disconcerting Crimes," in *The Black Book of Communism: Crimes, Terror, Repression,* ed. Stéphane Courtois et al., trans. Jonathan Murphy and Mark Kramer (Cambridge: Harvard University Press, 1999), 616.

57. Rourke, *International Politics.*

58. Rourke, *International Politics,* 145–146.

59. Helen Fein, "Accounting for Genocide after 1945: Theories and Some Findings," *International Journal on Group Rights* 1 (1993), 98.

60. Human Rights Watch/Middle East, *Iraq's Crime of Genocide: The Anfal Campaign against the Kurds* (New Haven: Yale University Press, 1995); Michael Kelly, *Martyrs' Day: Chronicle of a Small War* (New York: Random House, 1993).

61. Samary, *Yugoslavia Dismembered,* 90.

62. Zimmermann, *Origins of a Catastrophe,* 237.

63. David Held, *Political Theory and the Modern State* (Stanford: Stanford University Press, 1984).

64. Rummel, *Death by Government,* 13.

65. Dwight MacDonald, quoted in Tzvetan Todorov, *Facing the Extreme: Moral Life in the Concentration Camps,* trans. Arthur Denner and Abigail Pollak (New York: Metropolitan Books, 1996), 123.

66. For example, Eric Markusen and David Kopf, *The Holocaust and Strategic Bombing: Genocide and Total War in the Twentieth Century* (Boulder: Westview Press, 1995).

67. See for example Dane Archer and Rosemary Gartner, *Violence and Crime in Cross-National Perspective* (New Haven: Yale University Press, 1984).

68. See Markusen and Kopf, *The Holocaust and Strategic Bombing;* Ronald Schaffer, *Wings of Judgement: American Bombing in World War II* (New York: Oxford University Press, 1985).

69. Markusen and Kopf, *The Holocaust and Strategic Bombing,* 1–2.

70. Porter, *War and the Rise of the State,* 19.

71. For an excellent discussion of the role of history in the creation of the violence in the former Yugoslavia see Judah, *The Serbs.*

72. Eric Markusen, "Genocide and Warfare," in *Genocide, War, and Human Survival,* ed. Charles B. Strozier and Michael Flynn (Lanham, Md.: Rowman and Littlefield, 1996), 78.

73. For discussions of social disorganization theory see Frank P. Williams III and Marilyn D. McShane, *Criminological Theory,* 2nd ed. (Englewood Cliffs, N.J.: Prentice Hall, 1994); Ronald L. Akers, *Criminological Theories: Introduction and Evaluation* (Los Angeles: Roxbury Publishing, 1994).

74. Markusen, "Genocide and Warfare."

75. Rummel, *Death by Government.*

76. See Daniel Chirot, *Modern Tyrants: The Power and Prevalence of Evil in Our Age* (Princeton: Princeton University Press, 1994); Courtois et al., *The Black Book of Communism.*

77. Rummel, *Death by Government.*

78. Rummel, *Death by Government,* 1.

79. Ervin Staub, *The Roots of Evil: The Origins of Genocide and Other Group Violence* (Cambridge: Cambridge University Press, 1989), 47.

80. Archer and Gartner, *Violence and Crime,* 94.

81. This perspective is often termed "moral functionalist."

82. Austin T. Turk, "Law as a Weapon in Social Conflict," *Social Problems* 23 (1976), 279–280.

83. Turk, "Law As a Weapon," 280.

84. Martin Gilbert, *The Holocaust: A History of the Jews of Europe during the Second World War* (New York: Henry Holt, 1985), 32.

85. Karl A. Schleunes, *The Twisted Road to Auschwitz: Nazi Policy toward German Jews, 1933–1939* (Urbana: University of Illinois Press, 1990), 96.

86. Samuel Totten, William S. Parsons, and Israel W. Charny, eds., *Century of Genocide: Eyewitness Accounts and Critical Views* (New York: Garland Publishing, 1997), 337.

87. David Rieff, *Slaughterhouse: Bosnia and the Failure of the West* (New York: Touchstone Books, 1995).

88. Tom Gjelten, *Sarajevo Daily: A City and Its Newspaper under Siege* (New York: Harper Collins, 1995); Ed Vulliamy, *Seasons in Hell: Understanding Bosnia's War* (New York: St. Martin's Press, 1994).

89. Horowitz, *Taking Lives,* 168.

90. Ronald Headland, *Messages of Murder: A Study of the Reports of the Einsatzgruppen of the Security Police and the Security Service, 1941–1943* (Rutherford, N.J.: Fairleigh Dickinson University Press, 1992), 11.

91. Heinz Höhne, *The Order of the Death's Head: The Story of Hitler's SS,* trans. Richard Barry (London: Pan Books, 1969).

92. Cohen, *Hearts Grown Brutal.*

93. Judah, *The Serbs.*

94. Jan Willem Honig and Norbert Both, *Srebrenica: Record of a War Crime* (New York: Penguin Books, 1996); David Rohde, *Endgame: The Betrayal and Fall of Srebrenica: Europe's Worst Massacre since World War II* (New York: Farrar, Straus, and Giroux, 1997).

95. Goldhagen, *Hitler's Willing Executioners,* 11.

96. Raul Hilberg, *The Destruction of the European Jews* (New York: Holmes and Meier, 1985), 138.

97. See for example Joseph Borkin, *The Crime and Punishment of I. G. Farben* (New York: Free Press, 1978); Yisrael Gutman and Michael Berenbaum, eds., *Anatomy of the Auschwitz Death Camp* (Bloomington: Indiana University Press, 1994).

98. Judah, *The Serbs,* 242.

99. Vulliamy, *Seasons in Hell,* 130.

100. Cigar, *Genocide in Bosnia,* 83.

101. Gjelten, *Sarajevo Daily,* 137.

102. Noel Malcolm, *Bosnia: A Short History* (New York: New York University Press, 1996), 226.

103. Aryeh Neier, *War Crimes: Brutality, Genocide, Terror, and the Struggle for Justice* (New York: Times Books, 1998), 152–153.

104. Chuck Sudetic, *Blood and Vengeance* (New York: W. W. Norton, 1998), 155.

105. Gourevitch, *We Wish to Inform You,* 115.

106. Prunier, *The Rwanda Crisis,* 248.

107. Christopher Simpson, *The Splendid Blond Beast: Money, Law, and Genocide in the Twentieth Century* (Monroe, Maine: Common Courage Press, 1995), 29.

108. Marguerite Feitlowitz, *A Lexicon of Terror: Argentina and the Legacies of Torture* (New York: Oxford University Press, 1998).

109. Turk, "Law As a Weapon," 280.

110. Jeff Ferrell, "Confronting the Agenda of Authority: Critical Criminology, Anarchism, and Urban Graffiti," in *Varieties of Criminology: Readings from a Dynamic Discipline,* ed. Gregg Barak (Westport, Conn.: Praeger, 1994), 162.

111. Frank E. Hagan, *Political Crime: Ideology and Criminality* (Boston: Allyn and Bacon, 1997), 1.

112. Ray Surette, *Media, Crime, and Criminal Justice: Images and Realities,* 2nd ed. (Belmont, Calif.: West/Wadsworth Publishing, 1998).

113. Neil J. Kressel, *Mass Hate: The Global Rise of Genocide and Terror* (New York: Plenum Press, 1996), 200–201.

114. See for example Gourevitch, *We Wish to Inform You,* and Kressel, *Mass Hate.*

115. Cohen, *Hearts Grown Brutal,* 154.

116. Milan Milošević, "The Media Wars," in *Yugoslavia's Ethnic Nightmare: The Inside Story of Europe's Unfolding Ordeal,* ed. Jasminka Udovički and James Ridgeway (New York: Lawrence Hill Books, 1995), 107.

117. Robert D. Kaplan, *The Ends of the Earth: A Journey to the Frontiers of Anarchy* (New York: Vintage Books, 1996), 34.

118. Kressel, *Mass Hate,* 113.

119. Peter Maass, *Love Thy Neighbor: A Story of War* (New York: Vintage Books, 1996), 113–114.

120. Maass, *Love Thy Neighbor,* 229.

121. Hannah Arendt, *Eichmann in Jerusalem: A Report on the Banality of Evil* (New York: Penguin Books, 1964), 268.

122. Herbert C. Kelman and V. Lee Hamilton, *Crimes of Obedience: Toward a Social Psychology of Authority and Responsibility* (New Haven: Yale University Press, 1989), 46.

123. Gourevitch, *We Wish to Inform You,* 123.

124. Archer and Gartner, *Violence and Crime,* 63.

125. David Aikman, "O Nationalism! Yugoslavia Shows How Ancient Tensions Can Suddenly Boil Over," *Time,* October 24, 1988, 46–49.

126. Russell Watson, with Margaret Garrard Warner, Douglas Waller, Rod Nordland, and Karen Breslau, "Ethnic Cleansing," *Newsweek,* August 17, 1992, 18.

127. Rabia Ali and Lawrence Lifschultz, "Why Bosnia?" *Monthly Review* 45 (1994), 5.

128. Hagan, *Political Crime,* 31.

129. Ignatieff, *Blood and Belonging,* 21.

130. Cigar, *Genocide in Bosnia,* 12–13.

131. Maass, *Love Thy Neighbor,* 205.

132. Christopher made these remarks on the television show *Face the Nation.* See Cohen, *Hearts Grown Brutal,* 242–243.

133. Michael A. Sells, *The Bridge Betrayed: Religion and Genocide in Bosnia* (Berkeley: University of California Press, 1996), 124.

134. See Roy Gutman, *A Witness to Genocide* (New York: Macmillan Books, 1993), xxxii.

135. For an excellent overview of these factors see Cigar, *Genocide in Bosnia;* Laura Silber and Allan Little, *Yugoslavia: Death of a Nation* (New York: Penguin Books, 1997).

136. See for example Udovički and Ridgeway, *Yugoslavia's Ethnic Nightmare;* Silber and Little, *Yugoslavia.*

137. Maass, *Love Thy Neighbor,* 28.

138. Cigar, *Genocide in Bosnia,* 4.

139. Cigar, *Genocide in Bosnia,* 13.

140. Gutman, *A Witness to Genocide,* 157–163.

141. Cohen, *Hearts Grown Brutal,* 205.

142. John F. Burns, "Nationalist Leaders Twist History to Advance Their Own Aims," in *Macmillan Atlas of War and Peace* (New York: Macmillan, 1996), 4–5; Cohen, *Hearts Grown Brutal.*

143. Cohen, *Hearts Grown Brutal,* 192.

144. Cohen, *Hearts Grown Brutal.*

145. See for example Cigar, *Genocide in Bosnia;* Rieff, *Slaughterhouse.*

146. Doder and Branson, *Milosevic,* 101.

147. Doder and Branson, *Milosevic,* 102.

148. Judah, *The Serbs.*

149. Marguerite Michaels, "Central Africa: Descent into Mayhem," *Time,* April 18, 1994, posted on the Web at <http://www.time.com/time/magazine/archive/1994/940418/940418.centralafrica.html>, accessed May 31, 2000; Marguerite Michaels, "Rwanda: Streets of Slaughter," *Time,* April 25, 1994, posted on the Web at <http://www.time.com/time/magazine/archive/1994/940425/940425.rwanda.html>, accessed May 31, 2000.

150. Gourevitch, *We Wish to Inform You,* 59.

151. Rakiya Omaar and Alex de Waal, "U.S. Complicity by Silence: Genocide in Rwanda," *Covert Action Quarterly,* posted on the Web at <http://caq.com/CAQ52RW2.html>, accessed May 31, 2000.

152. Gourevitch, *We Wish to Inform You.*

153. Fergal Keane, *Season of Blood: A Rwandan Journey* (New York: Penguin Books, 1995), 8.

154. Rene Lemarchand, "The Rwanda Genocide," in Totten, Parsons, and Charny, *Century of Genocide*, 409.

155. Keane, *Season of Blood*, 24.

156. See for example Gourevitch, *We Wish to Inform You*; Keane, *Season of Blood*; Lemarchand, "The Rwanda Genocide"; Prunier, *The Rwanda Crisis.*

157. *Frontline*, "The Triumph of Evil," transcript posted on the Web at <http://www.pbs.org/wgbh/pages/frontline/shows/evil/interviews/marchal.html>, accessed April 8, 2000.

158. Lemarchand, "The Rwanda Genocide."

159. Rupert Butler, *An Illustrated History of the Gestapo* (Osceola, WI.: Motorbooks International, 1992).

160. For an excellent discussion of the Wannsee Conference see Gilbert; Leni Yahil, *The Holocaust: The Fate of European Jewry* (New York: Oxford University Press, 1987).

161. John Mendelsohn, ed., *The Holocaust: Selected Documents in Eighteen Volumes*, vol. 11, *The Wansee Protocol and a 1944 Report on Auschwitz by the Office of Strategic Services* (New York: Garland Publishing, 1982), 19.

162. Gilbert, *The Holocaust*, 283.

163. Mendelsohn, *The Holocaust*, 21.

4. Lethal Cogs

1. Stanley Milgram, *Obedience to Authority* (New York: Harper Torchbooks, 1969), 188.

2. Gerald E. Markle, *Meditations of a Holocaust Traveler* (Albany: State University of New York Press, 1995), 67.

3. C. P. Snow, "Either-Or," *Progressive* 24 (1961), 24.

4. Gerald Astor, *The "Last" Nazi: The Life and Times of Dr. Joseph Mengele* (New York: Donald I. Fine, 1985), 175.

5. Lord Russell of Liverpool, *The Trial of Adolf Eichmann* (London: Heinemann, 1962), 4–7.

6. See Hannah Arendt, *Eichmann in Jerusalem: A Report on the Banality of Evil* (New York: Penguin Books, 1964).

7. "Eichmann's Final Plea," in *In His Own Words: The Trial of Adolf Eichmann*, a Web site accompanying a documentary produced by ABC News Productions for the Public Broadcasting System. Premiered April 30, 1997. Posted on the Web at <http://www.pbs.org/eichmann/ownwords.htm>, accessed April 8, 2000.

8. See for example Jochen Von Lang with Claus Sibyll, eds., *Eichmann Interro-*

gated: *Transcripts from the Archives of the Israeli Police,* trans. Ralph Manheim (New York: Da Capo Press, 1999).

9. Eugenia Semyonovna Ginzburg, *Journey into the Whirlwind,* trans. Paul Stevenson and Max Hayward (New York: Harcourt, 1967), 171.

10. Vasily Grossman, *Forever Flowing,* trans. Thomas P. Whitney (New York: Harper and Row, 1972), 193.

11. Russell, *The Trial of Adolf Eichmann,* 9.

12. Henry L. Feingold, "How Unique is the Holocaust?" in *Genocide: Critical Issues of the Holocaust,* ed. Alex Grobman and Daniel Landes (Los Angeles: The Simon Wiesenthal Centre, 1983), 398.

13. Raul Hilberg, *The Destruction of the European Jews* (New York: Holmes and Meier, 1985), 994.

14. Hilberg, *The Destruction of the European Jews;* Richard L. Rubinstein, *The Cunning of History: The Holocaust and the American Future* (New York: Harper Colophon, 1975).

15. Hilberg, *The Destruction of the European Jews,* 1011.

16. See for example Vahakn N. Dadrian, *The History of the Armenian Genocide: Ethnic Conflict from the Balkans to Anatolia to the Caucasus* (Providence, R.I.: Berghahn Books, 1995).

17. Rouben P. Adalian, "The Armenian Genocide," in *Century of Genocide: Eyewitness Accounts and Critical Views,* ed. Samuel Totten, William S. Parsons, and Israel W. Charny (New York: Garland Publishing, 1997), 41–77.

18. The CUP (Committee of Union and Progress) was the ruling political clique in Turkey, known in the West as the Young Turks. Adalian, "The Armenian Genocide," 50.

19. Richard G. Hovannisian, "Etiology and Sequelae of the Armenian Genocide," in *Genocide: Conceptual and Historical Dimensions,* ed. George J. Andreopoulos (Philadelphia: University of Pennsylvania Press, 1994), 111–140; Donald E. Miller and Lorna Touryan Miller, *Survivors: An Oral History of the Armenian Genocide* (Berkeley: University of California Press, 1993).

20. Fred E. Katz, *Ordinary People and Extraordinary Evil: A Report on the Beguilings of Evil* (Albany: State University of New York Press, 1993), 11.

21. Katherine M. Jamieson, *The Organization of Corporate Crime: Dynamics of Antitrust Violation* (Thousand Oaks, Calif.: Sage Publications, 1994), 3.

22. "Eichmann's Final Plea."

23. Lang with Sibyll, *Eichmann Interrogated.*

24. Both are quoted in Arendt, *Eichmann in Jerusalem,* 127.

25. Philip Gourevitch, *We Wish to Inform You That Tomorrow We Will Be Killed with Our Families: Stories from Rwanda* (New York: Farrar, Straus, and Giroux, 1998), 309.

26. Tom Gjelten, *Sarajevo Daily: A City and Its Newspaper under Siege* (New York: Harper Collins, 1995), 145.

27. Michael P. Scharf, *Balkan Justice: The Story behind the First International War Crimes Trial since Nuremberg* (Durham, N.C.: Carolina Academic Press, 1997), 134.

28. Michael A. Sells, *The Bridge Betrayed: Religion and Genocide in Bosnia* (Berkeley: University of California Press, 1996), 73.

29. Neil J. Kressel, *Mass Hate: The Global Rise of Genocide and Terror* (New York: Plenum Press, 1996), 112.

30. Gourevitch, *We Wish to Inform You*, 307.

31. Heinz Höhne, *The Order of the Death's Head: The Story of Hitler's SS,* trans. Richard Barry (London: Pan Books, 1969).

32. Ben Kiernan, *The Pol Pot Regime: Race, Power, and Genocide in Cambodia under the Khmer Rouge, 1975–79* (New Haven: Yale University Press, 1996); Kenneth M. Quinn, "The Pattern and Scope of Violence," in *Cambodia 1975–1978: Rendezvous with Death,* ed. Karl D. Jackson (Princeton: Princeton University Press, 1989), 179–208.

33. Elizabeth Becker, *When the War Was Over: Cambodia and the Khmer Rouge Revolution* (New York: Public Affairs, 1998), 256.

34. Kressel, *Mass Hate.*

35. Gourevitch, *We Wish to Inform You*, 93; Kressel, *Mass Hate,* 111.

36. Roger Cohen, *Hearts Grown Brutal: Sagas of Sarajevo* 11 (New York: Random House, 1998), 11; Gjelten, *Sarajevo Daily,* 88–90.

37. Miller and Miller, *Survivors,* 43.

38. Richard Holmes, *Acts of War: The Behavior of Men in Battle* (New York: Free Press, 1985), 36.

39. Cohen, *Hearts Grown Brutal,* 410.

40. Kressel, *Mass Hate,* 111.

41. Richard A. Gabriel, *Military Psychiatry: A Comparative Perspective* (New York: Greenport Press, 1986).

42. Dave Grossman, *On Killing: The Psychological Cost of Learning to Kill in War and Society* (Boston: Little, Brown, 1995), 150; see also Holmes, *Acts of War;* John Keegan and Richard Holmes, *Soldiers: A History of Men in Battle* (New York: Elisabeth Sifton Books, 1986).

43. Cohen, *Hearts Grown Brutal,* 135–136.

44. Roy Gutman, *A Witness To Genocide* (New York: Macmillan Books, 1993), 66.

45. Ervin Staub, *The Roots of Evil: The Origins of Genocide and Other Group Violence* (Cambridge: Cambridge University Press, 1989), 130.

46. Christopher R. Browning, *Ordinary Men: Reserve Police Battalion 101 and the Final Solution in Poland* (New York: Aaron Asher Books, 1992), 57.

47. Staub, *The Roots of Evil,* 130.

48. Ernst Klee, Willi Dressen, and Volker Riess, eds., *The Good Old Days: The Holocaust As Seen by Its Perpetrators and Bystanders* (New York: Free Press, 1988), 78.

49. Tzvetan Todorov, *Facing the Extreme: Moral Life in the Concentration Camps,*

trans. Arthur Denner and Abigail Pollak (New York: Metropolitan Books, 1996), 165.

50.   Milgram, *Obedience to Authority.*

51.   See for example Irving Louis Horowitz, *Taking Lives: Genocide and State Power,* 4th ed. (New Brunswick: Transaction Publishers, 1997), 42.

52.   Holmes, *Acts of War,* 33.

53.   Milgram, *Obedience to Authority,* 188.

54.   Robert E. Conot, *Justice at Nuremberg* (New York: Carrol and Graf, 1983), 238.

55.   Christopher Simpson, *The Splendid Blond Beast: Money, Law, and Genocide in the Twentieth Century* (Monroe, Maine: Common Courage Press, 1995), 78.

56.   Gourevitch, *We Wish to Inform You,* 93.

57.   Ed Vulliamy, *Seasons in Hell: Understanding Bosnia's War* (New York: St. Martin's Press, 1994), 193.

58.   Gutman, *A Witness to Genocide,* 50.

59.   Sells, *The Bridge Betrayed.*

60.   Erna Paris, *Unhealed Wounds: France and the Klaus Barbie Affair* (New York: Grove Press), 42.

61.   Norman Cigar, *Genocide in Bosnia: The Policy of "Ethnic Cleansing"* (College Station: Texas A&M University Press, 1995), 65.

62.   Kressel, *Mass Hate,* 112.

63.   Staub, *The Roots of Evil,* 45.

64.   See chapter 11, "Bureaucracy," in Max Weber, *Economy and Society,* ed. Guenther Roth and Claus Wittich (Berkeley: University of California Press, 1978).

65.   Weber, *Economy and Society,* 973.

66.   Weber, *Economy and Society,* 975.

67.   Ralph P. Hummel, *The Bureaucratic Experience,* 3rd ed. (New York: St. Martin's Press, 1987), 6.

68.   Fred Katz, *Ordinary People and Extraordinary Evil,* 79.

69.   Hilberg, *The Destruction of the European Jews;* Rubenstein, *The Cunning of History.*

70.   Claude Lanzmann, *Shoah: An Oral History of the Holocaust* (New York: Pantheon Books, 1985), 135.

71.   Herbert C. Kelman and V. Lee Hamilton, *Crimes of Obedience: Toward a Social Psychology of Authority and Responsibility* (New Haven: Yale University Press, 1989).

72.   Omer Bartov, *Murder in our Midst: The Holocaust, Industrial Killing, and Representation* (New York: Oxford University Press, 1996), 97.

73.   John Lachs, *Responsibility of the Individual in Modern Society* (Brighton: Harvester, 1981), 58.

74.   Peter Maass, *Love Thy Neighbor: A Story of War* (New York: Vintage Books, 1996), 86.

75.   Arendt, *Eichmann in Jerusalem*.

76.   Katherine Jamieson writes, "There is some evidence to suggest that corporate criminal acts emanate from professional and business goals to produce profit margin" (*The Organization of Corporate Crime*, 8). Other research has also supported this position. See for example John Braithwaite, "White Collar Crime," *Annual Review of Sociology* 11 (1985): 1–25; E. D. Herlihy and T. A. Levine, "Corporate Crisis: the Overseas Payment Problem," in *Criminology Review Yearbook*, ed. E. Bittner and S. L. Messinger (Beverly Hills: Sage Publications, 1980), 221–242; R. E. Lane, "Why Businessmen Violate the Law," in *White Collar Crime*, ed. G. Geis and R. F. Meier, rev. ed. (New York: Free Press, 1977), 44.

77.   Lydia Voigt et al., *Criminology and Justice* (New York: McGraw Hill, 1994), 348.

78.   James William Coleman, *The Criminal Elite: The Sociology of White-Collar Crime*, 3rd ed. (New York: St. Martin's Press, 1994), 194–195.

79.   Vahakn Dadrian, "A Typology of Genocide," *International Review of Modern Sociology* 5 (1975): 201–212; Frank Chalk and Kurt Jonassohn, *The History and Sociology of Genocide: Analyses and Case Studies* (New Haven: Yale University Press, 1990).

80.   Robert K. Hitchcock and Tara M. Twedt, "Physical and Cultural Genocide of Various Indigenous Peoples," in Totten, Parsons, and Charny, *Century of Genocide*, 372–407.

81.   Shelton Davis, *Victims of the Miracle: Development and the Indians of Brazil* (Cambridge: Cambridge University Press, 1977); David Price, *Before the Bulldozer: The Nambiquara Indians and the World Bank* (Cabin John, Md.: Seven Locks Press, 1989).

82.   Horowitz, *Taking Lives*, 170–171.

83.   For example see Napoleon A. Chagnon, *Yanomamö: The Last Days of Eden* (San Diego: Harcourt Brace Jovanovich, 1992); Geoffrey O'Connor, *Amazon Journal: Dispatches from a Vanishing Frontier* (New York: Dutton Books, 1997); Ward Churchill, *A Little Matter of Genocide: Holocaust and Denial in the Americas, 1492 to the Present* (San Francisco: City Lights Books, 1997).

84.   CIMI—Indianist Missionary Council, "Chronology of the Yanomami Genocide," posted on the Web on August 27, 1993, at <http://bioc09.uthscsa.edu/natnet/archive/nl/9308/0275.html>, accessed April 8, 2000.

85.   Churchill, *A Little Matter of Genocide*, 111–112.

86.   Richard Arens, "Death Camps in Paraguay," *American Indian Journal* (July 1978): 2–13; Mark Münzel, *The Achè: Genocide Continues in Paraguay* (Copenhagen: International Workgroup for Indigenous Affairs, 1974).

87.   Roger W. Smith, "Human Destructiveness and Politics: The Twentieth Century As an Age of Genocide," in *Genocide and the Modern Age: Etiology and Case Studies of Mass Death*, ed. Isidor Walliman and Michael N. Dobkowski (New York: Greenwood Press, 1987), 25.

88.   O'Connor, *Amazon Journal*.

89.   Simpson, *The Splendid Blond Beast*, 65.

90. Shmuel Krakowski, "The Satellite Camps," in *Anatomy of the Auschwitz Death Camp,* ed. Yisrael Gutman and Michael Berenbaum (Bloomington: Indiana University Press, 1994), 50–60.

91. Franciszek Piper, "The System of Prisoner Exploitation 34–49," in Gutman and Berenbaum, *Anatomy,* 34–49.

92. Benjamin B. Ferencz, *Less Than Slaves: Jewish Forced Labor and the Quest for Compensation* (Cambridge: Harvard University Press, 1979), xix.

93. Piper, "The System of Prisoner Exploitation," 45.

94. Ferencz, *Less Than Slaves,* 36.

95. Ferencz, *Less Than Slaves,* 22.

96. Jean-Claude Pressac with Robert-Jan Van Pelt, "The Machinery of Mass Murder at Auschwitz," in Gutman and Berenbaum, *Anatomy,* 183–245.

97. See for example Marshall B. Clinard and Peter C. Yeager, *Corporate Crime* (New York: Free Press, 1980); P. Asch and J. J. Seneca, "Is Collusion Profitable?" *The Review of Economics and Statistics* 58 (1976): 1–12; Michael B. Blankenship, ed., *Understanding Corporate Criminality* (New York: Garland Publishing, 1993).

98. Neal Shover and Kevin M. Bryant, "Theoretical Explanations of Corporate Crime," in Blankenship, *Understanding Corporate Criminality,* 141–176.

99. Jamieson, *The Organization of Corporate Crime,* 12.

100. Todorov, *Facing the Extreme,* 154.

101. Jamieson, *The Organization of Corporate Crime,* 13.

102. Zygmunt Bauman, *Modernity and the Holocaust* (Ithaca: Cornell University Press, 1989), 100.

103. George M. Kren and Leon Rappoport, *The Holocaust and the Crisis of Human Behavior* (New York: Holmes and Meier, 1994), 153.

104. Katz, *Ordinary People and Extraordinary Evil,* 13.

105. Todorov, *Facing the Extreme,* 152.

106. Gitta Sereny, *Into That Darkness* (London: Andre Deutsch, 1974), 164, 200.

107. Sereny, *Into That Darkness,* 200.

108. Kermit Vandivier, "Why Should My Conscience Bother Me?" in *Corporate Violence: Injury and Death for Profit,* ed. Stuart L. Hills (Totowa, N.J.: Rowman and Littlefield, 1987), 154.

109. David Rieff, *Slaughterhouse: Bosnia and the Failure of the West* (New York: Touchstone Books, 1995), 171.

110. Coleman, *The Criminal Elite,* 209.

111. Coleman, *The Criminal Elite,* 211.

112. Raul Hilberg, *Perpetrators, Victims, Bystanders* (New York: Harper Perennial, 1992), 55.

113. Morton Mintz, "At Any Cost: Corporate Greed, Women, and the Dalkon Shield," in Hills, *Corporate Violence,* 31.

114. Mark Dowie, "Pinto Madness," in Hills, *Corporate Violence,* 16.

115.   Coleman, *The Criminal Elite*, 208–209.

116.   Coleman, *The Criminal Elite*, 209.

117.   Frederic S. Burin, "Bureaucracy and National Socialism: Reconsideration of Weberian Theory," in *Reader in Bureaucracy*, ed. Robert K. Merton et al. (New York: Free Press, 1952), 33–47.

118.   Klee, Dressen, and Riess, *The Good Old Days*, 78.

119.   Albert Breton and Ronald Wintrobe, "The Bureaucracy of Murder Revisited," *Journal of Political Economy* 94 (1986), 911.

120.   Pressac with Van Pelt, "The Machinery of Mass Murder," 187.

121.   William Manchester, *The Arms of Krupp, 1587–1968* (Boston: Little, Brown, 1968), 493.

122.   Ferencz, *Less Than Slaves*, 28.

5. Accommodating Genocide

1.   Tzvetan Todorov, *Facing the Extreme: Moral Life in the Concentration Camps*, trans. Arthur Denner and Abigail Pollak (New York: Metropolitan Books, 1996), 185.

2.   Anthony Storr, *Human Destructiveness* (New York: Ballantine Books, 1991), 11.

3.   Fergal Keane, *Season of Blood: A Rwandan Journey* (New York: Penguin Books, 1995).

4.   Philip Gourevitch, *We Wish to Inform You That Tomorrow We Will Be Killed with Our Families: Stories from Rwanda* (New York: Farrar, Straus, and Giroux, 1998), 18.

5.   Keane, *Season of Blood*, 73–93.

6.   Keane, *Season of Blood*, 80.

7.   S. E. Asch, "Opinions and Social Pressure," *Scientific American* 193 (1955): 31–35; S. E. Asch, "Studies of Independence and Conformity: A Minority of One against a Unanimous Majority," *Psychological Monographs* 70 (1956): 3–45 (whole of #416); Herbert C. Kelman and V. Lee Hamilton, *Crimes of Obedience: Toward a Social Psychology of Authority and Responsibility* (New Haven: Yale University Press, 1989); Stanley Milgram, *Obedience to Authority* (New York: Harper Torchbooks, 1969).

8.   S. L. A. Marshall found in his research on U.S. soldiers who had fought in World War Two that only 15 to 20 percent of them actually used their weapons and tried to kill the enemy. This conclusion appears in Dave Grossman, *On Killing: The Psychological Cost of Learning to Kill in War and Society* (Boston: Little, Brown, 1995), 29.

9.   I disagree with Daniel Goldhagen, who argues that the Germans were not *"rational, sober children of the Enlightenment . . . rooted in objective reality"* (*Hitler's Willing Executioners: Ordinary Germans and the Holocaust* [New York: Alfred A. Knopf, 1996], 27). While I agree with him that the type of anti-Semitism prevalent throughout Germany was a form of "magical thinking," the rational, objective, and civilized elements of German society cannot

simply be discounted. See Zygmunt Bauman, *Modernity and the Holocaust* (Ithaca: Cornell University Press, 1989); Michael Freeman, "The Theory and Prevention of Genocide," *Holocaust and Genocide Studies* 6 (1991): 185–199; Michael Freeman, "Genocide, Civilization, and Modernity," *British Journal of Sociology* 46 (1995): 207–223; Richard Rubenstein, *The Cunning of History: The Holocaust and the American Future* (New York: Harper Colophon, 1975).

10.   See for example Peter Maass, *Love Thy Neighbor: A Story of War* (New York: Vintage Books, 1996); Brian Hall, *The Impossible Country: A Journey through the Last Days of Yugoslavia* (New York: Penguin Books, 1994).

11.   Michael Bilton and Kevin Sim, *Four Hours in My Lai* (New York: Penguin Books, 1992).

12.   Richard Breitman, *The Architect of Genocide: Himmler and the Final Solution* (New York: Alfred A. Knopf, 1991); Michael Burleigh, *Death and Deliverance: "Euthanasia" in Germany, 1900–1945* (Cambridge: Cambridge University Press, 1994); Michael Burleigh and Wolfgang Wippermann, *The Racial State: Germany 1933–1945* (Cambridge: Cambridge University Press, 1991); Willi Dressen, "Euthanasia," in *Nazi Mass Murder: A Documentary History of the Use of Poison Gas,* ed. E. Kogon, H. Langbein, and A. Rückerl (New Haven: Yale University Press, 1993), 13–51; Henry Friedlander, *The Origins of Nazi Genocide: From Euthanasia to the Final Solution* (Chapel Hill: University of North Carolina Press, 1995); Goldhagen, *Hitler's Willing Executioners.*

13.   Goldhagen, *Hitler's Willing Executioners,* 119; Raul Hilberg, *Perpetrators, Victims, Bystanders* (New York: Harper Collins, 1992), 132.

14.   Goldhagen, *Hitler's Willing Executioners,* 119.

15.   Hilberg, *Perpetrators, Victims, Bystanders,* 95.

16.   Bauman, *Modernity and the Holocaust,* 185.

17.   Corrine Vanderwerff, *Kill Thy Neighbor* (Boise, Idaho: Pacific Press Publishing Association, 1996), 175–176.

18.   Gourevitch, *We Wish to Inform You,* 130.

19.   Bauman, *Modernity and the Holocaust,* 24.

20.   Gresham M. Sykes and David Matza, "Techniques of Neutralization: A Theory of Delinquency," *American Sociological Review* 22 (1957): 664–670.

21.   Kelman and Hamilton, *Crimes of Obedience.*

22.   Fred E. Katz, *Ordinary People and Extraordinary Evil: A Report on the Beguilings of Evil* (Albany: State University of New York Press, 1993), 38.

23.   Todorov, *Facing the Extreme,* 129.

24.   C. Wright Mills, "Situated Actions and Vocabularies of Motive," *American Sociological Review* 5 (1940): 904–913.

25.   These neutralizations most closely approximate Scott and Lyman's definition of justifications in relation to excuses. For Scott and Lyman, justifications are "accounts in which one accepts responsibility for the act in question, but denies the pejorative quality associated with it" (Marvin B. Scott and Stanford M. Lyman, "Accounts," *American Sociological Review* 33 [1968], 47).

26.   Sykes and Matza, "Techniques of Neutralization," 666.

27. Sykes and Matza, "Techniques of Neutralization," 667.

28. Sykes and Matza, "Techniques of Neutralization," 669.

29. Matza, for example, incorporated the concept of neutralization into his concept of "drift" (David Matza, *Delinquency and Drift* [New York: John Wiley, 1964]). He argued that the techniques of neutralization allow delinquents to "drift" in and out of delinquency. Minor developed two new techniques, which he called the Defense of Necessity (it is not a crime if it is a necessary act) and the Metaphor of the Ledger (even though you have committed crime, you have also done many good things) (William W. Minor, "Techniques of Neutralization: A Reconceptualization and Empirical Examination," *Journal of Research in Crime and Delinquency* 18 [1981]: 295–318). While Sykes and Matza used their work almost exclusively to understand the criminal actions of delinquent teenagers, others have applied the theory to the study of different types of criminality. Donald Cressey, for instance, found that embezzlers considered themselves to be decent, honest, law-abiding citizens even though they stole large amounts of money (Donald Cressey, *Other People's Money: A Study in the Social Psychology of Embezzlement* [Glencoe, Ill.: Free Press, 1953]). Overwhelmingly, the embezzlers had convinced themselves beforehand that they were not really stealing the money, but only "borrowing" it, and therefore their actions were acceptable and not in conflict with their conformist self-image. Gary Green asserts that Cressey's work is illustrative of neutralization theory (Gary S. Green, *Occupational Crime* [Chicago: Nelson Hall, 1990]). He argues that the justifications used by the embezzlers are examples of neutralization techniques, specifically the Denials of Injury, Victim, and Responsibility. Other studies have found similar techniques utilized by pilferers and other occupational criminals. See Donald M. Horning, "Blue Collar Theft: Conceptions of Property Attitudes toward Pilfering and Workgroup Norms in a Modern Industrial Plant," in *Crime Against Bureaucracy,* ed. Erwin Smigel and H. Lawrence Ross (New York: Van Nostrand Reinhold, 1979), 63–80; Gerald Mars, "Dock Pilferage: A Case Study in Occupational Theft," in *Deviance and Social Control,* ed. Paul Rock and Mary McIntosh (London: Tavistock, 1974), 89–101; Erwin O. Smigel, "Public Attitudes toward Stealing As Related to the Size of the Victim Organization," in Smigel and Ross, *Crime Against Bureaucracy,* 35–41; Lawrence Zeitlin, "A Little Larceny Can Do a Lot for Company Morale," *Psychology Today* 14 (1971): 22–26.

As for violent crime, Agnew found that a national sample of adolescents accepted neutralizations justifying violent behavior, and that utilization of these neutralizations contributed to adolescents' participating in violent behavior (Robert Agnew, "The Techniques of Neutralization and Violence," *Criminology* 32 [1994]: 555–580). Ferraro and Johnson applied neutralization theory in a novel way to intrafamilial violence and found that battered women utilized various neutralization techniques to rationalize and understand their experiences of being assaulted by their spouses (Kathleen J. Ferraro and John M. Johnson, "How Women Experience Battering: The Process of Victimization," *Social Problems* 30 [1983]: 325–339). By asking whether and how victims, rather than perpetrators, used techniques of neutralization, they essentially reversed the traditional application of this theory. In the same way that the theory has been used to understand the actions of violent delinquents, battered women, embezzlers, and occupational criminals, it can aid in understanding the process by which individuals participate in genocide.

30. Agnew, "Techniques"; Richard C. Hollinger, "Neutralizing in the Workplace: An Empirical Analysis of Property Theft and Production Deviance," *Deviant Behavior* 12 (1991): 169–202; J. A. Landsheer, J. T. Hart, and W. Kox, "Delinquent Values and Victim Damage: Exploring the Limits of Neutralization Theory," *British Journal of Criminology* 34 (1994): 44–53; Minor, "Techniques of Neutralization"; William W. Minor, "Neutralization As a Hardening Process: Considerations in the Modeling of Change," *Social Forces* 62 (1984): 995–1019; Jim Mitchell and Richard A. Dodder, "Types of Neutralization and Types of Delinquency," *Journal of Youth and Adolescence* 12 (1983): 307–318; Jim Mitchell, Richard A. Dodder, and Terry D. Norris, "Neutralization and Delinquency: A Comparison by Sex and Ethnicity," *Adolescence* 25 (1990): 488–497; Ian W. Shields and Georga C. Whitehall, "Neutralization and Delinquency among Teenagers," *Criminal Justice and Behavior* 21 (1994): 223–235.

31. Agnew, "Techniques."

32. Kelman and Hamilton, *Crimes of Obedience,* 16.

33. Yitzhak Arad, *Belzec, Sobibor, Treblinka: The Operation Reinhard Death Camps* (Bloomington: Indiana University Press, 1987), 186–187.

34. Hannah Arendt, *Eichmann in Jerusalem: A Report on the Banality of Evil* (New York: Penguin Books, 1964), 225–226.

35. Gourevitch, *We Wish to Inform You,* 303.

36. Kelman and Hamilton, *Crimes of Obedience,* 16.

37. Richard L. Rubenstein and J. K. Roth, *Approaches to Auschwitz* (Atlanta: John Knox, 1987), 137.

38. Norman Cigar, *Genocide in Bosnia: The Policy of "Ethnic Cleansing"* (College Station: Texas A&M University Press, 1995).

39. Michael Palaich, "Man or Monster: Confessions of a Serb War Criminal," *Soldier of Fortune* 18 (1993), 64.

40. Gourevitch, *We Wish to Inform You,* 307.

41. Arendt, *Eichmann in Jerusalem;* Christopher R. Browning, *Ordinary Men: Reserve Police Battalion 101 and the Final Solution in Poland* (New York: Aaron Asher Books, 1992); Goldhagen, *Hitler's Willing Executioners;* Ernst Klee, Willi Dressen, and Volker Riess, eds., *The Good Old Days: The Holocaust As Seen by Its Perpetrators and Bystanders* (New York: Free Press, 1988); Ervin Staub, *The Roots of Evil: The Origins of Genocide and Other Group Violence* (Cambridge: Cambridge University Press, 1989).

42. Klee, Dressen, and Riess, *The Good Old Days,* 76.

43. Rudolf Höss, *Death Dealer,* ed. Steven Paskuly, trans. Andrew Pollinger (Buffalo, N.Y.: Prometheus, 1992), 189.

44. Nachman Blumenthal, "On the Nazi Vocabulary," in *Yad Vashem Studies on the European Jewish Catastrophe and Resistance,* vol. 1, ed. Benzion Dimur and Shaul Esh (Jerusalem: Yad Vashem, 1957), 49–66; Nachman Blumental, "From

the Nazi Vocabulary," in *Yad Vashem Studies on the European Jewish Catastrophe and Resistance,* vol. 6, ed. Nathan Eck and Aryeh L. Kubovy (Jerusalem: Yad Vashem, 1967), 69–82; Shaul Esh, "Words and Their Meanings," in *Yad Vashem Studies on the European Jewish Catastrophe and Resistance,* vol. 5, ed. Nathan Eck and Aryeh L. Kubovy (Jerusalem: Yad Vashem, 1963), 133–167; Henry Friedlander, "The Manipulation of Language," in *The Holocaust: Ideology, Bureaucracy, and Genocide,* ed. Henry Friedlander and S. Milton (Millwood, N.Y.: Kraus International, 1980), 103–113; Beryl Lang, "Language and Genocide," in *Echoes From the Holocaust,* ed. A. Rosenberg and G. B. Myers (Philadelphia: Temple University Press, 1988), 341–361.

45.   Lang, "Language and Genocide."

46.   Hilberg, *Perpetrators, Victims, Bystanders,* 1012.

47.   Roger Cohen, *Hearts Grown Brutal: Sagas of Sarajevo* (New York: Random House, 1998), 32.

48.   Cigar, *Genocide in Bosnia,* 71.

49.   Gourevitch, *We Wish to Inform You;* Neil J. Kressel, *Mass Hate: The Global Rise of Genocide and Terror* (New York: Plenum Press, 1996); Gérard Prunier, *The Rwanda Crisis: History of a Genocide* (New York: Columbia University Press, 1995).

50.   Tina Rosenberg, *Children of Cain: Violence and the Violent in Latin America* (New York: Penguin Books, 1991), 90.

51.   Grossman, *On Killing,* 92.

52.   Carol Cohn, "Nuclear Language and How We Learned to Pat the Bomb," in *Making War, Making Peace: The Social Foundations of Violent Conflict,* ed. Francesca M. Cancian and James W. Gibson (Belmont, Calif.: Wadsworth Publishing, 1990), 120.

53.   David Rieff, *Slaughterhouse: Bosnia and the Failure of the West* (New York: Touchstone Books, 1995), 83.

54.   Lang, "Language and Genocide," 354.

55.   Claude Lanzmann, *Shoah: An Oral History of the Holocaust* (New York: Pantheon Books, 1985), 13.

56.   Gitta Sereny, *Into That Darkness* (London: Andre Deutsch, 1974), 201.

57.   Eugenia Semyonovna Ginzburg, *Within the Whirlwind,* trans. Ian Boland (New York: Harcourt, 1982), 71.

58.   Sheldon H. Harris, *Factories of Death: Japanese Biological Warfare, 1932–1945, and the American Coverup* (London: Routledge, 1994), 39.

59.   George M. Kren and Leon Rappoport, *The Holocaust and the Crisis of Human Behavior* (New York: Holmes and Meier, 1994), 150.

60.   Herbert Hirsch, *Genocide and the Politics of Memory: Studying Death to Preserve Life* (Chapel Hill: University of North Carolina Press, 1995), 85.

61.   Ed Vulliamy, *Seasons in Hell: Understanding Bosnia's War* (New York: St. Martin's Press, 1994), 48.

62.   Alexander Alvarez, "Trends and Patterns of Justifiable Homicide: A Comparative Analysis," *Violence and Victims* 7 (1992): 347–356; Cynthia K. Gillespie,

Justifiable Homicide (Columbus: Ohio State University Press, 1989); David D. Polsby, "Reflections on Violence, Guns, and the Defensive Use of Lethal Force," *Law and Contemporary Problems* 49 (1986): 89–111.

63. Kressel, *Mass Hate,* 109.

64. Cigar, *Genocide in Bosnia,* 78.

65. See for example Cohen, *Hearts Grown Brutal.*

66. Cigar, *Genocide in Bosnia,* 78.

67. Cohen, *Hearts Grown Brutal,* 169.

68. Cohen, *Hearts Grown Brutal,* 152.

69. Tom Gjelten, *Sarajevo Daily: A City and Its Newspaper under Siege* (New York: Harper Collins, 1995), 150.

70. Vulliamy, *Seasons in Hell,* 49.

71. Warren Zimmermann, *Origins of a Catastrophe* (New York: Times Books, 1999), 181.

72. Goldhagen, *Hitler's Willing Executioners.*

73. Sarah Gordon, *Hitler, Germans, and the "Jewish Question"* (Princeton: Princeton University Press, 1984), 151.

74. Staub, *The Roots of Evil.*

75. Klee, Dressen, and Riess, *The Good Old Days,* 158.

76. Klee, Dressen, and Riess, *The Good Old Days,* 163.

77. Höss, *Death Dealer,* 161.

78. Hilberg, *Perpetrators, Victims, Bystanders,* 1021.

79. Prunier, *The Rwanda Crisis,* 247.

80. Bill Berkeley, "Ethnicity and Conflict in Africa: The Methods behind the Madness," in *War Crimes: The Legacy of Nuremberg,* ed. Belinda Cooper (New York: TV Books, 1999), 190–191.

81. Cigar, *Genocide in Bosnia,* 95.

82. Bauman, *Modernity and the Holocaust,* 68.

83. Terrence Des Pres, *The Survivor: An Anatomy of Life in the Death Camps* (Oxford: Oxford University Press, 1976), 48.

84. Konnilyn G. Feig, *Hitler's Death Camps: The Sanity of Madness* (New York: Holmes and Meier, 1979); P. J. Haas, *Morality after Auschwitz* (Philadelphia: Fortress, 1988); Nora Levin, *The Holocaust: The Destruction of European Jewry, 1933–1945* (New York: Schocken Books, 1968); Richard Raschke, *Escape from Sobibor* (New York: Avon, 1982).

85. For an excellent discussion of this issue see Susan Zuccotti, *The Italians and the Holocaust: Persecution, Rescue, and Survival* (Lincoln: University of Nebraska Press, 1987).

86. Ward Churchill, *A Little Matter of Genocide: Holocaust and Denial in the Americas, 1492 to the Present* (San Francisco: City Lights Books, 1997), 52.

87. Staub, *The Roots of Evil,* 134.

88. Höss, *Death Dealer,* 185.

89. Arad, *Belzec, Sobibor, Treblinka,* 192.

90. Marguerite Feitlowitz, *A Lexicon of Terror: Argentina and the Legacies of Torture* (New York: Oxford University Press, 1998), 196, 212.

91. Rieff, *Slaughterhouse,* 103.

92. Cigar, *Genocide in Bosnia,* 65.

93. Rieff, *Slaughterhouse,* 86.

94. Klee, Dressen, and Riess, *The Good Old Days,* 57.

95. Kelman and Hamilton, *Crimes of Obedience.*

96. See for example Vamik Volkan, *Blood Lines: From Ethnic Pride to Ethnic Terrorism* (New York: Farrar, Straus, and Giroux, 1997).

97. Gourevitch, *We Wish to Inform You;* Prunier, *The Rwanda Crisis.*

98. Gourevitch, *We Wish to Inform You,* 114.

99. Tom Segev, *Soldiers of Evil* (New York: Berkeley Books, 1987), 81.

100. Vulliamy, *Seasons in Hell,* 133.

101. Cigar, *Genocide in Bosnia,* 100.

102. Michael A. Sells, *The Bridge Betrayed: Religion and Genocide in Bosnia* (Berkeley: University of California Press, 1996), xv.

103. James M. Glass, *"Life Unworthy of Life": Racial Phobia and Mass Murder in Hitler's Germany* (New York: Basic Books, 1997), 24.

104. Gerald Astor, *The "Last" Nazi: The Life and Times of Dr. Joseph Mengele* (New York: Donald I. Fine, 1985), 85.

105. W. Fitzhugh Brundage, *Lynching in the New South* (Urbana: University of Illinois Press, 1993); Stewart E. Tolnay and E. M. Beck, *A Festival of Violence* (Urbana: University of Illinois Press, 1995).

106. Ralph K. Andrist, *The Long Death: The Last Days of the Plains Indians* (New York: Collier, 1964); David E. Stannard, *American Holocaust: The Conquest of the New World* (New York: Oxford University Press, 1992); Ronald Takaki, *A Different Mirror: A History of Multicultural America* (Boston: Back Bay, 1993); R. A. Williams, *The American Indian in Western Legal Thought: Discourses of Conquest* (New York: Oxford University Press, 1990).

107. Ronald Takaki, *Strangers from a Different Shore: A History of Asian Americans* (New York: Penguin Books, 1987).

108. John W. Dower, *War without Mercy* (New York: Pantheon Books, 1986).

109. Helen Fein, *Genocide: A Sociological Perspective* (London: Sage Publications, 1993), 36.

110. Dower, *War without Mercy,* 89.

111. Samuel P. Oliner and Pearl M. Oliner, *The Altruistic Personality: Rescuers of Jews in Nazi Europe* (New York: Free Press, 1988).

112. Des Pres, *The Survivor,* 57.

113. Sereny, *Into That Darkness,* 101.

114. Segev, *Soldiers of Evil*, 203.

115. Sells, *The Bridge Betrayed*, 75.

116. Goldhagen, *Hitler's Willing Executioners*, 176.

117. Fred Katz, *Ordinary People and Extraordinary Evil*, 38.

118. Rubinstein and Roth, *Approaches to Auschwitz*, 137.

119. Primo Levi, *The Drowned and the Saved* (New York: Summit Books, 1986), 31.

6. Confronting Genocide

1. Primo Levi, *The Drowned and the Saved* (New York: Summit Books, 1986), 56.

2. Israel Charny, "Early Warning, Intervention, and Prevention of Genocide," in *Genocide in Our Time: An Annotated Bibliography with Analytical Introductions*, ed. Michael N. Dobkowski and Isidor Wallimann (Ann Arbor, Mich.: Pierian Press, 1992), 149.

3. Philip Hallie, *Lest Innocent Blood Be Shed: The Story of the Village of Le Chambon and How Goodness Happened There* (New York: Harper Perennial: 1979), xvii.

4. Rezak Hukanović, *The Tenth Circle of Hell: A Memoir of Life in the Death Camps of Bosnia* (New York: New Republic Books, 1993), 24.

5. Roger Cohen, *Hearts Grown Brutal: Sagas of Sarajevo* (New York: Random House, 1998), 27.

6. Tim Judah, *The Serbs: History, Myth, and the Destruction of Yugoslavia* (New Haven: Yale University Press, 1997), 117.

7. Fergal Keane, *Season of Blood: A Rwandan Journey* (New York: Penguin Books, 1995), 136.

8. Scholars of genocide also rely on metaphors of natural calamity. Books on Nazi Germany and the Holocaust sometimes have chapters titled "Before the Storm" or "Before the Deluge." See Richard Plant, *The Pink Triangle: The Nazi War against Homosexuals* (New York: Owl Books, 1986); a recent book on Bosnia has a chapter similarly titled "The Gathering Storm" (Sabrina Petra Ramet, *Balkan Babel: The Disintegration of Yugoslavia from the Death of Tito to Ethnic War*, 2nd ed. [Boulder: Westview Press, 1996]).

9. See for example Hallie, *Lest Innocent Blood Be Shed;* Philip Hallie, *Tales of Good and Evil, Help and Harm* (New York: Harper Perennial, 1997).

10. Susan Zuccotti, *The Italians and the Holocaust: Persecution, Rescue, and Survival* (Lincoln: University of Nebraska Press, 1987), xxv.

11. Samuel P. Oliner and Pearl M. Oliner, *The Altruistic Personality: Rescuers of Jews in Nazi Europe* (New York: Free Press, 1988), 13–48.

12. Oliner and Oliner, *The Altruistic Personality*, 13.

13. Zuccotti, *The Italians and the Holocaust*, 75.

14. Raul Hilberg, *The Destruction of the European Jews* (New York: Holmes and Meier, 1985).

15. David Callahan, *Unwinnable Wars* (New York: Hill and Wang, 1997), 53–54.

16. Helen Fein, "Accounting for Genocide after 1945: Theories and Some Findings," *International Journal of Group Rights* 1 (1993): 79–106.

17. Barbara Harff, "The Etiology of Genocides," in *Genocide and the Modern Age: Etiology and Case Studies of Mass Death,* ed. Isidor Wallimann and Michael N. Dobkowski (New York: Greenwood Press, 1987), 43.

18. Harff, "The Etiology of Genocides," 43.

19. Charny, "Early Warning."

20. Charny, "Early Warning," 153.

21. Charny, "Early Warning," 155.

22. Terrence Des Pres, *The Survivor: An Anatomy of Life in the Death Camps* (Oxford: Oxford University Press, 1976), 61.

23. Leo Kuper, "The Prevention of Genocide: Cultural and Structural Indicators of Genocidal Threat," *Ethnic and Racial Studies* 12 (1989), 158–160.

24. Dane Archer and Rosemary Gartner, *Violence and Crime in Cross-National Perspective* (New Haven: Yale University Press, 1984), 95.

25. Kurt Jonassohn and Karin Solveig Björnson, *Genocide and Gross Human Rights Violations in Comparative Perspective* (New Brunswick: Transaction Publishers, 1998), 95.

26. For a discussion of this issue see Richard B. Bilder, "An Overview of International Human Rights Law," in *Guide to International Human Rights Practice,* ed. Hurst Hannum (Philadelphia: University of Pennsylvania Press, 1992).

27. Louis René Beres, "Reason and Realpolitik: International Law and the Prevention of Genocide," in *Toward the Understanding and Prevention of Genocide,* ed. Israel W. Charny (Boulder: Westview Press, 1984), 306–323.

28. Michael P. Scharf, *Balkan Justice: The Story behind the First International War Crimes Trial since Nuremberg* (Durham, N.C.: Carolina Academic Press, 1997), 106.

29. Scharf, *Balkan Justice,* 106.

30. Callahan, *Unwinnable Wars,* 134.

31. Matthew Jardine, *East Timor: Genocide in Paradise* (Tucson: Odonian Press, 1995), 8.

32. Jardine, *East Timor,* 7.

33. *Frontline,* "The Triumph of Evil," transcript posted on the Web at <http://www.pbs.org/wgbh/pages/frontline/shows/evil/etc/script.html>, accessed April 8, 2000.

34. Norman Cigar, *Genocide in Bosnia: The Policy of "Ethnic Cleansing"* (College Station: Texas A&M University Press, 1995), 184.

35. Cigar, *Genocide in Bosnia,* 184.

36. Callahan, *Unwinnable Wars,* 164.

37. W. Michael Reisman and Chris T. Antoniou, eds., *The Laws of War: A Comprehensive Collection of Primary Documents on International Laws Governing Armed Conflict* (New York: Vintage Books, 1994), 6.

38. Reisman and Antoniou, *The Laws of War,* 90.

39. Ramsey Clark, *The Fire This Time: U.S. War Crimes in the Gulf* (New York: Thunder's Mouth Press, 1994).

40. Dusko Doder and Louise Branson, *Milosevic: Portrait of a Tyrant* (New York: Free Press, 1999), 217–221.

41. Cigar, *Genocide in Bosnia*, 148.

42. Hannah Arendt, *The Origins of Totalitarianism* (San Diego: Harvest Books, 1973), 341–364.

43. Henry Kamm, *Cambodia: Report from a Stricken Land* (New York: Arcade Publishing, 1998).

44. Lawrence Weschler, quoted in Adam Hochschild, *The Unquiet Ghost: Russians Remember Stalin* (New York: Penguin Books, 1994), 20.

45. Cigar, *Genocide in Bosnia*, 148.

46. Helen Fein, *Genocide: A Sociological Perspective* (London: Sage Publications, 1993), xiv.

47. Doder and Branson, *Milosevic*, 110.

48. Doder and Branson, *Milosevic*, 105.

49. Roger Smith, "The Armenian Genocide: Memory, Politics, and the Future," in *The Armenian Genocide: History, Politics, Ethics*, ed. Richard G. Hovannisian (New York: St. Martin's Press, 1992), 1–20.

50. Bazyler's ideas are reviewed in Leo Kuper, "Theoretical Issues Relating to Genocide: Uses and Abuses," in *Genocide: Conceptual and Historical Dimensions*, ed. George J. Andreopoulos (Philadelphia: University of Pennsylvania Press, 1994), 43.

51. Many of these concerns are discussed in Fein, *Genocide*.

52. Charny, "Early Warning," 150.

53. Luis Kutner and Ernest Katin, "World Genocide Tribunal: A Proposal for Planetary Preventive Measures Supplementing a Genocide Early Warning System," in *Toward the Understanding and Prevention of Genocide*, ed. Israel Charny (Boulder: Westview Press, 1984).

54. Callahan, *Unwinnable Wars*, 215.

55. Daniel S. Papp, *Contemporary International Relations: Frameworks for Understanding*, 4th ed. (New York: Macmillan College Publishing, 1994).

56. John T. Rourke, *International Politics on the World Stage*, 2nd ed. (Guilford, Conn.: Dushkin Publishing Group, 1989).

57. See for example Nicholas G. Onuf and V. Spike Peterson, "Human Rights from an International Rights Perspective," *Journal of International Affairs* 37 (1984): 334–337; A. H. Robertson, *Human Rights in the World* (New York: St. Martin's Press, 1982); Philip Alston, "The Alleged Demise of Political Human Rights at the U.N.," *International Organization* 37 (1983): 537–550.

58. Gérard Prunier, *The Rwanda Crisis: History of a Genocide* (New York: Columbia University Press, 1995).

59. Prunier, *The Rwanda Crisis*, 230.

60. Prunier, *The Rwanda Crisis*, 235.

61. This has been reported in a variety of places, such as Joe Kubert, *Fax From Sarajevo: A Story of Survival* (Milwaukie, Oreg.: Dark Horse Books, 1996), 132–135.

62. David Rohde, *Endgame: The Betrayal and Fall of Srebrenica, Europe's Worst Massacre Since World War II* (New York: Farrar, Straus, and Giroux, 1997).

63. Jan Willem Honig and Norbert Both, *Srebrenica: Record of a War Crime* (New York: Penguin Books, 1996); Rohde, *Endgame.*

64. Greg Campbell, *The Road To Kosovo: A Balkan Diary* (Boulder: Westview Press, 1999), 49.

65. Warren Zimmermann, *Origins of a Catastrophe* (New York: Times Books, 1999), 242.

66. Robert M. Bohm and Keith N. Haley, *Introduction to Criminal Justice* (New York: Glencoe, 1997), 32.

67. Information on Tadic is taken from Scharf, *Balkan Justice.*

68. Scharf, *Balkan Justice,* 94.

69. Scharf, *Balkan Justice,* 215.

70. Scharf, *Balkan Justice,* 215.

71. United Nations International Criminal Tribunal for the Former Yugoslavia, *Fact Sheet,* posted on the Web on August 25, 1999, at <http://www.un.org/icty/glance/fact.htm>, accessed September 15, 1999.

72. Christian Tomuschat, "International Criminal Prosecution: The Precedent of Nuremberg Confirmed," in *The Prosecution of International Crimes,* ed. Roger S. Clark and Madeleine Sann (New Brunswick: Transaction Publishers, 1996), 17–28.

73. William W. Horne, "The Real Trial of the Century," in *War Crimes: The Legacy of Nuremberg,* ed. Belinda Cooper (New York: TV Books, 1999), 124.

74. United Nations International Criminal Tribunal for the Former Yugoslavia, *Fact Sheet.*

75. Elizabeth Neuffer, "Mass Graves," in *Crimes of War: What the Public Should Know,* ed. Roy Gutman and David Rieff (New York: W. W. Norton, 1999), 240.

76. David Rohde, "Medico-Legal Investigations of War Crimes," in *Crimes of War: What the Public Should Know,* ed. Roy Gutman and David Rieff (New York: W. W. Norton, 1999), 245–247.

77. *Online NewsHour,* "Capturing Bosnian War Criminals," aired July 10, 1997; transcript posted on the Web at <http://www.pbs.org/newshour/bb/bosnia/july-dec97/war__criminals__7-10.html>, accessed March 25, 1998.

78. "NATO Soldiers Arrest Bosnian Serb Wartime Commander," posted on the Web on December 20, 1999, at <http://www.cnn.com/199 . . . 12/20/bc.bosnia.nato.ap/index.html>, accessed December 20, 1999.

79. United Nations International Criminal Tribunal for Rwanda, *Fact Sheet No. 1,* posted on the Web in November 1999 at <http://www.ictr.org/ENGLISH/factsheets/factshee.htm>, accessed December 10, 1999.

80. "Ex-Rwandan Militia Leader Convicted of Genocide, Crimes against Humanity," posted on the Web on December 6, 1999, at <http://www.cnn.com/199 . . . 2/06/rwanda.genocide.ap/index.html>, accessed on December 6, 1999.

81. Scharf, *Balkan Justice,* 85.

82. Neil J. Kritz, "War Crimes Trials: Who Should Conduct Them—and How," in *War Crimes: The Legacy of Nuremberg,* ed. Belinda Cooper (New York: TV Books, 1999), 168–182.

83. Corinne Dufka, "Rwanda Executes Genocide Convicts," Reuters, April 24, 1998; James C. McKinley Jr., "Firing Squads Execute Twenty-Two Convicted of Genocide in Rwanda," *New York Times,* April 25, 1998.

84. Kritz, "War Crimes Trials," 169.

85. Peter Maass, *Love Thy Neighbor: A Story of War* (New York: Vintage Books, 1996), 272.

86. Jonassohn and Björnson, *Genocide,* 98.

87. Charny, "Early Warning," 150.

88. Hochschild, *The Unquiet Ghost,* 9.

89. Hochschild, *The Unquiet Ghost,* 123.

90. Prunier, *The Rwanda Crisis,* 260.

91. Nora Levin, *The Holocaust: The Destruction of European Jewry, 1933–1945* (New York: Shocken Books, 1973), 325–326.

92. Oliner and Oliner, *The Altruistic Personality,* 2.

93. Hochschild, *The Unquiet Ghost,* 286.

Bibliography

Adalian, Rouben P. "The Armenian Genocide." In *Century of Genocide: Eyewitness Accounts and Critical Views,* ed. Samuel Totten, William S. Parsons, and Israel W. Charny, 41–77. New York: Garland Publishing, 1997.

Adorno, Theodore W., Else Frenkel-Brunswik, Daniel J. Levinson, and Nevitt Sanford. *The Authoritarian Personality.* New York: Harper and Row, 1950.

Agnew, Robert. "The Techniques of Neutralization and Violence." *Criminology* 32 (1994): 555–580.

Aikman, David. "O Nationalism! Yugoslavia Shows How Ancient Tensions Can Suddenly Boil Over." *Time,* October 24, 1988, 46–49.

Akers, Ronald L. *Criminological Theories: Introduction and Evaluation.* Los Angeles: Roxbury Publishing, 1994.

Ali, Rabia, and Lawrence Lifschultz. "Why Bosnia?" *Monthly Review* 45 (1994): 1–28.

Alston, Philip. "The Alleged Demise of Political Human Rights at the U.N." *International Organization* 37 (1983): 537–550.

Alvarez, Alexander. "Trends and Patterns of Justifiable Homicide: A Comparative Analysis." *Violence and Victims* 7 (1992): 347–356.

Aly, Götz, Peter Chroust, and Christian Pross. *Cleansing the Fatherland: Nazi Medicine and Racial Hygiene.* Trans. Belinda Cooper. Baltimore: The Johns Hopkins University Press, 1994.

Anderson, Benedict. *Imagined Communities: Reflections on the Origin and Spread of Nationalism.* London: Verso, 1983.

Andreopoulos, George J. *Genocide: Conceptual and Historical Dimensions.* Philadelphia: University of Pennsylvania Press, 1994.

Andrist, Ralph K. *The Long Death: The Last Days of the Plains Indians.* New York: Collier, 1964.

Anzulovic, Branimir. *Heavenly Serbia: From Myth to Genocide.* New York: New York University Press, 1999.

Arad, Yitzhak. *Belzec, Sobibor, Treblinka: The Operation Reinhard Death Camps.* Bloomington: Indiana University Press, 1987.

Archer, Dane, and Rosemary Gartner. *Violence and Crime in Cross-National Perspective.* New Haven: Yale University Press, 1984.

Archer, Dane, Rosemary Gartner, and M. Beittel. "Homicide and the Death Penalty: A Cross-National Test of a Deterrence Hypothesis." *The Journal of Criminal Law and Criminology* 3 (1983): 991–1013.

Arendt, Hannah. *Eichmann in Jerusalem: A Report on the Banality of Evil.* New York: Penguin Books, 1964.

———. *The Origins of Totalitarianism.* San Diego: Harvest Books, 1973.

Arens, Richard. "Death Camps in Paraguay." *American Indian Journal* (July 1978): 2–13.

Arkin, S. D. "Discrimination and Arbitrariness in Capital Punishment: An Analysis of

Post-Furman Murder Cases in Dade County, Florida, 1973–1976." *Stanford Law Review* 33 (1980): 75–101.

Asch, P., and J. J. Seneca. "Is Collusion Profitable?" *The Review of Economics and Statistics* 58 (1976): 1–12.

Asch, S. E. "Opinions and Social Pressure." *Scientific American* 193 (1955): 31–35.

——. "Studies of Independence and Conformity: A Minority of One against a Unanimous Majority." *Psychological Monographs* 70 (1956): 3–45 (whole of #416).

Astor, Gerald. *The "Last" Nazi: The Life and Times of Dr. Joseph Mengele.* New York: Donald I. Fine, 1985.

Bailey, William C. "Capital Punishment and Lethal Assaults against Police." *Criminology* 19 (1982): 608–625.

——. "Poverty, Inequality, and City Homicide Rates." *Criminology* 22 (1984): 531–550.

Bailey, William C., and R. D. Peterson. "Murder, Capital Punishment, and Deterrence: A Review of the Evidence and an Examination of Police Killings." *Journal of Social Issues* 50 (1994): 53–74.

——. "Police Killings and Capital Punishment: The Post-Furman Period." *Criminology* 25 (1987): 1–25.

Barak, Gregg. "Crime, Criminology, and Human Rights: Toward an Understanding of State Criminality." In *Varieties of Criminology: Readings from a Dynamic Discipline,* ed. Gregg Barak, 253–267. Westport, Conn.: Praeger, 1994.

——. "Newsmaking Criminology: Reflections on the Media, Intellectuals, and Crime." *Justice Quarterly* 5 (1988): 565–587.

Bartov, Omer. *Murder in Our Midst: The Holocaust, Industrial Killing, and Representation.* New York: Oxford University Press, 1996.

Bauer, Yehuda. *A History of the Holocaust.* New York: Franklin Watts, 1982.

——. "Is The Holocaust Explicable?" *Holocaust and Genocide Studies* 5 (1990): 145–155.

Bauman, Zygmunt. *Modernity and the Holocaust.* Ithaca: Cornell University Press, 1989.

Beck, Aaron T. *Prisoners of Hate: The Cognitive Basis of Anger, Hostility, and Violence.* New York: Harper Collins, 1999.

Becker, Elizabeth. *When the War Was Over: Cambodia and the Khmer Rouge Revolution.* New York: Public Affairs, 1998.

Beirne, Piers, and James Messerschmidt. *Criminology.* 2nd ed. Fort Worth: Harcourt Brace College Publishers, 1995.

Bell-Fialkoff, Andrew. *Ethnic Cleansing.* New York: St. Martin's Press/Griffin, 1999.

Beres, Louis René. "Reason and Realpolitik: International Law and the Prevention of Genocide." In *Toward the Understanding and Prevention of Genocide,* ed. Israel W. Charny, 306–323. Boulder: Westview Press, 1984.

van den Berghe, Pierre, ed. *State Violence and Ethnicity.* Boulder: University Press of Colorado, 1990.

Berkeley, Bill. "Ethnicity and Conflict in Africa: The Methods behind the Madness." In *War Crimes: The Legacy of Nuremberg,* ed. Belinda Cooper, 183–210. New York: TV Books, 1999.

Berkowitz, Sarah. *Where Are My Brothers?* New York: Helios, 1965.

Bettelheim, Bruno. *The Informed Heart.* New York: Free Press, 1966.

——. *Surviving.* New York: Alfred A. Knopf, 1979.

Bilder, Richard B. "An Overview of International Human Rights Law." In *Guide to International Human Rights Practice,* ed. Hurst Hannum, 3–18. Philadelphia: University of Pennsylvania Press, 1992.

Bilton, Michael, and Kevin Sim. *Four Hours in My Lai.* New York: Penguin Books, 1992.

Binder, Arnold, and Peter Scharf. "Deadly Force in Law Enforcement," *Crime and Delinquency* (1982): 1–23.

Bischoping, Katherine, and Natalie Fingerhut. "Border Lines: Indigenous Peoples in Genocide Studies." *Canadian Review of Sociology and Anthropology* 33 (1996): 481–506.

Blankenship, Michael B., ed. *Understanding Corporate Criminality.* New York: Garland Publishing, 1993.

Block, Alan A. "Violence, Corruption, and Clientelism: The Assassination of Jesús de Galíndez, 1956." *Social Justice* 16 (1989): 64–88.

Block, Carolyn R. "Race/Ethnicity and Patterns of Chicago Homicide, 1965 to 1981." *Crime and Delinquency* 31 (1985): 104–116.

Blumental, Nachman. "From the Nazi Vocabulary." In *Yad Vashem Studies on the European Jewish Catastrophe and Resistance,* vol. 6, ed. Nathan Eck and Aryeh L. Kubovy, 69–82. Jerusalem: Yad Vashem, 1967.

———. "On the Nazi Vocabulary." In *Yad Vashem Studies on the European Jewish Catastrophe and Resistance,* vol. 1, ed. Benzion Dimur and Shaul Esh, 49–66. Jerusalem: Yad Vashem, 1957.

Bobrick, Benson. *East of the Sun: The Epic Conquest and Tragic History of Siberia.* New York: Henry Holt, 1992.

Bohm, Robert M., and Keith N. Haley. *Introduction to Criminal Justice.* New York: Glencoe, 1997.

Borkin, Joseph. *The Crime and Punishment of I. G. Farben.* New York: Free Press, 1978.

Bowers, William J. *Legal Homicide.* Boston: Northeastern University Press, 1984.

Bowers, William J., and Glenn L. Pierce. "Arbitrariness and Discrimination under Post-Furman Capital Statutes." *Crime and Delinquency* 26 (1980): 563–635.

Boyle, Francis A. "The Hypocrisy and Racism behind the Formulation of U.S. Human Rights Foreign Policy: In Honor of Clyde Ferguson." *Social Justice* 16 (1989): 71–93.

Brackman, Arnold C. *The Other Nuremberg: The Untold Story of the Tokyo War Crimes Trials.* New York: Quill, 1987.

Braithwaite, John. "White Collar Crime." *Annual Review of Sociology* 11 (1985): 1–25.

Brannigan, Augustine. "Criminology and the Holocaust: Xenophobia, Evolution, and Genocide." *Crime and Delinquency* 44 (1998): 257–276.

Breitman, Richard. *The Architect of Genocide: Himmler and the Final Solution.* New York: Alfred A. Knopf, 1991.

Breton, Albert, and Ronald Wintrobe. "The Bureaucracy of Murder Revisited." *Journal of Political Economy* 94 (1986): 905–926.

Brieger, Gert H. "The Medical Profession." In *The Holocaust: Ideology, Bureaucracy, and Genocide,* ed. Henry Friedlander and Sybil Milton, 141–150. Millwood, N.Y.: Kraus International, 1980.

Brown, David. *The State and Ethnic Politics in South-East Asia.* London: Routledge, 1994.

Browning, Christopher R. *Ordinary Men: Reserve Police Battalion 101 and the Final Solution in Poland.* New York: Aaron Asher Books, 1992.

Brundage, W. Fitzhugh. *Lynching in the New South.* Urbana: University of Illinois Press, 1993.

Burg, Steven L., and Paul S. Shoup. *The War in Bosnia-Herzegovina: Ethnic Conflict and International Intervention.* Armonk, N.Y.: M. E. Sharpe, 1999.

Burin, Frederic S. "Bureaucracy and National Socialism: Reconsideration of Weberian Theory." In *Reader in Bureaucracy,* ed. Robert K. Merton, Ailsa P. Gray, Barbara Hockey, and Hanan C. Selvin, 33–47. New York: Free Press, 1952.

Burleigh, Michael. *Death and Deliverance: "Euthanasia" in Germany, 1900–1945.* Cambridge: Cambridge University Press, 1994.

Burleigh, Michael, and Wolfgang Wippermann. *The Racial State: Germany 1933–1945.* Cambridge: Cambridge University Press, 1991.

Burns, John F. "Nationalist Leaders Twist History to Advance Their Own Aims." In *Macmillan Atlas of War and Peace,* 4–5. New York: Macmillan, 1996.

Butler, Rupert. *An Illustrated History of the Gestapo.* Osceola, Wisc.: Motorbooks International, 1992.

Callahan, David. *Unwinnable Wars.* New York: Hill and Wang, 1997.

Campbell, Greg. *The Road to Kosovo: A Balkan Diary.* Boulder: Westview Press, 1999.

Carell, Paul. *Hitler Moves East, 1941–1943.* Winnepeg, Manitoba: J. J. Fedorowicz Publishing, 1991.

De Las Casas, Bartolomé. *The Devastation of the Indies: A Brief Account.* Baltimore: The Johns Hopkins University Press, 1974.

Caven, Brian. *The Punic Wars.* New York: Barnes and Noble Books, 1980.

Chagnon, Napoleon A. *Yanomamö: The Last Days of Eden.* San Diego: Harcourt Brace Jovanovich, 1992.

Chalk, Frank. "Redefining Genocide." In *Genocide: Conceptual and Historical Dimensions,* ed. George J. Andreopoulos, 47–63. Philadelphia: University of Pennsylvania Press, 1994.

Chalk, Frank, and Kurt Jonassohn. *The History and Sociology of Genocide: Analyses and Case Studies.* New Haven: Yale University Press, 1990.

Chambliss, William J. "State-Organized Crime." In *Making Law: The State, the Law, and Structural Contradictions,* ed. William J. Chambliss and Marjorie S. Zatz, 290–314. Bloomington: Indiana University Press, 1993.

Chandler, David P. *Brother Number One: A Political Biography of Pol Pot.* Boulder: Westview Press, 1992.

Charny, Israel. "Early Warning, Intervention, and Prevention of Genocide." In *Genocide in Our Time: An Annotated Bibliography with Analytical Introductions,* ed. Michael N. Dobkowski and Isidor Wallimann, 149–166. Ann Arbor, Mich.: Pierian Press, 1992.

———. "Toward a Generic Definition of Genocide." In *Genocide: Conceptual and Historical Dimensions,* ed. George J. Andreopoulos, 64–94. Philadelphia: University of Pennsylvania Press, 1994.

Cheatwood, Derral. "Capital Punishment and the Deterrence of Violent Crime in Comparable Counties." *Criminal Justice Review* 18 (1993): 165–181.

Chilton, Roland. "Twenty Years of Homicide and Robbery in Chicago: The Impact of the City's Changing Racial and Age Composition." *Journal of Quantitative Criminology* 3 (1987): 195–214.

Chirot, Daniel. *Modern Tyrants: The Power and Prevalence of Evil in Our Age.* Princeton: Princeton University Press, 1994.

Churchill, Ward. *Indians Are Us? Culture and Genocide in Native North America.* Monroe, Maine: Common Courage Press, 1994.

———. *A Little Matter of Genocide: Holocaust and Denial in the Americas, 1492 to the Present.* San Francisco: City Lights Books, 1997.

"CIA Says 'Most Ethnic Cleansing' Done by Serbs." *New York Times,* March 9, 1995.

Cigar, Norman. *Genocide in Bosnia: The Policy of "Ethnic Cleansing."* College Station: Texas A&M University Press, 1995.

CIMI—Indianist Missionary Council. "Chronology of the Yanomami Genocide." Posted August 27, 1993, on the Web at <http://bioc09.uthscsa.edu/natnet/archive/nl/9308/0275.html>. Accessed April 8, 2000.

Clark, Ramsey. *The Fire This Time: U.S. War Crimes in the Gulf.* New York: Thunder's Mouth Press, 1994.

Clinard, Marshall B., and Peter C. Yeager, *Corporate Crime.* New York: Free Press, 1980.

Cohen, Roger. *Hearts Grown Brutal: Sagas of Sarajevo.* New York: Random House, 1998.

Cohn, Carol. "Nuclear Language and How We Learned to Pat the Bomb." In *Making War, Making Peace: The Social Foundations of Violent Conflict,* ed. Francesca M. Cancian and James W. Gibson, 111–121. Belmont, Calif.: Wadsworth Publishing, 1990.

Coleman, James William. *The Criminal Elite: The Sociology of White-Collar Crime.* 3rd ed. New York: St. Martin's Press, 1994.

Connor, Walter. "Nation-Building or Nation-Destroying." In *The Theory and Practice of International Relations,* ed. Fred A. Sondermann, David S. McLellan, and William C. Olson, 55–66. Englewood Cliffs, N.J.: Prentice Hall, 1979.

Conot, Robert E. *Justice at Nuremberg.* New York: Carroll and Graf, 1983.

Conquest, Robert. *The Harvest of Sorrow: Soviet Collectivization and the Terror-Famine.* New York: Oxford University Press, 1986.

Courtois, Stéphane. "Introduction: The Crimes of Communism." In *The Black Book of Communism: Crimes, Terror, Repression,* ed. Stéphane Courtois, Nicolas Werth, Jean-Louis Panné, Andrzej Paczkowski, Karel Bartošek, and Jean-Louis Margolin, trans. Jonathan Murphy and Mark Kramer, 1–31. Cambridge: Harvard University Press, 1999.

Courtois, Stéphane, Nicolas Werth, Jean-Louis Panné, Andrzej Paczkowski, Karel Bartošek, and Jean-Louis Margolin, eds. *The Black Book of Communism: Crimes, Terror, Repression.* Trans. Jonathan Murphy and Mark Kramer. Cambridge: Harvard University Press, 1999.

Cressey, Donald. *Other People's Money: A Study in the Social Psychology of Embezzlement.* Glencoe, Ill.: Free Press, 1953.

Dadrian, Vahakn N. "The Documentation of the World War I Armenian Massacres in the Proceedings of the Turkish Military Tribunal." *International Journal of Middle East Studies* 23 (1991): 549–576.

———. "Genocide As a Problem of National and International Law: The World War I Armenian Case and Its Contemporary Legal Ramifications." *The Yale Journal of International Law* 14 (1989): 221–334.

———. *The History of the Armenian Genocide: Ethnic Conflict from the Balkans to Anatolia to the Caucasus.* Providence, R.I.: Berghahn Books, 1995.

———. "The Role of Turkish Physicians in the World War I Genocide of Ottoman Armenians." *Holocaust and Genocide Studies* 1 (1986): 169–192.

———. "A Typology of Genocide." *International Review of Modern Sociology* 5 (1975): 201–212.

Danner, Mark. *The Massacre at El Mozote.* New York: Vintage Books, 1993.

Davis, Shelton. *Victims of the Miracle: Development and the Indians of Brazil.* Cambridge: Cambridge University Press, 1977.

"Decoded German Reports Shed New Light on the Holocaust." *The Arizona Republic,* November 11, 1996.

Denitch, Bogdan. *Ethnic Nationalism: The Tragic Death of Yugoslavia.* Minneapolis: University of Minnesota Press, 1994.

Des Pres, Terrence. *The Survivor: An Anatomy of Life in the Death Camps.* Oxford: Oxford University Press, 1976.

Destexhe, Alain. *Rwanda and Genocide in the Twentieth Century.* New York: New York University Press, 1995.

Doder, Dusko, and Louise Branson. *Milosevic: Portrait of a Tyrant.* New York: Free Press, 1999.

Dower, John W. *War without Mercy.* New York: Pantheon Books, 1986.

Dowie, Mark. "Pinto Madness." In *Corporate Violence: Injury and Death for Profit,* ed. Stuart L. Hills, 13–29. (Totowa, N.J.: Rowman and Littlefield, 1987.

Dressen, Willi. "Euthanasia." In *Nazi Mass Murder: A Documentary History of the Use of Poison Gas,* ed. Eugen Kogon, Hermann Langbein, and Adalbert Rückerl, 13–51. New Haven: Yale University Press, 1993.

Dufka, Corinne. "Rwanda Executes Genocide Convicts." *Reuters,* April 24, 1998.

Egger, Steven A. *The Killers among Us: An Examination of Serial Murder and Its Investigation.* Upper Saddle River, N.J.: Prentice Hall, 1998.

"Eichmann's Final Plea." In *In His Own Words: The Trial of Adolf Eichmann.* Web site accompanying a documentary produced by ABC News Productions for the Public Broadcasting System. Premiered April 30, 1997. Posted on the Web at <http://www.pbs.org/eichmann/ownwords.htm>. Accessed April 8, 2000.

Elias, Norbert. *The Civilizing Process: The History of Manners.* New York: Urizen, 1978.

Esh, Shaul. "Words and Their Meanings." In *Yad Vashem Studies on the European Jewish Catastrophe and Resistance,* vol. 5, ed. Nathan Eck and Aryeh L. Kubovy, 133–167. Jerusalem: Yad Vashem, 1963.

Esson, D. M. R. *The Curse of Cromwell: A History of the Ironside Conquest of Ireland.* Totowa, N.J.: Rowman and Littlefield, 1971.

"Ex-Rwandan Militia Leader Convicted of Genocide, Crimes against Humanity." Posted on the Web on December 6, 1999, at <http://www.cnn.com/199 . . . 2/06/rwanda.genocide.ap/index.html>. Accessed December 6, 1999.

Ezell, Walter K. "Investigating Genocide: A Catalog of Known and Suspected Causes and Some Categories for Comparing Them." In *Remembering the Future: The Impact of the Holocaust on Jews and Christians,* vol. 3, ed. Yehuda Bauer et al., 2880–2892. Oxford: Pergamon Press, 1989.

Feig, Konnilyn G. *Hitler's Death Camps: The Sanity of Madness.* New York: Holmes and Meier, 1979.

Fein, Helen. "Accounting for Genocide after 1945: Theories and Some Findings." *International Journal on Group Rights* 1 (1993): 79–106.

———. *Accounting for Genocide: National Responses and Jewish Victimization during the Holocaust.* New York: Free Press, 1979.

———. *Genocide: A Sociological Perspective.* London: Sage Publications, 1993.

———. "Genocide, Terror, Life Integrity, and War Crimes: The Case for Discrimination." In *Genocide: Conceptual and Historical Dimensions,* ed. George J. Andreopoulos, 95–108. Philadelphia: University of Pennsylvania Press, 1994.

———. "Is Sociology Aware of Genocide? Recognition of Genocide in Introductory Sociology Texts in the U.S., 1947–1977." *Humanity and Society* (1979): 177–193.

Feingold, Henry L. "How Unique Is the Holocaust?" In *Genocide: Critical Issues of the Holocaust,* ed. Alex Grobman and Daniel Landes. Los Angeles: The Simon Wiesenthal Centre, 1983.

Feitlowitz, Marguerite. *A Lexicon of Terror: Argentina and the Legacies of Torture.* New York: Oxford University Press, 1998.

Ferencz, Benjamin B. *Less than Slaves: Jewish Forced Labor and the Quest for Compensation.* Cambridge: Harvard University Press, 1979.

Ferguson, R. Brian, and Neil L. Whitehead, eds. *War in the Tribal Zone: Expanding States and Indigenous Warfare.* Santa Fe: School of American Research Press, 1992.

Ferraro, Kathleen J., and John M. Johnson. "How Women Experience Battering: The Process of Victimization." *Social Problems* 30 (1983): 325–339.

Ferrell, Jeff. "Confronting the Agenda of Authority: Critical Criminology, Anarchism, and Urban Graffiti." In *Varieties of Criminology: Readings from a Dynamic Discipline,* ed. Gregg Barak, 161–178. Westport, Conn.: Praeger, 1994.

Fest, Joachim C. *The Face of the Third Reich.* New York: Pantheon Books, 1970.

Finkelstein, Norman G., and Ruth Bettina Birn. *A Nation on Trial: The Goldhagen Thesis and Historical Truth.* New York: Owl Books, 1998.

Fogelman, Eva. *Conscience and Courage: Rescuers of Jews during the Holocaust.* New York: Anchor Books, 1994.

Foucault, Michel. *Discipline and Punish: The Birth of the Prison.* New York: Vintage Books, 1977.

Freeman, Michael. "Genocide, Civilization, and Modernity." *British Journal of Sociology* 46 (1995): 207–223.

———. "The Theory and Prevention of Genocide." *Holocaust and Genocide Studies* 6 (1991): 185–199.

Friedlander, Henry. "The Manipulation of Language." In *The Holocaust: Ideology, Bureaucracy, and Genocide,* ed. Henry Friedlander and S. Milton, 103–113. Millwood, N.Y.: Kraus International, 1980.

———. *The Origins of Nazi Genocide: From Euthanasia to the Final Solution.* Chapel Hill: University of North Carolina Press, 1995.

Friedrichs, David O. "Criminological, Sociolegal, and Jurisprudential Dimensions of the Holocaust: A Pedagogical Approach." In *Proceedings of the Fourth Biennial Conference on Christianity and the Holocaust: The Fiftieth Anniversary of the Nuremberg War Crimes Trials: Their Effectiveness and Legacy.* Princeton, N.J.: Rider University, 1996.

———. "Governmental Crime, Hitler and White Collar Crime: A Problematic Relationship." *Caribbean Journal of Criminology and Social Psychology* 1 (1996): 44–63.

———, ed. *State Crime: Defining, Delineating, and Explaining State Crime.* Dartmouth: Ashgate, 1998.

Frontline. "The Triumph of Evil." Transcript posted on the Web at <http://www.pbs.org/wgbh/pages/frontline/shows/evil/etc/script.html>. Accessed April 8, 2000.

Fussell, Paul. *The Great War and Modern Memory.* New York: Oxford University Press, 1989.

Fyfe, James J. "Blind Justice: Police Shootings in Memphis." *The Journal of Criminal Law and Criminology* 73 (1982): 421–470.

Gabriel, Richard A. *Military Psychiatry: A Comparative Perspective.* New York: Greenport Press, 1986.

Galliher, John F. *Criminology: Human Rights, Criminal Law, and Crime.* Englewood Cliffs, N.J.: Prentice Hall, 1989.

Gellner, Ernest. *Thought and Change.* London: Weidenfeld and Nicholson, 1964.

Giddens, Anthony. *The Nation-State and Violence: A Contemporary Critique of Historical Materialism.* Vol. 2. Berkeley: University of California Press, 1985.

Gilbert, Martin. *The First World War: A Complete History.* New York: Henry Holt, 1994.
——. *The Holocaust: A History of the Jews of Europe during the Second World War.* New York: Henry Holt, 1985.
——. *Holocaust Journey: Travelling in Search of the Past.* New York: Columbia University Press, 1997.
Gillespie, Cynthia K. *Justifiable Homicide.* Columbus: Ohio State University Press, 1989.
Ginzburg, Eugenia Semyonovna. *Journey into the Whirlwind.* Trans. Paul Stevenson and Max Hayward. New York: Harcourt, 1967.
——. *Within the Whirlwind.* Trans. Ian Boland. New York: Harcourt, 1982.
Gjelten, Tom. *Sarajevo Daily: A City and Its Newspaper under Siege.* New York: Harper Collins, 1995.
Glass, James M. *"Life Unworthy of Life": Racial Phobia and Mass Murder in Hitler's Germany.* New York: Basic Books, 1997.
Goldhagen, Daniel. *Hitler's Willing Executioners: Ordinary Germans and the Holocaust.* New York: Alfred A. Knopf, 1996.
Gordon, Sarah. *Hitler, Germans, and the "Jewish Question."* Princeton: Princeton University Press, 1984.
Gourevitch, Philip. *We Wish to Inform You That Tomorrow We Will Be Killed with Our Families: Stories from Rwanda.* New York: Farrar, Straus, and Giroux, 1998.
Grant, Michael. *History of Rome.* New York: Charles Scribner's Sons, 1978.
Green, Gary S. *Occupational Crime.* Chicago: Nelson Hall, 1990.
Grossman, Dave. *On Killing: The Psychological Cost of Learning to Kill in War and Society.* Boston: Little, Brown, 1995.
Grossman, Vasily. *Forever Flowing.* Trans. Thomas P. Whitney. New York: Harper and Row, 1972.
Gutman, Roy. *A Witness to Genocide.* New York: Macmillan Books, 1993.
Gutman, Yisrael, and Michael Berenbaum, eds. *Anatomy of the Auschwitz Death Camp.* Bloomington: Indiana University Press, 1994.
Haas, P. J. *Morality after Auschwitz.* Philadelphia: Fortress, 1988.
Hackworth, David. *Hazardous Duty.* New York: Avon Books, 1996.
Hagan, Frank E. *Political Crime: Ideology and Criminality.* Boston: Allyn and Bacon, 1997.
Hall, Brian. *The Impossible Country: A Journey through the Last Days of Yugoslavia.* New York: Penguin Books, 1994.
Hallie, Philip. *Lest Innocent Blood Be Shed: The Story of the Village of Le Chambon and How Goodness Happened There.* New York: Harper Perennial, 1979.
——. *Tales of Good and Evil, Help and Harm.* New York: Harper Perennial, 1997.
Hamm, Mark S. "State-Organized Homicide: A Study of Seven CIA Plans to Assassinate Fidel Castro." In *Making Law: The State, the Law, and Structural Contradictions,* ed. William J. Chambliss and Marjorie S. Zatz, 315–343. Bloomington: Indiana University Press, 1993.
Harff, Barbara. "The Etiology of Genocides." In *Genocide and the Modern Age: Etiology and Case Studies of Mass Death,* ed. Isidor Wallimann and Michael N. Dobkowski, 41–59. New York: Greenwood Press, 1987.
Harff, Barbara, and Ted Robert Gurr. "Toward Empirical Theory of Genocides and Politicides: Identification and Measurement of Cases since 1945." *International Studies Quarterly* 32 (1988): 359–371.
Harris, Sheldon H. *Factories of Death: Japanese Biological Warfare, 1932–1945, and the American Coverup.* London: Routledge, 1994.

Hauptman, Laurence M. *Tribes and Tribulations*. Albuquerque: University of New Mexico Press, 1995.

Hayes, Peter. "Introduction." In *Lessons and Legacies: The Meaning of the Holocaust in a Changing World,* ed. Peter Hayes, 1–10. Evanston: Northwestern University Press, 1991.

Headland, Ronald. *Messages of Murder: A Study of the Reports of the Einsatzgruppen of the Security Police and the Security Service, 1941–1943.* Rutherford, N.J.: Fairleigh Dickinson University Press, 1992.

Held, David. *Political Theory and the Modern State.* Stanford: Stanford University Press, 1984.

Herlihy, E. D., and T. A. Levine. "Corporate Crisis: The Overseas Payment Problem." In *Criminology Review Yearbook,* ed. E. Bittner and S. L. Messinger, 221–242. Beverly Hills: Sage Publications, 1980.

Hickey, Eric W. *Serial Murderers and Their Victims.* 2nd ed. Belmont, Calif.: Wadsworth Publishing, 1997.

Hilberg, Raul. *The Destruction of the European Jews.* New York: Holmes and Meier, 1985.

———. *Perpetrators, Victims, Bystanders.* New York: Harper Perennial, 1992.

Hildinger, Erik. *Warriors of the Steppe: A Military History of Central Asia, 500 B.C. to 1700 A.D.* New York: Sarpedon Press, 1997.

Hills, Stuart L., ed. *Corporate Violence: Injury and Death for Profit.* Totowa, N.J.: Rowman and Littlefield, 1987.

Hirsch, Herbert. *Genocide and the Politics of Memory: Studying Death to Preserve Life.* Chapel Hill: University of North Carolina Press, 1995.

Hitchcock, Robert K., and Tara M. Twedt. "Physical and Cultural Genocide of Various Indigenous Peoples." In *Century of Genocide: Eyewitness Accounts and Critical Views,* ed. Samuel Totten, William S. Parsons, and Israel W. Charny, 372–407. New York: Garland Publishing, 1997.

Hobbes, Thomas. *Leviathan.* New York: Macmillan, 1947. Originally published 1651.

Hobsbawm, E. J. *Nations and Nationalism since 1780: Programme, Myth, Reality.* 2nd ed. Cambridge: Cambridge University Press, 1990.

Hochschild, Adam. *The Unquiet Ghost: Russians Remember Stalin.* New York: Penguin Books, 1994.

Höhne, Heinz. *The Order of the Death's Head: The Story of Hitler's SS.* Trans. Richard Barry. London: Pan Books, 1969.

Hollinger, Richard C. "Neutralizing in the Workplace: An Empirical Analysis of Property Theft and Production Deviance." *Deviant Behavior* 12 (1991): 169–202.

Holmes, Richard. *Acts of War: The Behavior of Men in Battle.* New York: Free Press, 1985.

Holmes, Ronald M., and James De Burger. *Serial Murder.* Newbury Park, Calif.: Sage Publications, 1988.

Honig, Jan Willem, and Norbert Both. *Srebrenica: Record of a War Crime.* New York: Penguin Books, 1996.

Horne, Alistair. *The Price of Glory: Verdun 1916.* London: Penguin Books, 1962.

Horne, William W. "The Real Trial of the Century." In *War Crimes: The Legacy of Nuremberg,* ed. Belinda Cooper, 120–138. New York: TV Books, 1999.

Horning, Donald M. "Blue Collar Theft: Conceptions of Property Attitudes toward Pilfering and Workgroup Norms in a Modern Industrial Plant." In *Crime Against Bureaucracy,* ed. Erwin Smigel and H. Lawrence Ross, 63–80. New York: Van Nostrand Reinhold, 1979.

Horowitz, Irving Louis. *Genocide: State Power and Mass Murder.* New Brunswick: Transaction Publishers, 1976.

———. *Taking Lives: Genocide and State Power.* 4th ed. New Brunswick: Transaction Publishers, 1997.

Höss, Rudolph. *Death Dealer: The Memoirs of the SS Kommandant at Auschwitz.* Ed. Steven Paskuly. Trans. Andrew Pollinger. Buffalo, N.Y.: Prometheus, 1992.

Hovannisian, Richard G. "Etiology and Sequelae of the Armenian Genocide." In *Genocide: Conceptual and Historical Dimensions,* ed. George J. Andreopoulos, 111–140. Philadelphia: University of Pennsylvania Press, 1994.

Hughes, Everett C. "Good People and Dirty Work." *Social Problems* 10 (1962): 3–11.

Hukanović, Rezak. *The Tenth Circle of Hell: A Memoir of Life in the Death Camps of Bosnia.* New York: Basic Books, 1993.

Human Rights Watch/Middle East. *Iraq's Crime of Genocide: The Anfal Campaign against the Kurds.* New Haven: Yale University Press, 1995.

Human Rights Watch/Africa. "Zaire: Forced to Flee: Violence against the Tutsis in Zaire." Report. Vol. 8, no. 2 (A) (July 1996).

Human Rights Watch. *Slaughter among Neighbors: The Political Origins of Communal Violence.* New Haven: Yale University Press, 1995.

Hummel, Ralph P. *The Bureaucratic Experience.* 3rd ed. New York: St. Martin's Press, 1987.

Hynes, Samuel. *The Soldiers' Tale: Bearing Witness to Modern War.* New York: Penguin Books, 1997.

Ignatieff, Michael. *Blood and Belonging: Journeys into the New Nationalism.* New York: Noonday Press, 1993.

Jacobs, David, and David Britt. "Inequality and Police Use of Deadly Force: An Empirical Assessment of a Conflict Hypothesis." *Social Problems* 26 (1979): 403–411.

Jacobs, S. L. *Raphael Lemkin's Thoughts on Nazi Genocide.* Lewiston, Maine: Edwin Mellen, 1992.

Jamieson, Katherine M. *The Organization of Corporate Crime: Dynamics of Antitrust Violation.* Thousand Oaks, Calif.: Sage Publications, 1994.

Jardine, Matthew. *East Timor: Genocide in Paradise.* Tucson: Odonian Press, 1995.

Johnson, Eric A., and Eric H. Monkkonen, eds. *The Civilization of Crime: Violence in Town and Country since the Middle Ages.* Urbana: University of Illinois Press, 1996.

Jonassohn, Kurt, and Karin Solveig Björnson. *Genocide and Gross Human Rights Violations in Comparative Perspective.* New Brunswick: Transaction Publishers, 1998.

Jones, Susanne. *The Battle for Guatemala: Rebels, Death Squads, and U.S. Power.* Boulder: Westview Press, 1991.

Judah, Tim. *The Serbs: History, Myth and the Destruction of Yugoslavia.* New Haven: Yale University Press, 1997.

Kamm, Henry. *Cambodia: Report from a Stricken Land.* New York: Arcade Publishing, 1998.

Kane, Joe. *Savages.* New York: Vintage Books, 1995.

Kaplan, Robert D. *The Ends of the Earth: A Journey to the Frontiers of Anarchy.* New York: Vintage Books, 1996.

Katz, Fred E. *Ordinary People and Extraordinary Evil: A Report on the Beguilings of Evil.* Albany: State University of New York Press, 1993.

Katz, Steven. *The Holocaust in Historical Context.* Vol. 1, *The Holocaust and Mass Death before the Modern Age.* New York: Oxford University Press, 1992.

——. "Ideology, State Power, and Mass Murder/Genocide." In *Lessons and Legacies: The Meaning of the Holocaust in a Changing World*, ed. Peter Hayes, 47–89. Evanston: Northwestern University Press, 1991.

——. "The Uniqueness of the Holocaust: The Historical Dimension." In *Is The Holocaust Unique: Perspectives on Comparative Genocide*, ed. Alan S. Rosenbaum, 19–38. Boulder: Westview Press, 1996.

Keane, Fergal. *Season of Blood: A Rwandan Journey.* New York: Penguin Books, 1995.

Keegan, John, and Richard Holmes. *Soldiers: A History of Men in Battle.* New York: Elisabeth Sifton Books, 1986.

Keil, T. J., and Gennaro F. Vito. "Race, Homicide Severity, and Application of the Death Penalty: A Consideration of the Barnett Scale." *Criminology* 27 (1989): 511–535.

Kelly, Michael. *Martyrs' Day: Chronicle of a Small War.* New York: Random House, 1993.

Kelman, Herbert C. "Violence without Moral Restraint: Reflections on the Dehumanization of Victims and Victimizers." *Journal of Social Issues* 29 (1973): 25–61.

Kelman, Herbert C., and V. Lee Hamilton. *Crimes of Obedience: Toward a Social Psychology of Authority and Responsibility.* New Haven: Yale University Press, 1989.

Kennedy, Leslie W., and Robert A. Silverman. "The Elderly Victim of Homicide: An Application of the Routine Activities Approach." *The Sociological Quarterly* 31 (1990): 307–319.

Kiernan, Ben. *The Pol Pot Regime: Race, Power, and Genocide in Cambodia under the Khmer Rouge, 1975–79.* New Haven: Yale University Press, 1996.

Kleck, Gary. "Racial Discrimination in Criminal Sentencing: A Critical Evaluation of the Evidence with Additional Evidence on the Death Penalty." *American Sociological Review* 46 (1981): 783–805.

Klee, Ernst, Willi Dressen, and Volker Riess, eds. *The Good Old Days: The Holocaust As Seen by Its Perpetrators and Bystanders.* New York: Free Press, 1988.

Korman, Gerd. "The Holocaust in Historical Writing." *Societas* 2 (1972): 15–16.

Krakowski, Shmuel. "The Satellite Camps." In *Anatomy of the Auschwitz Death Camp*, ed. Yisrael Gutman and Michael Berenbaum, 50–60. Bloomington: Indiana University Press, 1994.

Kren, George M., and Leon Rappoport. *The Holocaust and the Crisis of Human Behavior.* New York: Holmes and Meier, 1994.

Kressel, Neil J. *Mass Hate: The Global Rise of Genocide and Terror.* New York: Plenum Press, 1996.

Kritz, Neil J. "War Crimes Trials: Who Should Conduct Them——and How." In *War Crimes: The Legacy of Nuremberg*, ed. Belinda Cooper, 168–182. New York: TV Books, 1999.

Kubert, Joe. *Fax From Sarajevo: A Story of Survival.* Milwaukie, Oreg.: Dark Horse Books, 1996.

Kuper, Leo. *Genocide.* New Haven: Yale University Press, 1981.

——. "The Prevention of Genocide: Cultural and Structural Indicators of Genocidal Threat." *Ethnic and Racial Studies* 12 (1989): 157–173.

——. "Theoretical Issues Relating to Genocide: Uses and Abuses." In *Genocide: Conceptual and Historical Dimensions*, ed. George J. Andreopoulos, 31–46. Philadelphia: University of Pennsylvania Press, 1994.

Kutner, Luis, and Ernest Katin. "World Genocide Tribunal: A Proposal for Planetary Preventive Measures Supplementing a Genocide Early Warning System." In *Toward the Understanding and Prevention of Genocide*, ed. Israel Charny, 330–346. Boulder: Westview Press, 1984.

Kuykendall, Jack. "Trends in the Use of Deadly Force by Police." *Journal of Criminal Justice* 9 (1981): 359–366.

Lachs, John. *Responsibility of the Individual in Modern Society.* Brighton: Harvester, 1981.

Land, Kenneth C., Patricia L. McCall, and Lawrence E. Cohen. "Structural Covariates of Homicide Rates: Are There Any Invariances across Time and Social Space?" *American Journal of Sociology* 95 (1990): 922–963.

Landsheer, J. A., J. T. Hart, and W. Kox. "Delinquent Values and Victim Damage: Exploring the Limits of Neutralization Theory." *British Journal of Criminology* 34 (1994): 44–53.

Lane, R. E. "Why Businessmen Violate the Law." In *White Collar Crime,* rev. ed., ed. G. Geis and R. F. Meier, 44. New York: Free Press, 1977.

Lang, Beryl. "Language and Genocide." In *Echoes from the Holocaust,* ed. A. Rosenberg and G. B. Myers, 341–361. Philadelphia: Temple University Press, 1988.

Lang, Jochen Von, with Claus Sibyll, eds. *Eichmann Interrogated: Transcripts from the Archives of the Israeli Police.* Trans. Ralph Manheim. New York: Da Capo Press, 1999.

Lanzmann, Claude. *Shoah: An Oral History of the Holocaust.* New York: Pantheon Books, 1985.

Legters, Lyman H. "The American Genocide." *Policy Studies Journal* 16 (1988): 768–777.

Lemarchand, Rene. "The Rwanda Genocide." In *Century of Genocide: Eyewitness Accounts and Critical Views,* ed. Samuel Totten, William S. Parsons, and Israel Charny, 317–333. New York: Garland Publishing, 1997.

Lemkin, Raphael. *Axis Rule in Occupied Europe.* Washington, D.C.: Carnegie Endowment for International Peace, 1944.

———. "Genocide as a Crime under International Law." *American Journal of International Law* 41 (1947): 145–151.

Lempert, R. "The Effect of Executions on Homicides: A New Look in an Old Light." *Crime and Delinquency* 29 (1983): 88–115.

Levi, Primo. *The Drowned and the Saved.* New York: Summit Books, 1986.

———. *The Periodic Table,* Trans. Raymond Rosenthal. New York: Schocken Books, 1984.

———. *The Reawakening.* New York: Collier, 1965.

Levin, Nora. *The Holocaust: The Destruction of European Jewry, 1933–1945.* New York: Shocken Books, 1968.

Lewin, Moshe. *Russian Peasants and Soviet Power.* London: George Allen and Unwin, 1968.

Lifton, Robert J. *The Nazi Doctors: Medical Killing and the Psychology of Genocide.* New York: Basic Books, 1986.

Lifton, Robert J., and Eric Markusen. *The Genocidal Mentality: Nazi Holocaust and Nuclear Threat.* New York: Basic Books, 1990.

Lincoln, W. Bruce. *The Conquest of a Continent: Siberia and the Russians.* New York: Random House, 1994.

Lipstadt, Deborah. *Denying the Holocaust: The Growing Assault on Truth and Memory.* New York: Plume, 1993.

Lopate, Phillip. "Resistance to the Holocaust." *Tikkun* 4 (1989): 55–65.

Maass, Peter. *Love Thy Neighbor: A Story of War.* New York: Vintage Books, 1996.

Mace, James E. "Genocide by Famine: Ukraine in 1932–1933." In *State Violence and Ethnicity,* ed. Pierre L. van den Berghe, 53–71. Niwot, Colo.: University Press of Colorado, 1990.

———. "Soviet Man-Made Famine in the Ukraine." In *Century of Genocide: Eyewitness*

Accounts and Critical Views, ed. Samuel Totten, William S. Parsons, and Israel W. Charny, 78–89. New York: Garland Publishing, 1997.

Macionis, John J. *Sociology.* 5th ed. Englewood Cliffs, N.J.: Prentice Hall, 1995.

Malcolm, Noel. *Bosnia: A Short History.* New York: New York University Press, 1996.

Manchester, William. *The Arms of Krupp, 1587–1968.* Boston: Little, Brown, 1968.

Margolin, Jean-Louis. "Cambodia: The Country of Disconcerting Crimes." In *The Black Book of Communism: Crimes, Terror, Repression,* ed. Stéphane Courtois, Nicolas Werth, Jean-Louis Panné, Andrzej Paczkowski, Karel Bartošek, and Jean-Louis Margolin, trans. Jonathan Murphy and Mark Kramer, 577–635. Cambridge: Harvard University Press, 1999.

Markle, Gerald E. *Meditations of a Holocaust Traveler.* Albany: State University of New York Press, 1995.

Markusen, Eric. "Genocide and Total War." In *Genocide and the Modern Age: Etiology and Case Studies of Mass Death,* ed. Isidor Wallimann and Michael N. Dobkowski, 97–123. New York: Greenwood Press, 1987.

———. "Genocide and Warfare." In *Genocide, War, and Human Survival,* ed. Charles B. Strozier and Michael Flynn, 75–86. Lanham, Md.: Rowman and Littlefield, 1996.

Markusen, Eric, and David Kopf. *The Holocaust and Strategic Bombing: Genocide and Total War in the Twentieth Century.* Boulder: Westview Press, 1995.

Mars, Gerald. "Dock Pilferage: A Case Study in Occupational Theft." In *Deviance and Social Control,* ed. Paul Rock and Mary McIntosh, 89–101. London: Tavistock, 1974.

Matza, David. *Delinquency and Drift.* New York: John Wiley, 1964.

McDowell, Robin. "Pol Pot Shows No Remorse for Cambodian Genocide." *Associated Press,* October, 1997. Posted on the Web at <http://www.jrnl.net/news/97/oct/jrn179231097.html>. Accessed February 12, 1998.

McKinley, James C., Jr. "Firing Squads Execute Twenty-Two Convicted of Genocide in Rwanda." *New York Times,* April 25, 1998.

Melson, Robert. "Revolution and Genocide: On the Causes of the Armenian Genocide and the Holocaust." In *The Armenian Genocide: History, Politics, Ethics,* ed. Richard G. Hovannisian, 80–102. New York: St. Martin's Press, 1992.

———. *Revolution and Genocide: On the Origins of the Armenian Genocide and the Holocaust.* Chicago: University of Chicago Press, 1992.

Mendelsohn, John, ed., *The Holocaust: Selected Documents in Eighteen Volumes.* Vol. 11, *The Wansee Protocol and a 1944 Report on Auschwitz by the Office of Strategic Services.* New York: Garland Publishing, 1982.

Messner, Steven F. "Regional Differences in the Economic Correlates of the Urban Homicide Rate: Some Evidence on the Importance of Cultural Context." *Criminology* 21 (1983): 477–488.

Michaels, Marguerite. "Central Africa: Descent into Mayhem." *Time,* April 18, 1994. Posted on the Web at <http://www.time.com/time/magazine/archive/1994/940418/940418.centralafrica.html>. Accessed May 31, 2000.

———. "Rwanda: Streets of Slaughter." *Time,* April 25, 1994. Posted on the Web at <http://www.time.com/time/magazine/archive/1994/940425/940425.rwanda.html>. Accessed May 31, 2000.

Milgram, Stanley. *Obedience to Authority.* New York: Harper Torchbooks, 1969.

Miller, Donald E., and Lorna Touryan Miller. *Survivors: An Oral History of the Armenian Genocide.* Berkeley: University of California Press, 1993.

Miller, Richard L. *Nazi Justiz: Law of the Holocaust.* Westport, Conn.: Praeger, 1995.

Mills, C. Wright. "Situated Actions and Vocabularies of Motive." *American Sociological Review* 5 (1940): 904–913.

Milošević, Milan. "The Media Wars." In *Yugoslavia's Ethnic Nightmare: The Inside Story of Europe's Unfolding Ordeal,* ed. Jasminka Udovički and James Ridgeway, 105–122. New York: Lawrence Hill Books, 1995.

Minor, William W. "Neutralization As a Hardening Process: Considerations in the Modeling of Change." *Social Forces* 62 (1984): 995–1019.

———. "Techniques of Neutralization: A Reconceptualization and Empirical Examination." *Journal of Research in Crime and Delinquency* 18 (1981): 295–318.

Mintz, Morton. "At Any Cost: Corporate Greed, Women, and the Dalkon Shield." In *Corporate Violence: Injury and Death for Profit,* ed. Stuart L. Hills, 30–40. Totowa, N.J.: Rowman and Littlefield, 1987.

Mitchell, Jim, and Richard A. Dodder. "Types of Neutralization and Types of Delinquency." *Journal of Youth and Adolescence* 12 (1983): 307–318.

Mitchell, Jim, Richard A. Dodder, and Terry D. Norris. "Neutralization and Delinquency: A Comparison by Sex and Ethnicity." *Adolescence* 25 (1990): 488–497.

Morris, Donald R. *The Washing of the Spears.* New York: Simon and Schuster, 1965.

Mostert, Noel. *Frontiers: The Epic of South Africa's Creation and the Tragedy of the Xhosa People.* New York: Alfred A. Knopf, 1992.

Münzel, Mark. *The Achè: Genocide Continues in Paraguay.* Copenhagen: International Workgroup for Indigenous Affairs, 1974.

"NATO Soldiers Arrest Bosnian Serb Wartime Commander." Posted on the Web on December 20, 1999, at <http://www.cnn.com/199 . . . 12/20/bc.bosnia.nato.ap/index.html>. Accessed December 20, 1999.

Neier, Aryeh. *War Crimes: Brutality, Genocide, Terror, and the Struggle for Justice.* New York: Times Books, 1998.

Neuffer, Elizabeth. "Mass Graves." In *Crimes of War: What the Public Should Know,* ed. Roy Gutman and David Rieff, 288–291. New York: W. W. Norton, 1999.

Nyiszli, Miklos. *Auschwitz: A Doctor's Eyewitness Account.* New York: Arcade Publishing, 1960.

O'Connor, Geoffrey. *Amazon Journal: Dispatches from a Vanishing Frontier.* New York: Dutton Books, 1997.

Oldenbourg, Zoé. *Massacre at Montségur.* London: Phoenix Giant, 1959.

Oliner, Samuel P., and Pearl M. Oliner. *The Altruistic Personality: Rescuers of Jews in Nazi Europe.* New York: Free Press, 1988.

Omaar, Rakiya, and Alex de Waal. "U.S. Complicity by Silence: Genocide in Rwanda." *Covert Action Quarterly.* Posted on the Web at <http://caq.com/CAQ52RW2.html>. Accessed May 31, 2000.

Online NewsHour. "Capturing Bosnian War Criminals." Aired July 10, 1997. Transcript posted on the Web at <http://www.pbs.org/newshour/bb/bosnia/july–dec97/war__criminals__7-10.html>. Accessed March 25, 1998.

Onuf, Nicholas G., and V. Spike Peterson. "Human Rights from an International Rights Perspective." *Journal of International Affairs* 37 (1984): 334–337.

Palaich, Michael. "Man or Monster: Confessions of a Serb War Criminal." *Soldier of Fortune* 18 (1993): 64.

Papp, Daniel. *Contemporary International Relations: Frameworks for Understanding.* 4th ed. New York: Macmillan College Publishing, 1994.

Paris, Erna. *Unhealed Wounds: France and the Klaus Barbie Affair.* New York: Grove Press, 1985.

Parker, Robert N. "Poverty, Subculture of Violence, and Type of Homicide." *Social Forces* 67 (1989): 983–1007.

Payne, Robert. *The Dream and the Tomb: A History of the Crusades.* New York: Dorset Press, 1984.

Perel, Solomon. *Europa, Europa.* Trans. Margot Bettauer Denbo. New York: John Wiley and Sons, 1997.

Peterson, R. D., and William C. Bailey. "Felony Murder and Capital Punishment: An Examination of the Deterrence Question." *Criminology* 29 (1991): 367–395.

———. "Murder and Capital Punishment in the Evolving Context of the Post-*Furman* Era." *Social Forces* 66 (1988): 774–807.

Phillips, C. D. "Exploring Relations among Forms of Social Control: The Lynching and Execution of Blacks in North Carolina, 1889–1918." *Law and Society Review* 21 (1987): 361–374.

Piper, Franciszek. "The System of Prisoner Exploitation." In *Anatomy of the Auschwitz Death Camp,* ed. Yisrael Gutman and Michael Berenbaum, 34–49. Bloomington: Indiana University Press, 1994.

Plant, Richard. *The Pink Triangle: The Nazi War against Homosexuals.* New York: Owl Books, 1986.

Polsby, David D. "Reflections on Violence, Guns, and the Defensive Use of Lethal Force." *Law and Contemporary Problems* 49 (1986): 89–111.

Polybius. *The Rise of the Roman Empire.* Trans. I. Scott-Kilvert. New York: Penguin Books, 1979.

Porter, Bruce D. *War and the Rise of the State: The Military Foundations of Modern Politics.* New York: Free Press, 1994.

Porter, Jack Nusan. "Introduction: What is Genocide? Notes toward a Definition." In *Genocide and Human Rights: A Global Anthology,* ed. Jack Nusan Porter, 9–10. Lanham: University Press of America, 1982.

Pressac, Jean-Claude, with Robert-Jan Van Pelt. "The Machinery of Mass Murder at Auschwitz." In *Anatomy of the Auschwitz Death Camp,* ed. Yisrael Gutman and Michael Berenbaum, 183–245. Bloomington: Indiana University Press, 1994.

Price, David. *Before the Bulldozer: The Nambiquara Indians and the World Bank.* Cabin John, Md.: Seven Locks Press, 1989.

Prunier, Gérard. *The Rwanda Crisis: History of a Genocide.* New York: Columbia University Press, 1995.

Quinn, Kenneth M. "The Pattern and Scope of Violence." In *Cambodia 1975–1978: Rendezvous with Death,* ed. Karl D. Jackson, 179–208. Princeton: Princeton University Press, 1989.

Radelet, Michael L. "Racial Characteristics and the Imposition of the Death Penalty." *American Sociological Review* 46 (1981): 918–927.

Ramet, Sabrina Petra. *Balkan Babel: The Disintegration of Yugoslavia from the Death of Tito to Ethnic War.* 2nd ed. Boulder: Westview Press, 1996.

Raschke, Richard. *Escape from Sobibor.* New York: Avon, 1982.

Ray, James Lee. *Global Politics.* 4th ed. Boston: Houghton Mifflin, 1990.

Reisman, W. Michael, and Chris T. Antoniou, eds. *The Laws of War: A Comprehensive Collection of Primary Documents on International Laws Governing Armed Conflict.* New York: Vintage Books, 1994.

Rieff, David. *Slaughterhouse: Bosnia and the Failure of the West.* New York: Touchstone Books, 1995.

Riley-Smith, Jonathan. *The Crusades: A Short History.* New Haven: Yale University Press, 1987.

Ritter, E. A. *Shaka Zulu.* New York: Penguin Books, 1955.

Robertson, A. H. *Human Rights in the World.* New York: St. Martin's Press, 1982.

Robinson, John J. *Dungeon, Fire, and Sword: The Knights Templar in the Crusades.* New York: M. Evans, 1991.

Rohde, David. *Endgame: The Betrayal and Fall of Srebrenica: Europe's Worst Massacre since World War II.* New York: Farrar, Straus, and Giroux, 1997.

——. "Medico-Legal Investigations of War Crimes." In *Crimes of War: What the Public Should Know,* ed. Roy Gutman and David Rieff, 245–247. New York: W. W. Norton, 1999.

Rosenbaum, Alan S. *Prosecuting Nazi War Criminals.* Boulder: Westview Press, 1993.

Rosenberg, Tina. *Children of Cain: Violence and the Violent in Latin America.* New York: Penguin Books, 1991.

Ross, Jeffrey Ian. "Controlling State Crime: Toward an Integrated Structural Model." In *Controlling State Crime: An Introduction,* ed. Jeffrey Ian Ross, 3–34. New York: Garland Publishing, 1995.

Rourke, John T. *International Politics on the World Stage.* 2nd ed. Guilford, Conn.: Dushkin Publishing Group, 1989.

Rubenstein, Richard L. *The Cunning of History: The Holocaust and the American Future.* New York: Harper Colophon, 1975.

Rubenstein, Richard L., and J. K. Roth. *Approaches to Auschwitz.* Atlanta: John Knox, 1987.

Rummel, R. J. *China's Bloody Century: Genocide and Mass Murder since 1900.* New Brunswick: Transaction Publishers, 1991.

——. *Death by Government.* New Brunswick: Transaction Publishers, 1994.

——. "Democracy, Power, Genocide, and Mass Murder." *Journal of Conflict Resolution* 39 (1995): 3–26.

Russell, Lord, of Liverpool. *The Trial of Adolf Eichmann.* London: Heinemann, 1962.

Sabrin, B. F., ed. *Alliance For Murder: The Nazi-Ukrainian Nationalist Partnership in Genocide.* New York: Sarpedon, 1991.

Samaha, Joel. *Criminal Law.* 3rd ed. St. Paul, Minn.: West Publishing, 1990.

Samary, Catherine. *Yugoslavia Dismembered.* Trans. Peter Drucker. New York: Monthly Review Press, 1995.

Schaffer, Ronald. *Wings of Judgement: American Bombing in World War II.* New York: Oxford University Press, 1985.

Scharf, Michael P. *Balkan Justice: The Story behind the First International War Crimes Trial since Nuremberg.* Durham, N.C.: Carolina Academic Press, 1997.

Schleunes, Karl A. *The Twisted Road to Auschwitz: Nazi Policy toward German Jews, 1933–1939.* Urbana: University of Illinois Press, 1990.

Scott, Marvin B., and Stanford M. Lyman. "Accounts." *American Sociological Review* 33 (1968): 46–62.

Segev, Tom. *Soldiers of Evil.* New York: Berkeley Books, 1987.

Seidelman, William E. "Medical Selection: Auschwitz Antecedents and Effluent." *Holocaust and Genocide Studies* 4 (1989): 435–448.

Sells, Michael A. *The Bridge Betrayed: Religion and Genocide in Bosnia.* Berkeley: University of California Press, 1996.

Sereny, Gitta. *Into That Darkness.* London: Andre Deutsch, 1974.

Sesser, Stan. *The Lands of Charm and Cruelty: Travels in Southeast Asia.* New York: Vintage Books, 1989.

Seton-Watson, Hugh. *Nations and States: An Enquiry into the Origins of Nations and the Politics of Nationalism.* Boulder: Westview Press, 1977.

Shields, Ian W., and Georga C. Whitehall. "Neutralization and Delinquency among Teenagers." *Criminal Justice and Behavior* 21 (1994): 223–235.

Shover, Neal, and Kevin M. Bryant. "Theoretical Explanations of Corporate Crime." In *Understanding Corporate Criminality,* ed. Michael B. Blankenship, 141–176. New York: Garland Publishing, 1993.

Silber, Laura, and Allan Little. *Yugoslavia: Death of a Nation.* New York: Penguin Books, 1997.

Simpson, Christopher. *The Splendid Blond Beast: Money, Law, and Genocide in the Twentieth Century.* Monroe, Maine: Common Courage Press, 1995.

Smigel, Erwin O. "Public Attitudes toward Stealing As Related to the Size of the Victim Organization." In *Crime Against Bureaucracy,* ed. Erwin O. Smigel and H. Lawrence Ross, 35–41. New York: Van Nostrand Reinhold, 1979.

Smith, Bradley F. *Reaching Judgement at Nuremberg.* New York: Basic Books, 1977.

Smith, Roger. "The Armenian Genocide: Memory, Politics, and the Future." In *The Armenian Genocide: History, Politics, Ethics,* ed. Richard G. Hovannisian, 1–20. New York: St. Martin's Press, 1992.

———. "Human Destructiveness and Politics: The Twentieth Century As an Age of Genocide." In *Genocide and the Modern Age: Etiology and Case Studies of Mass Death,* ed. Isidor Wallimann and Michael N. Dobkowski, 21–39. New York: Greenwood Press, 1987.

Smith, Roger W., Eric Markusen, and Robert Jay Lifton. "Professional Ethics and the Denial of Armenian Genocide." *Holocaust and Genocide Studies* 9 (1995): 1–22.

Snow, C. P. "Either-Or." *Progressive* 24 (1961), 24.

Sowell, Thomas. "Middleman Minorities." *The American Enterprise* (1993), 30–41.

Stannard, David E. *American Holocaust: The Conquest of the New World.* New York: Oxford University Press, 1992.

Staub, Ervin. *The Roots of Evil: The Origins of Genocide and Other Group Violence.* New York: Cambridge University Press, 1989.

Steele, Ian K. *Warpaths: Invasions of North America.* New York: Oxford University Press, 1994.

Stein, H. F. "The International and Group Milieu of Ethnicity: Identifying Generic Group Dynamic Issues." *Canadian Review of Studies in Nationalism* 17 (1990): 107–130.

Storr, Anthony. *Human Destructiveness.* New York: Ballantine Books, 1991.

Strayer, Joseph R. *On the Medieval Origins of the Modern State.* Princeton: Princeton University Press, 1970.

Sudetic, Chuck. *Blood and Vengeance.* New York: W. W. Norton, 1998.

Surette, Ray. *Media, Crime, and Criminal Justice: Images and Realities.* 2nd ed. Belmont, Calif.: West/Wadsworth, 1998.

Sykes, Gresham M., and David Matza. "Techniques of Neutralization: A Theory of Delinquency." *American Sociological Review* 22 (1957): 664–670.

Takaki, Ronald. *A Different Mirror: A History of Multicultural America.* Boston: Back Bay, 1993.

———. *Strangers from a Different Shore: A History of Asian Americans.* New York: Penguin Books, 1987.

Thayer, Nate. "Second Thoughts for Pol Pot: Fallen Tyrant Defends His Brutal Regime but Now Wants Cambodia Tied to West." *The Washington Post,* October 28, 1997.

Thompson, Warren K. "Ethics, Evil, and the Final Solution." In *Echoes From the Holocaust,* ed. Alan Rosenberg and Gerald E. Myers, 181–200. Philadelphia: Temple University Press, 1988.

Thurston, Robert W. *Life and Terror in Stalin's Russia, 1934–1941.* New Haven: Yale University Press, 1996.

Todorov, Tzvetan. *Facing the Extreme: Moral Life in the Concentration Camps.* Trans. Arthur Denner and Abigail Pollak. New York: Metropolitan Books, 1996.

Tolnay, Stewart E., and E. M. Beck. *A Festival of Violence.* Urbana: University of Illinois Press, 1995.

Tomuschat, Christian. "International Criminal Prosecution: The Precedent of Nuremberg Confirmed." In *The Prosecution of International Crimes,* ed. Roger S. Clark and Madeleine Sann, 17–28. New Brunswick: Transaction Publishers, 1996.

Totten, Samuel, and William S. Parsons. "Introduction." In *Century of Genocide: Eyewitness Accounts and Critical Views,* ed. Samuel Totten, William S. Parsons, and Israel W. Charny, xxi–xxxix. New York: Garland Publishing, 1997.

Totten, Samuel, William S. Parsons, and Israel W. Charny, eds. *Century of Genocide: Eyewitness Accounts and Critical Views.* New York: Garland Publishing, 1997.

Tunnell, Kenneth D. "Political Crime and Pedagogy: A Content Analysis of Criminology and Criminal Justice Texts." *Journal of Criminal Justice Education* 4 (1993): 101–114.

———. "Prologue." In *Political Crime in Contemporary America: A Critical Approach,* ed. Kenneth D. Tunnell, xi–xix. New York: Garland Publishing, 1993.

Turk, Austin T. "Law as a Weapon in Social Conflict." *Social Problems* 23 (1976): 276–291.

Udovički, Jasminka, and James Ridgeway, eds. *Yugoslavia's Ethnic Nightmare: The Inside Story of Europe's Unfolding Ordeal.* New York: Lawrence Hill Books, 1995.

United States Holocaust Memorial Museum. *Historical Atlas of the Holocaust.* New York: Macmillan Publishing, 1996.

United Nations International Criminal Tribunal for Rwanda. *Fact Sheet No. 1.* Posted on the Web in November 1999 at <http://www.ictr.org/ENGLISH/factsheets/factshee.htm>. Accessed December 10, 1999.

United Nations International Criminal Tribunal for the Former Yugoslavia. *Fact Sheet.* Posted on the Web on August 25, 1999, at <http://www.un.org/icty/glance/fact.htm>. Accessed September 13, 1999.

Vanderwerff, Corrine. *Kill Thy Neighbor.* Boise, Idaho: Pacific Press Publishing Association, 1996.

Vandivier, Kermit. "Why Should My Conscience Bother Me?" In *Corporate Violence: Injury and Death for Profit,* ed. Stuart L. Hills, 145–162. Totowa, N.J.: Rowman and Littlefield, 1987.

Voigt, Lydia, William E. Thornton Jr., Leo Barrile, and Jerrol M. Seaman. *Criminology and Justice.* New York: McGraw Hill, 1994.

Volkan, Vamik. *Blood Lines: From Ethnic Pride to Ethnic Terrorism.* New York: Farrar, Straus, and Giroux, 1997.

Vulliamy, Ed. *Seasons in Hell: Understanding Bosnia's War.* New York: St. Martin's Press, 1994.

Waegel, William B. "How Police Justify the Use of Deadly Force." *Social Problems* 32 (1984): 144–155.

Waite, Robert G. L. "The Holocaust and Historical Explanation." In *Genocide and the Modern Age: Etiology and Case Studies of Mass Death,* ed. Isidor Wallimann and Michael N. Dobkowski, 163–184. New York: Greenwood Press, 1987.

Wallace, Harvey. *Victimology: Legal, Psychological, and Social Perspectives.* Boston: Allyn and Bacon, 1998.

Wallimann, Isidor, and Michael N. Dobkowski, eds. *Genocide and the Modern Age: Etiology and Case Studies of Mass Death.* New York: Greenwood Press, 1987.

Warmington, B. H. *Carthage: A History.* New York: Barnes and Noble Books, 1960.

Watson, Russell, with Margaret Garrard Warner, Douglas Waller, Rod Nordland, and Karen Breslau. "Ethnic Cleansing." *Newsweek,* August 17, 1992, 16–20.

Weber, Max. *Economy and Society.* Ed. Guenther Roth and Claus Wittich. Berkeley: University of California Press, 1978.

———. *The Theory of Social and Economic Organization.* New York: Oxford University Press, 1947.

Williams, Frank P., III. "The Demise of the Criminological Imagination: A Critique of Recent Criminology." *Justice Quarterly* 1 (1984): 91–106.

Williams, Frank P., III., and Marilyn D. McShane. *Criminological Theory.* 2nd ed. Englewood Cliffs, N.J.: Prentice Hall, 1994.

Williams, R. A. *The American Indian in Western Legal Thought: Discourses of Conquest.* New York: Oxford University Press, 1990.

Wilson, James Q. *Thinking About Crime.* New York: Basic Books, 1975.

Wistrich, Robert S. *Antisemitism: The Longest Hatred.* New York: Schocken Books, 1991.

Wolfgang, Marvin E., and Mark Riedel. "Race, Judicial Discretion, and the Death Penalty." *The Annals of the American Academy of Political and Social Science* 407 (1973): 119–133.

Woodward, Susan L. *Balkan Tragedy: Chaos and Dissolution after the Cold War.* Washington, D.C.: The Brookings Institute, 1995.

Wright, R. A., and David Friedrichs. "White-Collar Crime in the Criminal Justice Curriculum." *Journal of Criminal Justice Curriculum* 2 (1991): 96–121.

Yahil, Leni. *The Holocaust: The Fate of European Jewry.* New York: Oxford University Press, 1987.

de Zayas, Alfred M. *The Wehrmacht War Crimes Bureau, 1939–1945.* Lincoln: University of Nebraska Press, 1989.

Zeisel, H. "Race Bias in the Administration of the Death Penalty: The Florida Experience." *Harvard Law Review* 95 (1981): 456–468.

Zeitlin, Lawrence. "A Little Larceny Can Do a Lot for Company Morale." *Psychology Today* 14 (1971): 22–26.

Zimmermann, Warren. *Origins of a Catastrophe.* New York: Times Books, 1999.

Zuccotti, Susan. *The Italians and the Holocaust: Persecution, Rescue, and Survival.* Lincoln: University of Nebraska Press, 1987.

Index

Lon Nol government, 30, 72–73
loyalty, appeal to, 115, 124–25
Lyman, Stanford M., 185n25

Maass, Peter, 20, 25, 77, 80, 99–100
Mace, James, 22
Manjača, 13, 19–20
Marchal, Luc, 83
Margolin, Jean-Louis, 66
Markusen, Eric, 3, 6, 7, 16–17, 48; mecha-
   nisms of genocide, 69–71
Marshall, S. L. A., 184n8
maruta, 119–20
mass graves, 148
mass killing, governmental, 68, 78
mass murder, 46–47, 50
massacres, 48
Matza, David, 112, 113, 114–15, 123, 186n29
Mazowiecki, Tadeusz, 145
media, 2, 9, 134–35; electronic jamming, 140–
   41; ideological power and, 76–78, 123
mediation, 138
Mehemedović, Alija, 130
Melson, Robert, 13, 41, 50
mens rea, 51–52
Mfecane, 29
middleman minority groups, 49–50
Mihailović, Draža, 130
Milgram, Stanley, 16, 95
military action as intervention, 139–40
militias. *See* paramilitary groups
Mills, C. Wright, 4, 113
Milošević, Milan, 77
Milošević, Slobodan, 13, 60, 77, 80–82, 121,
   140–41, 148
Minor, William W., 186n29
Mintz, Morton, 107
Mladić, Ratko, 74, 123, 137, 148
modernity, 30–33
morality, 95, 106–107, 112
Mouvement Révolutionaire National pour le
   Développement (MRND), 83
multinational states, 66
murder, 7–9, 46–47, 50
Muslims, 13, 19–20, 49–50, 53–54, 61, 75; bu-
   reaucracy and, 99–100; as middleman mi-
   nority group, 49; stereotypes, 121–22
My Lai, 111

Nagasaki, 35, 39–40
nationalism, 9, 11, 60–61; as cultural ideal, 62–
   63; history and, 64–66, 80–81; minor differ-

ences and, 63–64; victimization and, 65–66;
   war and, 68–69
nation-state, 66
Native Americans, 5
NATO. *See* North Atlantic Treaty Organization
natural disaster metaphor, 130–31, 191n8
Nazis, 21, 36, 64, 72, 122; denial of humanity,
   126–27; European support for, 22–23; euthanasia program, 11, 24, 111, 158n9. *See also*
   Holocaust
Nebe, Artur, 23
Netherlands, 131
Neuffer, Elizabeth, 148
neutralization, 112–13, 160n29, 185n25,
   186n29; appeal to higher loyalties, 115, 124–
   25; condemnation of condemners, 114–15,
   123–24; defining situation, 128–29; denial
   of humanity, 125–28; denial of injury, 114,
   117–20; denial of responsibility, 114, 115–
   17; denial of victim, 114, 120–23; techniques, 113, 114–15, 128–29
newsmaking criminology, 2
NGOs (nongovernmental organizations),
   142–43
Niyitegeka, Félicité, 151
Nobel, Alfred, 10
nongovernmental organizations (NGOs),
   142–43
noninterference, 59
Noriega, Manuel, 5
normality of perpetrators, 21–22, 90, 112, 129
North Atlantic Treaty Organization (NATO),
   5, 139–40
Nuremburg trials, 11–12, 22, 36, 136, 146
Nyarabuye church, 109–10

Ohlendorf, Otto, 95
Oliner, Pearl M., 151
Oliner, Samuel P., 151
Omarska, 13, 19, 24
one-sided killing, 41–42, 43
optimal genocide, 40
Oradour-sur-glane, 131
organizational crime, 8, 100–101
organizations. *See* bureaucracy
out-groups, 16

Palaich, Michael, 116
Paraguay, 52, 53, 102
paramilitary groups, 73–75, 82, 90, 91–97,
   117; identity and, 93–95; indoctrination,
   93, 95–96
Parsons, William S., 3

Volkan, Vamik, 65
Vulliamy, Ed, 120
vulnerability, 40, 42, 49, 70, 73, 135

Waite, Robert, 18–19
Wallimann, Isidor, 51–52
Wannsee conference, 84, 95–96
war, 9, 30, 58, 68–71
War Academy, 93
war crimes tribunals, 9, 36–37, 86–87, 142,
    145–50; International Criminal Tribunal
    for the Former Yugoslavia, 39, 93, 136,
    146–48; International Criminal Tribunal
    for Rwanda, 147, 148–49
war/police power, 72
Weber, Max, 2, 15, 97
Westphalia, Peace of, 57, 58
White Eagle militia, 82, 117
Wiesel, Elie, 27
Williams, Frank, 4
Wilson, James Q., 7
Woods, James, 137
world genocide early warning system, 133–34

World War I, 11, 31–32, 68
World War II, 36, 39–40, 68, 131. *See also*
    Holocaust
Wright, R., 6

xenophobic genocides, 47

Yanomamö people, 101, 102
Young Turks, 11, 99, 179n18
youth crime, 112, 114, 186n29
Yugoslav National Army (JNA), 53
Yugoslavia, former, 9, 12; historical animosi-
    ties as explanation, 79–81; sovereignty, 60–
    63; war crimes tribunals, 39, 93, 136, 146–
    48. *See also* Bosnia

Zaïdl, Motke, 119
Zaire, 5
Zepa, 139
Zimmerman, Warren, 61, 67
Zuccotti, Susan, 132
Zulu nation, 29

224 *Index*

ALEX ALVAREZ earned his Ph.D. in Sociology from the University of New Hampshire in 1991 and is currently Associate Professor in the Department of Criminal Justice at Northern Arizona University. His primary areas of study are minorities, crime, and criminal justice, as well as collective and interpersonal violence. He has published on Native Americans, Latinos, and African Americans, fear of crime, sentencing, justifiable and criminal homicide, and genocide. He is currently writing a book on patterns of American murder.